Arabic for Life

Arabic for Life

A Textbook for Beginning Arabic

With Online Media

Bassam K. Frangieh
Claremont McKenna College

Yale UNIVERSITY PRESS
New Haven and London

This book was originally accompanied by a DVD. The video and audio files are now available online at yalebooks.com/arabicforlife.

Yale University Press books may be purchased in quantity for educational, business, or promotional use. For information, please e-mail sales.press@yale.edu (U.S. office) or sales@yaleup.co.uk (U.K. office).

Publisher: Mary Jane Peluso
Editor: Tim Shea
Publishing Assistant: Ashley E. Lago
Manuscript Editor: Debra Morris Smith
Production Editor: Ann-Marie Imbornoni
Production Controller: Aldo Cupo

Printed in the United States of America.

Library of Congress Control Number: 2011928096
ISBN: 978-0-300-14131-3 (DVD edition)
ISBN: 978-0-300-23383-4 (online media edition)

A catalogue record for this book is available from the British Library.

This paper meets the requirements of ANSI/NISO Z39.48-1992 (Permanence of Paper).

10 9 8 7 6 5 4 3 2

إرضـــاء الناس غـــايـــة لا تــــدركه

Pleasing people is an impossible task.

- Arabic Proverb

Table of Contents

Preface
توطئــة

Arabic for Life is a beginning-level textbook for the serious student of Modern Standard Arabic. It is for students who are eager to learn the language, as challenging as it can be, and it is designed to be taught during one academic year. Arabic is a complicated language, and students must be given the necessary tools to grasp the structure and basic grammar of the language. *Arabic for Life* utilizes a developmental-skills approach to teach listening comprehension, reading, writing, and speaking to beginners. This approach focuses on the order of linguistic need, and each chapter becomes the basis for the next to ensure that the acquisition of Arabic is systematic.

Arabic for Life was written with input from three generations of enthusiastic students of Arabic at Georgetown University, Yale University, and The Claremont Colleges. Many of my students have bemoaned the complexity of Arabic grammar and usage, and the amount of dedication required to memorize the voluminous Arabic vocabulary. Therefore, my objective in this textbook is to provide solid training in all of the basic skills, and in Arabic grammar and structure, to prepare students for their second year of study. I began conducting research for this book while teaching at Yale University. After I moved to Claremont, California, in 2008, I made major revisions and updates to the structure and content of the book in order to make it even more interactive and useful for today's students of Arabic.

The book endeavors to strike a balance between the proficiency-oriented approach and the grammar-oriented approach in teaching the Arabic language. I have attempted to use a style that is as straightforward and easy to use as possible. *Arabic for Life* strives to provide students with intensive training in reading, writing, speaking, and listening comprehension, and an introduction to Arabic grammar. It also provides the necessary background in Arabic phonology, morphology and syntax, the backbone components to the study of Arabic.

We have included a DVD with some eighty videos of native speakers reciting the vocalized texts in the book. *Arabic for Life* also includes a DVD with dozens of audio recordings covering vocabulary and expressions, drills on Arabic sounds and letters, and various exercises and activities. In addition to presenting Arabic vocabulary, idioms and expressions, the book also includes basic and comprehensive texts, grammar, drills and exercises, and speaking and writing activities. The texts in the book were written or selected to be meaningful and interesting to read, but above all true representations of Arab life, thought, and culture. All of the texts were written by me unless stated otherwise.

Acknowledgments   شـــكر وتقديــر

I am indebted to the many individuals who joined me on this project and whose contributions have greatly improved the quality of *Arabic for Life*. I would especially like to thank my students at Yale University and The Claremont Colleges. It has been a real joy these past two years to get to know the students at Claremont McKenna College, Pomona College, Pitzer College, Scripps College, and Harvey Mudd College. They have indeed reinforced what I had learned from students at Yale and Georgetown – that Arabic may be a difficult language to learn, but it can also be a great deal of fun. These students gave me the support that I needed, which is much appreciated.

Olivia Uranga, a Claremont McKenna College student, was the first to offer to help with the textbook when she was only a freshman and a first-year Arabic student. She spent countless hours conducting research and working on the book's design and layout. She devoted her time to tiny, but critically important, details. Rio Fischer, another Claremont McKenna College student, joined the project soon after, and he provided technical assistance, conducted research, and compiled the glossaries. Both students have also dedicated large amounts of time to filming, recording, and editing the audio and video recordings.

I am also indebted to Rebekah Binns for proofreading some of the early chapters, and for providing editorial assistance and valuable suggestions. Claremont Graduate University doctoral student Dorothea Kahena Viale was a valuable editor throughout this project, as well as a friend and supporter. CMC's Krysten Hartman spent long hours putting together vocabulary lists, obtaining copyright permissions, and composing drills for the conversational section. Melissa Carlson conducted helpful research for the book, and ably assisted with the final layout. Pomona College student Camille Cole composed conversation drafts for "Let's Speak Arabic," and Jake Scruggs helped to proofread the manuscript and offered useful editorial suggestions. Valuable advice and assistance were also provided by David Franzel, Matthew Wissa, and Yuri Pacheco. Brian Davidson provided technical support throughout the project, and he helped select the software and gave advice on technical applications and audiovisual devices. Joo Park carried on the task of putting together and finalizing the production of the audios and videos. Dr. Seth Lobis provided helpful advice.

I am deeply grateful to the many friends who agreed to be filmed for the book. My special heartfelt thanks go to Joumana Namour, Salma Chehabi, Mahmoud Harmoush, Majda Hourani, Simon Samoeil, Huda al-Jord, Dany Doueiri, Ayman Ramadan, Mohamad Saadoun, Abdulwahab Qadri, and Mike Masri, the Manager of Dahesh Heritage Bookstore in New York City. I would also like to extend my appreciation and sincere thanks to the Arab students in Claremont who offered to help by narrating texts or reading dialogues, including Pitzer College student Juman Nijim, CMC students Noor Haddad and Amer Shalan, Claremont Graduate University student Abdulaziz Abu Sag, and students Faisal Al-Salloum, Dhekra Toumi, and Hala Nazzal.

I am of course deeply grateful to the poets, authors, journalists, singers, and writers whose works are included in the textbook, and especially to those who personally provided me with excerpts of their work for the book. I deeply appreciate their contributions and permission to use their work in *Arabic for Life*. Professor Fayeq Oweis, a well-known calligrapher and artist based in San Francisco, made his extensive collection of calligraphy works available to me, and he also designed the title of the book. I offer him my heartfelt thanks for allowing me to utilize his exquisite work throughout *Arabic for Life*.

I am very grateful to Dr. Abdul Latif Kanoo, founder and chairman of Bahrain's Beit Al Qur`an, for granting permission to use the beautiful image on the cover of the textbook. A special thanks goes to Ms. Hind al-Harithi, head librarian of Beit Al Qur`an in Bahrain, for her continous help and support.

My wife, Aleta Wenger, has been a great supporter throughout the project. She proofread the entire manuscript, corrected mistakes, and provided advice and valuable editorial assistance. To my children, Marguerite, Tariq, and Jawad Frangieh, I am indebted to them for putting up with the endless hours I spent on the book, and for their good humor and kindhearted advice.

I would also like to thank Professor Devin Stewart of Emory University and Professor Walid Harmarneh of Swarthmore College for thoroughly reviewing the manuscript and for making excellent suggestions. They have my deepest appreciation for their valuable contributions to this textbook.

At Yale University Press, this project was met with great enthusiasm. I particularly appreciate the hard work of Tim Shea, Mary Jane Peluso, Ann-Marie Imbornoni, Elise Panza, Debra Morris Smith, Ashley Lago, and Aldo Cupo, along with the entire staff of Yale University Press. This book would not have come to fruition without their kind help and support. To all those mentioned above, I offer my salutations, gratitude, and love. Any shortcomings in this work are my responsibility alone.

Introduction
مقدمـــة

The goal of *Arabic for Life* is for the beginning student to learn to read, write, speak, and comprehend Arabic, and to learn about Arab culture and society. The book begins with an extensive introduction to all of the letters and sounds of the Arabic alphabet. The phonological system of the Arabic language is covered comprehensively, including reading and writing all consonants and vowels, and learning their distinct function in words and sentences. Drills and exercises are included after each individual letter of the Arabic alphabet to provide students with needed practice and repetition, and additional practice audios are contained on the accompanying DVD. The vocabulary words, phrases, and sentences are vocalized, and vocabulary terms and idioms are included on the DVD.

Qur'anic scripts, several different calligraphy styles, prose style scripts, and handwritten personal letters from well-known Arab literary figures, are included to familiarize the students with the various styles and scripts of Arabic writing. *Arabic for Life* contains numerous excerpts, texts, and examples from the works of Arab intellectuals, authors, poets, and educators. These examples will provide the students with insights into Arab history, society, culture, and traditions. The book encourages active student involvement in the language through repetition, oral communication, and actively reading and reciting texts.

Through a direct and comprehensive style of instruction, students using this textbook will find both technical and language-specific explanations, coupled with examples of Arab culture, in order to elucidate the true source of the language. Each chapter includes a coherent structure for the lesson plan, in which vocabulary, words, and expressions are introduced as the lesson's foundation. This foundational information is followed by the basic text, a short piece focused on an important aspect of the Arab World. After reviewing key vocabulary and expressions, the student examines the usage in order to have a more concrete understanding of how words and expressions are used in the language. The texts were selected or written to provide the student with varied perspectives from the Arab World.

Each lesson includes a grammar section that explains specific aspects of the Arabic language and its grammar. By focusing on a few inter-related elements of Arabic grammar in each lesson, there is a more gradual, retainable comprehension. Each lesson provides additional grammatical instruction, and the student learns Arabic in a way that ensures full comprehension. The comprehension text is a more nuanced type of basic text, and it reinforces the vocabulary included in the lesson's grammar section. In this way, the student encounters additional examples of the real usage of learned principles of the Arabic language. The comprehension text also serves to enhance the student's knowledge about the Arab World with excerpts and examples from Arab society, history, traditions, and culture.

Each lesson contains a short component called "Let's Speak Arabic" to encourage students to learn to converse in Arabic early in their study of the language. Each chapter includes exercises to read aloud that will help the students with their basic conversation skills. Straightforward topics like the weather, family, and types of food, are presented early in the book to promote conversation. Each lesson ends with a section on Arab culture that features an audiovisual recording of a poem, song, speech, or text.

Arabic for Life presents vocabulary, idioms, grammatical rules, and cultural perspectives. The book includes approximately fifteen hundred vocabulary words presented along with the English meanings that fit precisely within the context of the text. Each lesson includes drills to reinforce what is taught, and each text reinforces what is taught while presenting a snapshot of the Arab World. The book also provides the necessary background in Arabic grammar.

The final chapter of the book, Lesson Twenty-One, presents twenty readings in Arabic poetry and prose, literature and thought; eighteen selections are from the modern period and two are from the classical period. The first twenty lessons in the book are structured to prepare students to be able to read, comprehend, and appreciate the varied selections in the final lesson.

For the student's convenience, the book includes two glossaries, English-Arabic, and Arabic-English. The Appendix contains several vocabulary lists, verb and grammar charts, and other resources that will be helpful to students. The Appendix also includes hand-written letters by Arab intellectuals, and a few letters from students of Arabic.

It is my sincere hope that this book will help students to enjoy studying the Arabic language, and to better understand and appreciate Arab culture and society.

This book was originally accompanied by a DVD.

The video and audio files are now available online at yalebooks.com/arabicforlife.

Section One
القسم الأول

Sounds and Letters of the Arabic Language

حروف اللغة العربية وأصواتها

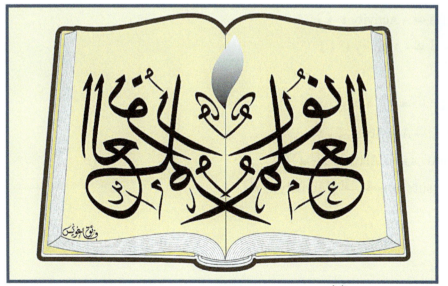

Arabic calligraphy: Knowledge is light - العلم نور

Section One
Sounds and Letters of the Arabic Language
Contents

Unit Five - الوحدة الخامسة

   I.   The Letter ه - Activity 1 🎧

   II.   Taa` Marbouta (ة) التاء المربوطة - Activity 1 🎧

   III.   Letters ع غ - Activity 1 – 3 🎧

Unit Six - الوحدة السادسة

   I.   Letters ص ض - Activity 1 – 2 🎧

   II.   Letters ط ظ - Activity 1 – 4 🎧

   III.   Emphatic Letters (ص ض ط ظ)

Unit Seven - الوحدة السابعة

   I.   Double Consonants (ـّ) الشَّدّة - Activity 1 – 2 🎧

   II.   Hamza (ء) الهمزة - Activity 1 – 2 🎧

   III.   Madda (آ) المـدّة - Activity 1 🎧

   IV.   Dagger Alif الألف القصيرة

   V.   Hamzat al-Wasl or Wasla همزة الوصل أو الوصلة - Activity 1 🎧

Unit Eight - الوحدة الثامنة

   I.   The Definite Article (الـ) أداة التعريف

   II.   Moon Letters الحروف القمريَّة - Activity 1 🎧

   III.   Sun Letters الحروف الشَّمسيَّة - Activity 1 🎧

Unit Nine - الوحدة التاسعة

   I.   Arabic Script and Calligraphy 💿

   II.   Printed Styles of Arabic Script

   III.   Handwriting Samples

   IV.   Arabic Calligraphy

   V.   Reading Practice

Unit One
الوحدة الأولى

This section introduces the Arabic sounds, letters, and scripts and covers the basic phonological system of the Arabic language.

Arabic has twenty-eight characters: Twenty-five are consonants and three are long vowels. Arabic also has several symbols, signs written above or below the letters, that affect pronunciation and grammatical structures.

Arabic is written from right to left, and there are no capital letters. Below is a chart of the Arabic alphabet. Look at it as a whole, and listen to the accompanying audio of the alphabet being read. After you listen to the alphabet several times, click on the disk to watch and listen to a student sing the alphabet.

I. The Arabic Alphabet
الحروف الهجائية

خ	ح	ج	ث	ت	ب	ا
ص	ش	س	ز	ر	ذ	د
ق	ف	غ	ع	ظ	ط	ض
ي	و	ه	ن	م	ل	ك

Now, look at the chart below, the name of each letter, and the way each letter is written. Letters are written in four positions: initial, medial, final position (connected), and final position (unconnected).

Letters are connected in both printed and handwritten forms. They are joined by connecting strokes with the preceding and/or following letters.

When we begin a word in Arabic we write the first letter in initial form and the last letter in final form. Any letters between them appear in medial form. Medial and final letters may or may not be connected to the letter preceding them, depending on whether the preceding letter is a connector. There are six letters ا د ذ ر ز و that are not connectors; they do not connect on the the left side. If the final letter is not connected, then the letter is written in its independent isolated form.

The Arabic Alphabet in Its Traditional Order
الحروف الهجائية

Final		Medial	Initial	Name of Letter	Independent
Unconnected	Connected				
ا	ـا	ـا	ا	ألف	ا
ب	ـب	ـبـ	بـ	باء	ب
ت	ـت	ـتـ	تـ	تاء	ت
ث	ـث	ـثـ	ثـ	ثاء	ث
ج	ـج	ـجـ	جـ	جيم	ج
ح	ـح	ـحـ	حـ	حاء	ح
خ	ـخ	ـخـ	خـ	خاء	خ
د	ـد	ـد	د	دال	د
ذ	ـذ	ـذ	ذ	ذال	ذ
ر	ـر	ـر	ر	راء	ر
ز	ـز	ـز	ز	زاي	ز
س	ـس	ـسـ	سـ	سين	س
ش	ـش	ـشـ	شـ	شين	ش
ص	ـص	ـصـ	صـ	صاد	ص
ض	ـض	ـضـ	ضـ	ضاد	ض
ط	ـط	ـطـ	طـ	طاء	ط
ظ	ـظ	ـظـ	ظـ	ظاء	ظ
ع	ـع	ـعـ	عـ	عين	ع
غ	ـغ	ـغـ	غـ	غين	غ
ف	ـف	ـفـ	فـ	فاء	ف
ق	ـق	ـقـ	قـ	قاف	ق
ك	ـك	ـكـ	كـ	كاف	ك
ل	ـل	ـلـ	لـ	لام	ل
م	ـم	ـمـ	مـ	ميم	م
ن	ـن	ـنـ	نـ	نون	ن
ه	ـه	ـهـ	هـ	هاء	ه
و	ـو	ـو	و	واو	و
ي	ـي	ـيـ	يـ	ياء	ي

II. Letters

Calligraphic image of the letter ب

The letter ب is similar to the English letter <u>b</u> in pronunciation, as in 'bat.'

This is how the letter ب is written by hand:

Calligraphic image of the letter ت

The letter ت is similar to the English <u>t</u> in pronunciation, as in 'tab.'

This is how the letter ت is written by hand:

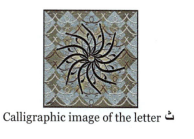

Calligraphic image of the letter ث

The letter ث is pronounced like the English <u>th,</u> as in 'thunder.'

ث	ـث	ـثـ	ثـ

This is how the letter ث is written by hand:

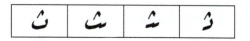

These three letters have the same shape in all positions: initial, medial, and final. They differ in the number of dots and the placement of these dots. The ب has one dot below, the ت has two dots above it, and the ث has three dots above. In handwritten form, any two dots can run together to form a short line and any three dots can run together to form a triangle, as you see in the examples above.

These letters are connectors, which means they connect on both sides with other letters.

Look at the shapes and examples of the letters. Read aloud.

ث	
Example	Shape
ثاب	ثـ
بثاب	ـثـ
بث	ـث
باث	ث

ت	
Example	Shape
تاب	تـ
بتاب	ـتـ
بت	ـت
تات	ت

ب	
Example	Shape
باب	بـ
بباب	ـبـ
بب	ـب
باب	ب

Compare letters and words in their printed and handwritten forms.

ثاب	تاب	باب	بث	بت	بب
ثاب	تاب	باب	بث	بت	بب

بايب	بباب	بتاب	بثاب	تات	باث
بابب	بباب	بتاب	بثاب	تات	باث

III. The Long Vowels ا و ي

There are three long vowels: the ا and و and ي. Keep in mind, the و and the ي can be used as both vowels and consonants.

Calligraphic image of the letter ا

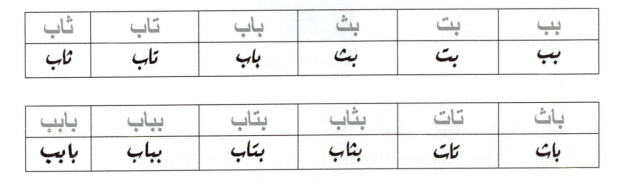

The alif (ا) is the first character in the Arabic alphabet. It is a long vowel and sounds like a long <u>aa</u>, as in 'cat.' The ا is also the bearer of the hamza (ء), as in أ and إ (we will learn more on this later). The long vowel alif (ا), which is pronounced as a long <u>aa</u>, is written from top to bottom.

ا	ـا	ـا	ا

This is how the letter ا is handwritten:

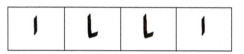

ا	ـا	ـا	ا

Calligraphic image of the letter و

و و و و و و و و و و و و و و و و و و و و

The و is a long vowel. It is similar to the English pronunciation oo as in 'boot.'

و	ـو	ـو	و

This is how the letter و is handwritten:

و	ـو	ـو	و

Calligraphic image of the letter ي

ي ي ي ي ي ي ي ي ي ي ي

The ي is a long vowel. It sounds like ee and is similar in pronunciation to the English word 'street.'

This is how the letter ي is handwritten:

Again, to repeat, the ا sounds like <u>aa</u>, the و sounds like <u>oo</u>, and the ي sounds like <u>ee</u>.

These three vowels have different abilities to connect with other letters. The ي is a connector that connects on both sides, but the vowels ا and و are not connectors (they do not connect on the left side). When they fall in the middle of the word, the letter after the ا or و must be written in the initial position.

Look at the shapes and examples of the vowels (ا و ي). Read aloud.

ي	
Example	Shape
ياب	يـ
بياب	ـيـ
بيبي	ـي
بودي	ي

و	
Example	Shape
واب	و
بوت	ـو
بوبو	ـو
بودو	و

ا	
Example	Shape
اب	ا
بابب	ـا
ويبا	ـا
بيدا	ا

❖

Drill 1: Copy. Pronounce the letters and each word as you write.

بابيت	باب	بوبو	بيب	بابا	ب
_____	_____	_____	_____	_____	_____
توتا	تات	توتو	تيت	تاتا	ت
_____	_____	_____	_____	_____	_____
ثوتابا	ثاث	ثوثو	ثيث	ثاثا	ث
_____	_____	_____	_____	_____	_____

🎧 **Activity 1**: Read each word aloud then click, listen, and repeat.

بيب	بي	بوب	بو	باب	با
تيت	تي	توت	تو	تات	تا
ثيث	ثي	ثوث	ثو	ثاث	ثا

❖

🎧 **Activity 2**: Read each word aloud then click, listen, and repeat.

ثي	ثو	ثا
ثيثي	ثوثو	ثاثا
ثيث	ثوث	ثاث

تي	تو	تا
تيتي	توتو	تاتا
تيت	توت	تات

بي	بو	با
بيبي	بوبو	بابا
بيت	بوت	بات

❖

Drill 2: Copy the handwriting style below and read aloud as you write.

ويبا	بيبي	بوبو	ثاب	تات	باب
ــــــ	ــــــ	ــــــ	ــــــ	ــــــ	ــــــ
بوت	بثاب	بهاب	ياب	واب	اب
ــــــ	ــــــ	ــــــ	ــــــ	ــــــ	ــــــ

❖

Drill 3: Copy. Pronounce the letters and each word as you write.

باث	تات	ثاث	بوث	باب	ا
ــــــ	ــــــ	ــــــ	ــــــ	ــــــ	ــــــ
تابو	ثوب	توت	توتا	بوث	و
ــــــ	ــــــ	ــــــ	ــــــ	ــــــ	ــــــ

يابي	تيت	ثيثا	بيت يوت	ي
_____	_____	_____	_____	_____

❖

Drill 4: Copy the handwriting style below and read aloud as you write.

ويبا	بيبي	بوبو	بوت
_____	_____	_____	_____
تات	ياب	اب	بياب
_____	_____	_____	_____

IV. The Short Vowels: *fatha, damma, kasra*
الحركات: الفتحة والضمة والكسرة

In addition to the three long vowels (ي و ا), there are also three short vowels. These short vowels are not letters. They are signs placed above or below the letters. Their pronunciation is equal to half the long vowels' pronunciation. These short vowels are *fatha* (‑), *damma* (‑), and *kasra* (‑). Each short vowel corresponds to a long vowel: *fatha* corresponds to الألف, *damma* corresponds to الواو, and *kasra* corresponds to الياء.

Fatha - الفتحة

The *fatha* (ـَ) is a sign placed above a letter to represent the short vowel <u>a</u>. The combination of the letter ب and the *fatha* sign (ـَ) above it is pronounced بَ 'ba.' The long vowel *alif* (ا) represents the long vowel <u>aa</u>. Thus, the combination of the letter ب and the long vowel ا is pronounced بَا 'baa.'

❖

🎧   **Activity 1:** Read each word aloud then click, listen, and repeat.

تَاتَ	تَا	تَ	بَابَ	بَا	بَ
وَاوَ	وَا	وَ	ثَاثَ	ثَا	ثَ
بابو	بابا	باب	واوو	واوي	واوا

❖

Drill 1: Copy.

بَا	ثَ	تَ	بَ
_____	_____	_____	_____
ثِيَبَ	بَوَتَ	يَابَ	يَا
_____	_____	_____	_____

❖

Damma - الضمة

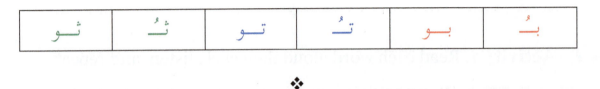

The *damma* (ُ) is a sign placed over a letter to represent the short vowel <u>u</u>. The combination of the letter ب plus the *damma* sign (ُ) is pronounced بُ 'bu,' as in 'put.' The long vowel و represents the long vowel <u>uu</u>. Thus, the combination of the letter ب plus the long vowel و is pronounced بو 'buu' as in 'boot.'

ثُو	ثُ	تو	تُ	بو	بُ

❖

🎧 **Activity 2**: Read each word aloud then click, listen, and repeat.

بُوبُو	بُوبُ	بو	بُ
تُوتُو	تُوتُ	تو	تُ
ثُوثُو	ثُوثُ	ثو	ثُ
يُوبُو	يُوبُ	يُو	يُ

❖

Drill 2: Copy.

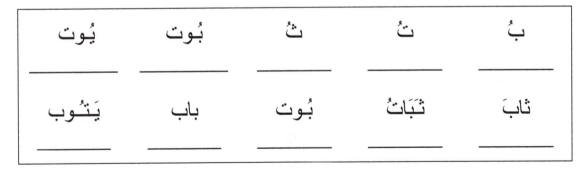

يُوت	بُوت	ثُ	تُ	بُ
____	____	____	____	____
يَتُوب	باب	بُوت	ثَبَاتُ	ثابَ
____	____	____	____	____

❖

Kasra - الكسرة

The *kasra* (ِ) is a sign placed below a letter to represent the short vowel i. The combination of the letter ب and the *kasra* sign (ِ) is pronounced 'bi' as in 'bit.' The long vowel ي represents the long vowel ee. Thus, the combination of the letter ب and the long vowel ي is pronounced بِي 'bee' as in 'bead.'

ثِي	ثِـ	تِي	تِـ	بِـي	بِـ

🎧 **Activity 3**: Read each word aloud then click, listen, and repeat.

وي	وِ	ثِي	ثِـ	تِي	تِـ	بي	بِ
ثِيثِي	بيتي	وابُ	واوي	بَابِـي	تـوت	يَـاثِي	ياتِي

❖

Drill 3: Copy.

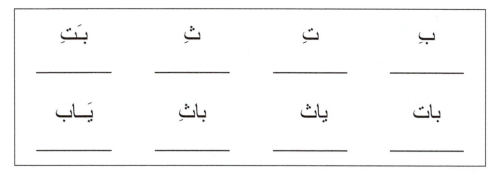

بَتِ	ثِ	تِ	بِ
___	___	___	___
يَـاب	باثِ	ياث	بات
___	___	___	___

V. Sukuun السكُون

Sukuun (سكون) means 'silence.' It is a sign placed above a letter to indicate the absence of any vowel. For example the letter ب sounds 'ba' with *fatha*, 'bu' with *damma*, and 'bi' with *kasra*. But with sukuun, the 'b' has no vowels.

Drill 1: See the short vowels and sukuun. Repeat out loud.

وَ	ثَ	تَ	بَ	ـَ	فَتْحَة
وُ	ثُ	تُ	بُ	ـُ	ضَمَّة
وِ	ثِ	تِ	بِ	ـِ	كَسْرَة
وْ	ثْ	تْ	بْ	ـْ	سُكُون

❖

Drill 2: Copy and read aloud as you write.

بُوتْ	ثْ	تْ	بْ
_____	_____	_____	_____
بُوتُ	بَثاثْ	ثَبَاتْ	يَاوِي
_____	_____	_____	_____

❖

Drill 3: Copy the handwriting style below and read aloud as you write.

بِياب	بثاب	ثاب	بثاب
_____	_____	_____	_____

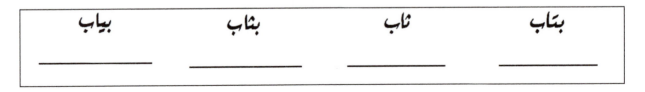

بودو	ثاب	تاب	بوت
_____	_____	_____	_____

❖

Drill 4: Join the letters into words. Include the vowels.

6- بَ + يْ + ت =	1- بُ + ثْ + و + ثْ =
7- تَ + ا + بَ =	2- تُ + و + تُ =
8- بَ + ا + بُ =	3- ثَ + وْ + بِ + ي =
9- وَ + ا + وِ + ي =	4- ثَ + ا + بِ + تُ =
10- ب + ا + ب + ي =	5- بُ + يُ + و + تْ =

❖

🎧 **Activity 1**: Read each word aloud then click, listen, and repeat.

بَابَا	بَابُو	بَابِي	بَابُ	بَيْتُ	بُوتْ	بَاتْ
ثَابِتُ	بَاتُ	ثُبُوت	واثي	باوي	بَوابي	بُيُوتِي
ثَابَ	ثَوْبِي	ثَوْبِ	ثَوْبَ	ثَوْبُ	ثِيَابْ	ثَوَابْ

الحُب - Love

Unit Two
الـوحدة الثانية

I. Letters د ذ

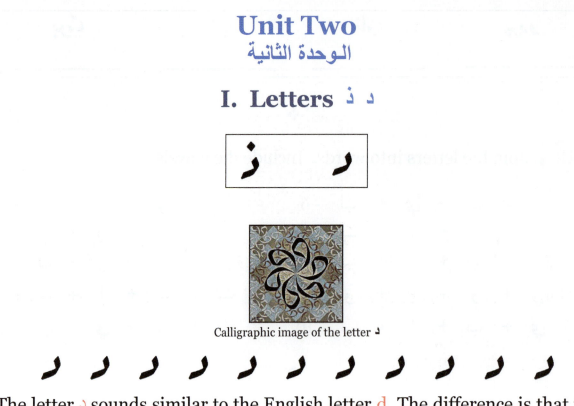

Calligraphic image of the letter د

The letter د sounds similar to the English letter <u>d</u>. The difference is that the tip of the tongue touches the upper teeth to pronounce properly.

This is how the handwritten letter looks:

❖

Drill 1: Copy and read aloud as you write. Read aloud.

داد	دِ	دُ	دَ	ذْ
ــــــــــ	ــــــــــ	ــــــــــ	ــــــــــ	ــــــــــ
داثْ	دَيْبَ	بَيْدَ	بُودُ	ديد
ــــــــــ	ــــــــــ	ــــــــــ	ــــــــــ	ــــــــــ

بَدَوَ	دوبا	دودو	دُوتُ	ديبا
_____	_____	_____	_____	_____

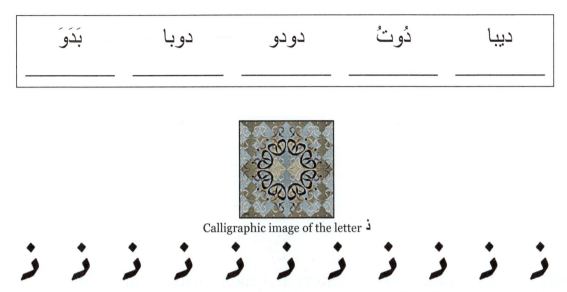

Calligraphic image of the letter ذ

The letter ذ represents the same sound of the voiced English <u>th</u>, as in 'this.'

Both letters د and ذ are not connectors (they do not connect on the left side). Therefore, when they are in a middle position the letter that follows must be in the initial position.

Both letters are similar in writing and have the same shape. The only difference between them is the dot on the top of the letter ذ.

This is how the handwritten ذ looks:

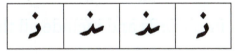

Look at the shapes and examples of letters د and ذ. Read aloud.

ذ	
Example	Shape
ذاب	ذ
بـذود	ـذ
بيذ	ـذ
باذ	ذ

د	
Example	Shape
داب	د
بـُدود	ـد
بيد	ـد
باد	د

19

🎧   **Activity 1**: Read each word aloud then click, listen, and repeat.

ديدِ	دودُ	دادَ	دِ	دُ	دَ
دادي	دُوبا	دَوْدُ	ديدي	دودو	دادا

ذاذي	ذوذ	ذاذ	ذِ	ذُ	ذَ
ذي	ذو	ذُبابُ	ذيذي	ذوذو	ذاذا

❖

Drill 2: Copy. Pronounce the letters and each word as you write.

بُذ	بَذ	ذو	ذا	ذِي
____	____	____	____	____
يَذ	يَذِ	يَاذِ	باذُ	ذيذي
____	____	____	____	____
دوذي	ذاذا	يَذوي	وَدادُ	بَوادِي
____	____	____	____	____

❖

Drill 3: Join the letters into words and include all the vowels.

6- د + ي + د + ي =   1- دَ + ا + و + دُ =

7- ذ + ا + بَ =   2- دُ + و + د =

8- بَ + ا + دَ =   3- ذ + و + ب =

9- وَ + ا + دِ + ي =   4- ذُ + بَ + ا + ب =

10- ب + ا + ب + ا =   5- ب + ي + د =

❖

Drill 4: Copy the following handwritten words. Read aloud as you write.

بيدا	بودي	بُدود	بذوذ
ــــــــــ	ــــــــــ	ــــــــــ	ــــــــــ
بودو	بيذ	ذاب	داب
ــــــــــ	ــــــــــ	ــــــــــ	ــــــــــ

II. Letters ر ز

Calligraphic image of the letter ر

The Arabic consonant ر is not like the English <u>r</u>. It is produced by a quick succession of several flaps with the tip of the tongue turned back. It is similar in pronunciation to the Spanish 'r' as in '*caro*' (expensive).

This is how the handwritten ر looks:

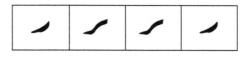

Drill 1: Copy and read aloud as you write.

رُ	رَ	رُ	ر	رار
___	___	___	___	___
رير	رَوْرُ	رَيَبَ	رورو	رابا
___	___	___	___	___

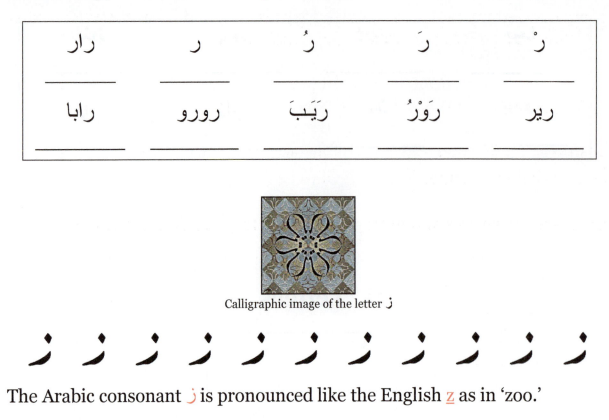

Calligraphic image of the letter ز

ز ز ز ز ز ز ز ز ز ز ز

The Arabic consonant ز is pronounced like the English z as in 'zoo.'

ز	ـز	ـزـ	زـ

This is how the handwritten ز looks:

ز	ـز	ـزـ	زـ

Drill 2: Copy and read each word aloud.

زَيْد	زير	زو	زا	زي
___	___	___	___	___
باز	زيز	زُرْ	زور	زازا
___	___	___	___	___

Both letters ر and ز do not connect on the left side. They are like the non-connector letters ا ذ د and و; when they are in a middle position they must be followed by a letter written in the initial position.

Both ر and ز are similar in writing and have the same shape. The only difference between the two letters is the dot on top of ز.

While the د and ذ turn down and finish along the line, the tail of the letters ر and ز is below the line.

Compare the shapes and examples of the letters ر and ز. Read aloud.

ز	
Example	Shape
زاب	ز
بُزوز	ـز
بيز	ـز
باز	ز

ر	
Example	Shape
راب	ر
بُرور	ـر
بير	ـر
بار	ر

❖

🎧 **Activity 1**: Read each word aloud then click, listen, and repeat.

رير	رور	رار	رِ	رُ	رَ
راري	رُوبا	رَوْرُ	ريري	رورو	رارا

زازي	زوز	زاز	زِ	زُ	زَ
زي	زو	زُوربا	زيزي	زوزو	زازا

❖

Drill 3: Join the letters into words and include all vowels.

6- رَ + ا + زَ =	1- ر + ا + ر =
7- ذ + ا + بَ =	2- ز + و + ر =
8- ز + ا + دَ =	3- زَ + وْ + ر =
9- ز + ا + ز =	4- بَ + ا + ز =
10- ز + ا + ت =	5- ز + ي + ز =

❖

Drill 4: Copy the handwriting style below and read aloud as you write.

بيز	بُزوز	برور	زاب	راب
_____	_____	_____	_____	_____
بار	بيد	بذوذ	بُدود	بيذ
_____	_____	_____	_____	_____

III. Letters ج ح خ

خ ح ج

Calligraphic image of the letter ج

The letter ج is pronounced like the English letter 'j' as in 'judge.' However, there is a slight variation in the pronunciation. The pronunciation of the letter ج is found in a mix of the English letters 'j' as in 'judge,' 's' as in 'pleasure,' and 'z' as in 'azure.' In most parts of Egypt ج is pronounced 'g' as in 'girl.'

See how the letter is handwritten:

Drill 1: Copy and read each word aloud.

داجي	جورج	جو	جاري	جا
_____	_____	_____	_____	_____

Calligraphic image of the letter ح

The letter ح has no equivalent in English. It is a voiceless consonant, in which the vocal cords do not vibrate. The <u>h</u> in English is closest in sound to the letter ح. The ح is referred by students as the 'big h' because it is similar to the letter 'h' but starts further back in the throat.

25

See how the letter is handwritten:

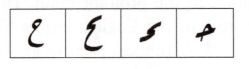

❖

Drill 2: Copy.

حا	حاد	حو	حوت	داحي
_____	_____	_____	_____	_____

Calligraphic image of the letter خ

The letter خ has no equivalent in English. It is similar to the German 'ch' as in 'Bach.' It is formed in the uvula and the back of the tongue.

خ	خ	خ	خ

See how the letter is handwritten:

خ	خ	خ	خ

Drill 3: Copy.

خا	خاخ	خو	خور	داخي
_____	_____	_____	_____	_____

Compare the shapes and examples of the letters خ ح and ج.

خ	
Example	Shape
خار	خـ
بخـر	ـخـ
ديـخ	ـخ
داخ	ـخ

ح	
Example	Shape
حار	حـ
بحـر	ـحـ
ديج	ـح
داح	ـح

ج	
Example	Shape
جار	جـ
بجـر	ـجـ
ديج	ـج
جاج	ـج

❖

🎧 **Activity 1:** Read each word aloud then click, listen, and repeat.

جورج	جاجو	بوج	جوب	جاب	جا
بَحْر	حاحي	توح	حوت	حات	حا
خوري	خيخي	ثوخ	خوث	خاث	خا

❖

Drill 4: Join the letters into words and include all vowels.

6- خُ + و + ر + ي =   1- جَ + ا + ر + ي =
7- جَ + حَ + ا + ب =   2- جُ + و + ر + ج =
8- حَ + رَ + ثَ =   3- حُ + و + ت =
9- خَ + يْ + رُ =   4- خَ + بِ + ي + ر =
10- رَ + ا + حَ =   5- دَ + جَ + ا + ج =

❖

27

Drill 5: Copy the handwriting style below and read aloud as you write.

بجبر	بجر	خار	حار	جار
ديج	ديج	داخ	داح	جاج

Passion - محبة

Unit Three
الوحدة الثالثة

I. Letters ش س

Calligraphic image of the letter س

The letter س is pronounced the same as the letter s in English, as in 'so' and 'sit.'

ـسـ	ـس	س

See how the letter is handwritten:

ـ	ـ	س	ـس

❖

Drill 1: Copy.

سْ	سَ	سُ	سِ س	ساس
_____	_____	_____	_____	_____
سوس	سي	سُور	سيري	راس
_____	_____	_____	_____	_____

Calligraphic image of the letter ش

ش ش ش ش ش ش ش ش ش

The letter ش is pronounced the same as <u>sh</u> in English, as in 'she' and 'rush.'

See how the letter is handwritten:

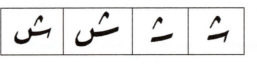

❖

Drill 2: Copy.

شادي	بَاشِي	شُ	شَ	شْ
شاذ	شَوَاذ	شوت	شوش	شاش
شاي	رُشْد	رَشاد	شارد	شُرْب

Look at the printed letters. Notice that س and ش have the same shape. The only difference is that ش has three dots above it, while the س has no dots. And both have three 'teeth' at the beginning of the letter. Their last part is rounded and is below the line. As the handwriting example shows, both س and ش are handwritten with a single, smooth line instead of the three 'teeth' of the printed version.

30

Compare the shapes and examples of the letters س and ش. Read aloud.

<table>
<tr><td colspan="2" align="center">ش</td></tr>
<tr><td>Example</td><td>Shape</td></tr>
<tr><td>شاب</td><td>شـ</td></tr>
<tr><td>يَشيب</td><td>ـشـ</td></tr>
<tr><td>بَش</td><td>ـش</td></tr>
<tr><td>راش</td><td>ش</td></tr>
</table>

<table>
<tr><td colspan="2" align="center">س</td></tr>
<tr><td>Example</td><td>Shape</td></tr>
<tr><td>سار</td><td>سـ</td></tr>
<tr><td>يَسير</td><td>ـسـ</td></tr>
<tr><td>بَس</td><td>ـس</td></tr>
<tr><td>راس</td><td>س</td></tr>
</table>

❖

Drill 3: Repeat out loud.

شَ	شُ	شِ
شاش	شوش	شيش
شادي	شوشو	شيراز

سَ	سُ	سِ
ساس	سوس	سيس
دَرَسَ	دَرْسٌ	دارسٌ

❖

Drill 4: Join the letters into words and include all vowels.

1 - شَ + يْ + خ =
2 - حَ + سَ + ا + ب =
3 - وَ + سْ + وَ + سَ =
4 - دُ + رُ + و + س =
5 - شَ + ا + ب =

6 - سَ + ا + رَ + ت =
7 - شَ + ا + و + ي =
8 - بَ + شَ + ر =
9 - سَ + بَ + ر =
10 - شُ + رُ + و + ش =

❖

Drill 5: Copy the handwriting style below and read aloud as you write.

بَس	يَسير	راس	سار
_____	_____	_____	_____
بش	يشيب	شاب	راش
_____	_____	_____	_____

II. Letters ف ق

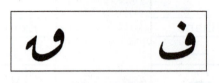

Calligraphic image of the letter ف

The letter ف is the same as the sound of the letter f in English, as in 'fan.'

The letter in handwritten form:

ف	ـف	ـفـ	فـ

❖

Drill 1: Copy.

فَ	فُ	فِ	فْ	فار
_____	_____	_____	_____	_____
فور	ريف	تَرَف	رُفوف	فراري
_____	_____	_____	_____	_____

Calligraphic image of the letter ق

The letter ق is an emphatic letter pronounced similar to the sound of the letter c , as in 'cot' (but pronounced further back in the throat). Your teacher will help you with the correct pronunciation.

ق	ﻖ	ﻘ	ﻗ

Compare the printed form above with this handwritten form:

❖

Drill 2: Copy.

قور	قاف	قُ	قَ	قْ
_____	_____	_____	_____	_____
شارق	دفيق	بُروق	قِرْد	وَرَق
_____	_____	_____	_____	_____

Both letters connect on both sides. ف has one dot above it and the ق has two dots above it (the dots are next to each other).

The shape of the ف and ق are similar in their initial and medial positions but different in their final connected and independent positions. While the ف is written on the line in all positions, the ق descends below the line in its final connected and independent positions.

Compare the shapes and examples of the letters ف and ق. Read aloud.

ق	
Example	Shape
قَاد	قـ
يَقـود	ـقـ
ريق	ـق
فاروق	ق

ف	
Example	Shape
فَاد	فـ
يَفـور	ـفـ
ريف	ـف
زفاف	ـف

❖

🎧 **Activity 1:** Read each word aloud then click, listen, and repeat.

قِ	قُ	قَ
شَفيف	شَوْق	قاس
دقيق	رفيف	رفيق
فَقير	رقيق	ورَق

فِ	فُ	فَ
فيق	فوق	فاق
بَرْق	فريق	قريب
بَقَر	يَقود	وافَقَ

❖

Drill 3: Join the letters into words and include all vowels.

6- سَ + فِ + ي + ر =   1- ق + ر + ي + ب =
7- ر + فَ + ي + د =   2- بَ + ر + ي + ق =
8- فَ + ر + ي + ق =   3- وَ + ق + و + د =
9- فُ + سُ + و + ر =   4- وُ + فُ + و + د =
10- قُ + رُ + و + د =   5- ز + ف + ا + ف =

❖

Drill 4: Copy the handwriting style below and read aloud as you write.

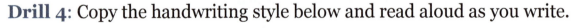

يَقود	يفور	قاد	فاد
_____	_____	_____	_____
زفاف	فاروق	ريف	ريق
_____	_____	_____	_____

III. Letters ك ل

Calligraphic image of the letter ك

The letter ك in Arabic is similar to the <u>k</u> in English, as in 'kind.' The ك connects on both sides. When in the initial and medial positions, the ك takes the shape ﻛ as shown below.

كـ	ـكـ	ـكـ	كـ

Compare the printed ك with this handwritten form:

ك	ـكـ	ـكـ	كـ

❖

Drill 1: Copy.

كال	كاف	كِ	كُ	كَ
ـــــــــ	ـــــــــ	ـــــــــ	ـــــــــ	ـــــــــ

سواك	رفيق	كوكا	كفيف	كيل
_____	_____	_____	_____	_____

Calligraphic image of the letter ل

ل ل ل ل ل ل ل ل ل ل ل ل ل

The letter ل is essentially the English l, as in 'lamb.' The ل can change slightly in pronunciation depending upon its use. It becomes semi-emphatic when it occurs in the word الله 'God' and when it is followed or preceded by the emphatic consonants (ص ض ط ظ).

As you see in both the printed and written forms the ل is written above the line, but it curves downward below the line leftward then again upward to meet a point on the line.

ل	ـل	ـلـ	ـل

Compare the printed form of letter ل with this handwritten form:

ل	ـل	ـلـ	ـل

❖

Drill 2: Copy

لولو	كيل	لْ	لُ	لَ
_____	_____	_____	_____	_____

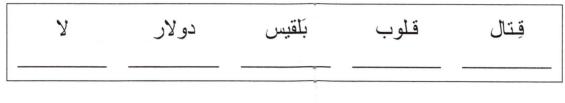

لا	دولار	بَلقيس	قلوب	قِتال
_____	_____	_____	_____	_____

❖

Compare the shapes and examples of the letters ك and ل. Read aloud.

ل	
Example	Shape
لبيب	ـل
قلب	ـلـ
جليل	لـ
جداول	ل

ك	
Example	Shape
كتاب	كـ
يكـاد	ـكـ
ركيك	ـك
شُكوك	ك

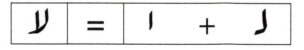

When ل is followed by ا, it is printed لا:

لا	=	ا	+	ـل

In handwritten form, the لا is written لا:

لا	=	ا	+	ل

If ل is connected with a preceding letter, it is printed ـلا:

بلاغ	ـلا	=	ا	+	ـلـ

In handwritten form, the ـلا is written: ـلا as in بلاغ

❖

37

🎧 **Activity 1:** Read each word aloud then click, listen, and repeat.

كَ	كُ	كِ
باك	كابول	كبير
كُروش	بُكور	بليل
وابِل	يَلوذ	كابوس

لَ	لُ	لِ
قال	قيل	حَلال
سليب	سِلال	سُلوك
كلب	فول	فيـل

❖

Drill 3: Join the letters into words and include all vowels.

1 - قَ + ا + لَ =

2 - ج + د + ا + ل =

3 - و + ف + ا + ق =

4 - رَ + ف + ي + ق =

5 - لَ + يْ + ل =

6 - ق + ا + لَ + ت =

7 - فَ + ر + ي + د =

8 - سَ + كَ + ا + د =

9 - فُ + لْ + فُ + لْ =

10 - رَ + وْ + نَ + ق =

❖

Drill 4: Copy the handwriting style below and read aloud as you write.

كتاب	قلب	يكاد	لبيب
_____	_____	_____	_____
ركيك	شُكوك	جداول	جليل
_____	_____	_____	_____

❖

Unit Four
الوحدة الرابعة

I. Letters م ن

Calligraphic image of the letter م

The letter م is pronounced like the letter <u>m</u> in English, as in 'mate.' This letter has a small loop written on the line with its tail drawn down below the line. The loop in the initial position can be written as a loop from the top or bottom. The م in medial position comes from the top to loop counter-clockwise. The loop of the final connected م also comes from the top to be drawn counterclockwise. But the loop of the final unconnected form begins from the bottom and is drawn clockwise.

Compare the printed form of letter م with this handwritten form:

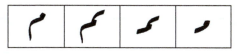

Drill 1: Copy.

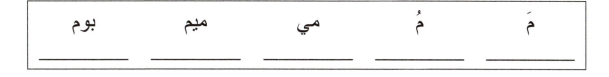

39

سَمَر	سُموم	لكمْ	لمْ	ماما
ـــــــــ	ـــــــــ	ـــــــــ	ـــــــــ	ـــــــــ

Calligraphic image of the letter ن

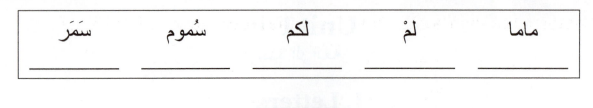

The letter ن is pronounced like the letter <u>n</u> in English, as in 'no.' The ن is written partly below the line. The letter starts above the line but its tail goes below.

Compare the printed form of letter ن with this handwritten form:

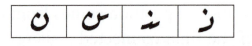

❖

Drill 2: Copy.

لـنا	نون	ن	نُ	نَ
ـــــــــ	ـــــــــ	ـــــــــ	ـــــــــ	ـــــــــ
نانسي	لن	تونس	ناس	نبيل
ـــــــــ	ـــــــــ	ـــــــــ	ـــــــــ	ـــــــــ

❖

Compare the shapes and examples of the letters م and ن. Read aloud.

ن	
Example	Shape
نور	ـنـ
جُنون	ـنـ
تنوين	ـن
زَيْتون	ن

م	
Example	Shape
مات	مـ
جميل	ـمـ
ريم	ـم
رام	م

❖

🎧 **Activity 1:** Read each word aloud then click, listen, and repeat.

نِ	نُ	نَ
فنون	تين	نال
بيان	سنين	بنات
مُبين	رنين	نون

مِ	مُ	مَ
ميـل	ميم	دام
مريم	سمير	كُروم
سليم	نِيام	قلم

❖

Drill 3: Join the letters into words and include all vowels.

6 - جُ + م + ا + ن =	1 - سَ + ا + مِ + ر =
7 - مُ + ن + ي + ر =	2 - مُ + ب + ي + ن =
8 - كَ + ن + ا + ن =	3 - نْ + ذِ + ر =
9 - حُ + سَ + ا + م =	4 - ح + رَ + ي + م =
10 - حَ + ن + ا + ن =	5 - ل + ا + مَ + س =

❖

Drill 4: Copy the handwriting style below and read aloud as you write.

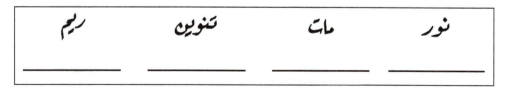

ريم   تنوين   مات   نور

_____ _____ _____ _____

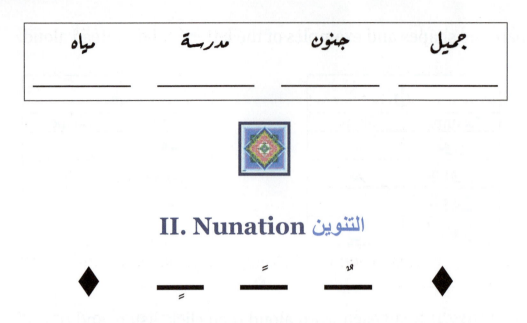

مياه	مدرسة	جنون	جميل
_____	_____	_____	_____

II. Nunation التنوين

◆   ــً   ــٌ   ــٍ   ◆

Nunation (التنوين) is a term means doubling the short vowels that are above or below the last letter in a word. The second or doubled vowel is pronounced 'n.' Thus, ــٌ is pronounced *un* like بابٌ 'baab*un*' , (ــً) is pronounced *an* like باباً 'baab*an*', and (ــٍ) is pronounced *in* like بابٍ 'baab*in*'.

With (تنوين الفتح) that is with the *fathataan* (ــً) an *alif* must be added, but this *alif* is not pronounced. The *alif* (ا) acts as a 'seat' for the *fathataan* (ــً). This *alif* (ا) is not required if the word ends in taa` marbouta (ة) or hamza (ء).

❖

Compare the short vowels and nunation signs. Then read the examples out loud:

Example	With Consonant	Vowels And Nunation	Name
البابُ	بُ	ــُ	ضمة
البابَ	بَ	ــَ	فتحة
البابِ	بِ	ــِ	كسرة
بابٌ	بٌ	ــٌ	تنوين الضم
باباً	بً	ــً	تنوين الفتح
بابٍ	بٍ	ــٍ	تنوين الكسر

🎧 **Activity 1:** Read each word aloud then click, listen, and repeat.

كتابٌ	كتاب	نارٌ	نار
نورٌ	نور	بنتٌ	بنت
دارٌ	دار	بَيْتٌ	بَيْت
جميلٌ	جميل	كبيرٌ	كبير

❖

🎧 **Activity 2:** Read each word aloud then click, listen, and repeat.

كتاباً	كتاب	ناراً	نار
نوراً	نور	بنتاً	بنت
داراً	دار	بَيْتاً	بَيْت
جميلاً	جميل	كبيراً	كبير

❖

🎧 **Activity 3:** Read each word aloud then click, listen, and repeat.

كتابٍ	كتاب	نارٍ	نار
نورٍ	نور	بنتٍ	بنت
دارٍ	دار	بَيْتٍ	بَيْت
جميلٍ	جميل	كبيرٍ	كبير

❖

🎧 **Activity 4:** Read each word aloud then click, listen, and repeat.

فريدِ	فريدَ	فريدٌ	فريدْ
فريدٍ	فريداً	فريدٌ	فريدٌ
قلمِ	قلمَ	قلمٌ	قلمْ
قلمٍ	قلماً	قلمٌ	قلمْ
مساءِ	مساءَ	مساءٌ	مساءْ
مساءٍ	مساءً	مساءٌ	مساءٌ

Drill 1: Join the letters into words and include all vowels.

6 - بِ + ي + لَ + حَ =	1 - مُّ + ا + لَ + س =
7 - دٍ + رُ + وُ =	2 - بُ + ا + بَ + رَ =
8 - لٌّ + وُ + سُ + كَ =	3 - رٌّ + ي + دِ + مُ =
9 - سٌّ + ا + مَ + حَ =	4 - أ + حَ + مَ + رَ =
10 - دِ + ي + رَ + بَ =	5 - أ + دَ + لَ + بَ =

❖

Drill 2: Copy. Pronounce the letters and each word as you write.

مريمُ	سميرٌ	باباً	وفـدٍ	سلامٌ
_____	_____	_____	_____	_____
شُـكراً	بَرْداً	خـيْـرٌ	دَجاجٌ	ممتازاً
_____	_____	_____	_____	_____
شَمَسٌ	البابُ	سَمَـكاً	سمادٌ	سريراً
_____	_____	_____	_____	_____

44

III. Alif Maqsura ألف مقصورة

ى

ى ى ى ى ى ى ى ى ى ى ى

Alif maqsura ى is a variant form of the letter alif (ا). The ى occurs only in the final connected or unconnected form. It is pronounced as the regular alif and does take nunation, as in هُدىً 'hudan.' Grammatical rules determine which alif at the end of a word should be used. You could learn to recognize or even memorize most of the words ending in ى. But ا is more commonly used than ى in the Arabic language.

Alif maqsura ى looks like the letter ي but without the two dots. Some write a small alif above ى to distinguish it from the ي.

Compare the shapes of the two alifs:

Final		Medial	Initial	Name of letter
Unconnected	Connected			
ا	ـا	ـا	ا	ألف مَمْـدودة
ى	ـى	-	-	ألف مَقصورة

Compare the printed form of the ى with the handwritten one:

ى	ـى	-	-
ى	ـى	-	-

When we add a suffix to a word that ends in ى, the alif maqsura is no longer the last letter in that word. The ى changes to a regular alif or to a medial ي. Examples:

قُراكَ	=	كَ	+	قُرى
ليلاي	=	ي	+	ليلى
رَماكِ	=	كِ	+	رمى
لدينا	=	نا	+	لدى
بنَاهُ	=	هُ	+	بنى

🎧 **Activity 1:** Read each word aloud then click, listen, and repeat.

قضى	جَرَى	نَدَى	مدَى	هُدَى
مُنى	بكى	لَدَى	نَجْوَى	بَنى
لَيْلى	سَلْوَى	سلْمَى	بَرَدَى	كُبْرَى

❖

Drill 1: Copy. Pronounce the letters and each word as you write.

شجى	لدى	سرى	رمى
_____	_____	_____	_____
شذاكَ	لديكَ	يَرانا	بكى
_____	_____	_____	_____

❖

Drill 2: Join the letters into words and include all vowels.

6- حَ + لْ + وَ + ى + هُ =   1- س + لْ + وَ + ى =

7- فَ + د + ى + هُ =   2- سَ + لْ + و + ى + كَ =

8- فَ + د + ى + كَ =   3- مُ + ن + ى =

9- عَ + ل + ى + هُ =   4- مُ + ن + ى + ي =

10- عَ + ل + ى + كَ =   5- حَ + لْ + وَ + ى =

Unit Five
الوحدة الخامسة

I. The Letter ه

Calligraphic image of the letter ه

The letter ه is pronounced similar to the English letter <u>h</u>, as in 'hot,' but with more force. The ه can occur in all positions in a word, and connects on both sides.

ه	ـه	ـهـ	هـ

Compare the printed ه with the handwritten form:

ه	ـه	ـهـ	هـ

See the shape of the letter with these examples. Read aloud.

ه	
Example	Shape
هام	هـ
شهر	ـهـ
بيته	ـه
مياه	ه

47

🎧 **Activity 1:** Read each word aloud then click, listen, and repeat.

فوهُ	فوهَ	فيهِ	هاءُ	هادي	سَهْلٌ
سُهُولٌ	هِلالٌ	بَهْلُولٌ	بهاءُ	بهائي	رفاه
هِشام	سِهام	بائهُ	بهِ	فقيهٍ	هُناكَ

❖

Drill 1: Join the letters into words and include all vowels.

6- سَ + مَ + ا + ه =   1- هَ + رَ + م =

7- مَ + لَ + هَ + ىً =   2- بِ + هِ + ي + لَ =

8- هَ + ز + ي + ل =   3- مُ + هَ + مَ + ل =

9- حَ + مَ + ا + ه =   4- رَ + هِ + ي + ب =

10- سَ + و + ا + ه =   5- رَ + ا + هِ + ب =

❖

Drill 2: Copy. Pronounce the letters and each word as you write.

هَمَسَ	يَهْدي	نَهْر	هادي
_____	_____	_____	_____
هَجْر	شِفاه	أهْلاً	مِياه
_____	_____	_____	_____
كِتابُهُ	هُناك	هُنا	مَشهور
_____	_____	_____	_____

❖

Drill 3: Copy the handwriting style below and read aloud as you write.

مِياه	شاه	فيه	شهْر	هاء
_____	_____	_____	_____	_____

48

II. Taa` Marbouta (ة)
التاء المربوطة

Taa` marbouta ة is a variant of the letter 'taa` maftouha' ت. The taa` marbouta (ة) is used instead of the taa` maftouha (ت) when it is the last letter in certain words. The ة comes only in the final position. The ة usually indicates feminine nouns and adjectives.

Compare the printed ة with the handwritten form in the following words:

مدرسة	فضيحة	والدة	بيئة	فتاة
مدرسة	فضيحة	والدة	بيئة	فتاة

The ة has the same shape as ه but has two dots above it. It takes nunation like other letters. The ة is always preceded by a *fatha*. The ة is not pronounced in the pause form (when the ة is at the end of the last word in a sentence).

Final		Medial	Initial	Letter
Not Connected	Connected			
ة	ـة	-	-	تاء مربوطة
ه	ـه	ـهـ	هـ	هاء

Compare the shapes and examples of the letters ة and ه. Read aloud.

ة	
Example	Shape
-	-
-	-
مدرسة	ـة
والدة	ة

ه	
Example	Shape
هاء	هـ
شهْر	ـهـ
فيه	ـه
مياه	ه

❖

Drill 1: Read aloud and pay attention to the pause form of the letter ة.

The Pause Form	Full Form	Full Form
مدرسة	مدرسةٌ	مدرسةُ
madrasah	madrasatun	Madrasatu
مدرسة	مدرسةً	مدرسةَ
madrasah	madrasatan	Madrasata
مدرسة	مدرسةٍ	مدرسةِ
madrasah	madrasatin	Madrasati

❖

🎧 **Activity 1:** Read the following sentences composed of two words. Make sure to pronounce the ة fully in the first word.

4 - والدةُ سمير   1 - مدينةُ دمشق

5 - سفارةُ روسيا   2 - مدرسةُ تونس

6 - زيارةُ والدي   3 - شهادةُ الماجستير

❖

Drill 2: Read the ة in the following words, once fully pronounced and once in the pause form.

قرية	قريةٌ	جريدة	جريدةُ

شجرة	شجرةٍ	سورة	سورةً
وردة	وردةٌ	زوجة	زوجةٌ

❖

Drill 3: Join the letters into words and include all vowels.

6- مُ + ف + ي + دَ + ة =   1- مَ + دِ + ي + نَ + ة =

7- مُ + دِ + ي + رَ + ة =   2- دَ + وْ + رَ + ة =

8- زَ + وْ + جَ + ة =   3- وَ + ز + ي + رَ + ة =

9- كَ + ا + تِ + بَ + ة =   4- كَ + ب + ي + رَ + ة =

10 - جَ + ا + مَ + دَ + ة =   5- رَ + ف + ي + قَ + ة =

❖

Drill 4: Copy. Pronounce the letters and each word as you write.

حَليمة	سَميرة	وَزيرة	مُديرة	سَفيرة
ــــــ	ــــــ	ــــــ	ــــــ	ــــــ
هِجْرة	سِياحة	مَهارة	سَفارة	والِدة
ــــــ	ــــــ	ــــــ	ــــــ	ــــــ
شَريفة	مَحبوبة	مَهَمَّة	مَفهومة	مَشهورة
ــــــ	ــــــ	ــــــ	ــــــ	ــــــ

❖

Drill 5: Copy the handwriting style below and read aloud as you write.

قِراءَة	فَضيحة	فتاة	مدرسة
ــــــ	ــــــ	ــــــ	ــــــ
فتاة	والدة	قِراءَة	بيئَة
ــــــ	ــــــ	ــــــ	ــــــ

III. Letters ع غ

Calligraphic image of the letter ع

ع ع ع ع ع ع ع ع ع ع ع ع

The letter ع has no equivalent in English. As a pronounced consonant, the ع vibrates the vocal cords. It is mastered after many repetitions.

Compare the printed ع with this handwritten form:

❖

Drill 1: Copy. Pronounce the letters and each word as you write.

عَرَفَة	عَرَفات	عَ	عُ
ــــــــ	ــــــــ	ــــــــ	ــــــــ
عُلُوم	عَجَلات	بَعْلٌ	مَعْلوم
ــــــــ	ــــــــ	ــــــــ	ــــــــ

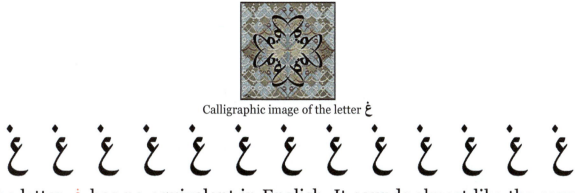

Calligraphic image of the letter غ

The letter غ has no equivalent in English. It sounds almost like the sound one makes when gargling water. This consonant also vibrates the vocal cords when pronounced.

Compare the printed غ with this handwritten form:

❖

Drill 2: Copy. Pronounce the letters and each word as you write.

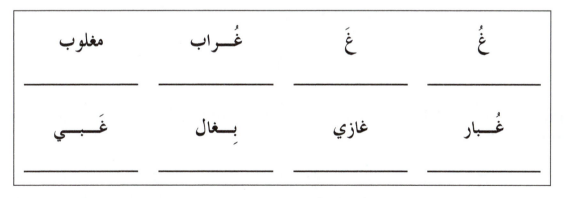

❖

Compare the shapes and examples of the letters ع and غ. Read aloud.

غ	
Example	Shape
غرب	غـ
نَغم	ـغـ
نابغ	ـغ
بلاغ	ـغ

ع	
Example	Shape
عرب	عـ
نعم	ـعـ
نافع	ـع
شارع	ـع

❖

🎧 **Activity 1:** Read each word aloud then click, listen, and repeat.

13 - عَسَـل	9 - عَبير	5 - عُلوم	1 - عَرَبي
14 - مَطعَم	10 - نعيم	6 - نَعَم	2 - بَعيد
15 - سَمِيع	11 - شَريعة	7 - سَابع	3 - نابـع
16 - مُـذِيع	12 - سُعاد	8 - مَشروع	4 - شَارع

🎧 **Activity 2:** Read each word aloud then click, listen, and repeat.

10 - غَرْب	7 - غُرْفة	4 - غَريد	1 - غَريب
11 - يَغيب	8 - بَغداد	5 - يُغري	2 - يُغِير
12 - بَليغ	9 - بَلاغ	6 - تَبْغ	3 - دِمَاغ

❖

Drill 3: Join the letters into words, include all vowels, and read aloud as you write them.

6 - لـ + بَ + ي + غ =	1 - مَ + ذْ + عُ + و =
7 - غ + يَ + ا + ب =	2 - ة + وَ + غْ + دَ =
8 - غ + رْ + بَ + ة =	3 - زز + ي + زز + عَ =
9 - م + يُ + و + غ =	4 - بّ + ا + ل + كِ =
10 - مَ + غْ + ي + ب =	5 - عَ + ر + ب + ي =

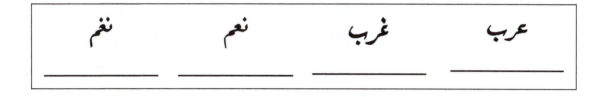 **Activity 3**: Read each word aloud then click, listen, and repeat.

5 - كِتَابُ عدنَان.   1 - غُرْفَةُ عادل.

6 - لُغتي العربية.   2 - سَاعَةُ مسْعود.

7 - جَامعةُ بغْداد.   3 - عُامِلُ المطعم.

8 - المُجْتَمعُ العربي.   4 - شَارعُ شِعْلان.

❖

Drill 4: Copy the handwriting style below and read aloud as you write.

نَغَم	نعم	غرب	عرب
_____	_____	_____	_____

Beauty - جمال

Unit Six
الوحدة السادسة

I. Letters ص ض

Calligraphic image of the letter ص

The letter ص is the emphatic equivalent of the letter س. It is produced further back in the mouth. The sound of the letter ص is similar to the sound of English letter s as in 'sod.'

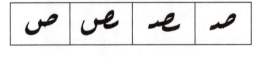

Compare the printed form of the letter ص with this handwritten one:

Drill 1: Copy.

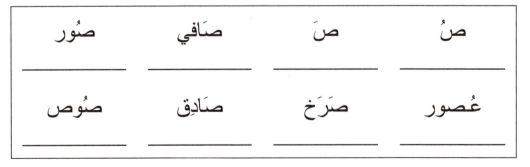

Calligraphic image of the letter ض

The letter ض is the emphatic equivalent of the letter د. It has no English equivalent.

Both ص and ض connect on both sides and have the same shape. ض has a dot above it, and ص has none.

Compare the printed form of the letter ض with this handwritten one:

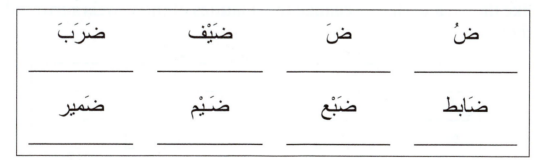

❖

Drill 2: Copy.

ضَرَبَ	ضَيْف	ضَ	ضُ
_____	_____	_____	_____
ضَمِير	ضَيْم	ضَبْع	ضَابط
_____	_____	_____	_____

❖

57

Compare the shapes and examples of the letters ص and ض. Read aloud.

ض	
Example	Shape
ضاد	ضـ
فضيحة	ـضـ
رافِض	ـض
رياض	ـض

ص	
Example	Shape
صباح	صـ
بصل	ـصـ
بصيص	ـص
رصاص	ـص

Emphatic letters like the ص and the ض change the qualities of the vowels surrounding them.

❖

Drill 3: Read aloud.

13 - مِصْرُ	9 - قَصْري	5 - صَديق	1 - صَبْري
14 - راضِي	10 - ضَرَبَ	6 - رَقْصٌ	2 - قُصُور
15 - ضَبْعٌ	11 - ضَيْعَة	7 - رِضا	3 - رَضْوَانُ
16 - ضَيْفٌ	12 - رافِضٌ	8 - فاضِل	4 - ضَريرٌ

❖

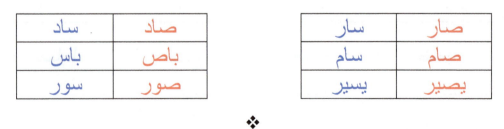 **Activity 1**: Repeat out loud and compare س and ص. Emphatic letters like the ص and the ض change the qualities of the vowels surrounding them.

ساد	صاد
باس	باص
سور	صور

سار	صار
سام	صام
يسير	يصير

❖

Activity 2: Repeat out loud and contrast ض and د. Remember that emphatic letters like the ص and ض change the qualities of vowels surrounding them.

رياد	رياض
دام	ضام
دروع	ضروع

باد	باض
مدى	مضى
دروب	ضروب

❖

Drill 4: Repeat out loud.

4 - فَيْصَل مصري
5 - صُورَة صَابر
6 - بابُ قصْري

1 - صَديقي في صَيْدَا
2 - فاضِل في الرياض
3 - صَابُون مِصْري

❖

Drill 5: Join the letters into words, include all vowels, and read aloud as you write.

6 - صُ + و + رَ + ة =
7 - فَ + ا + ضِ + ل =
8 - رَ + وْ + ضَ + ة =
9 - غ + ا + ضِ + ب =
10 - ة + ضَ + يْ + بَ =

1 - ضَ + يْ + ف + ي =
2 - ض + ا + هِ + ر =
3 - صَ + دِ + ي + ق =
4 - سَ + م + يْ + ك =
5 - س + ي + رَ + ة =

❖

Drill 6: Copy the handwriting style below and read aloud as you write.

رافِض	بصيص	ضاد	صباع
_____	_____	_____	_____
رياض	رصاص	فضيّة	بصل
_____	_____	_____	_____

❖

II. Letters ظ ط

Calligraphic image of the letter ط

ط ط ط ط ط ط ط ط ط ط ط ط ط

The letter ط is an emphatic letter pronounced with the teeth and tongue touching. It is the emphatic equivalent of the letter ت.

Compare the printed form with this handwritten one:

ط ط ط ط

❖

Drill 1: Copy.

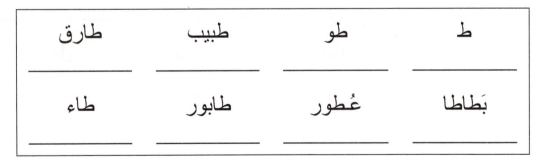

❖

Calligraphic image of the letter ظ

ظ ظ ظ ظ ظ ظ ظ ظ ظ ظ ظ ظ

The letter ظ is the emphatic equivalent of the letter ذ. Both ط and ظ connect on both sides. Both are emphatic, thus they change the quality of the vowels surrounding them. Both have the same shape. The ط does not have a dot, and the ظ has one dot above the body of the letter.

ظ	ظ	ظ	ظ

Compare to this handwritten form:

❖

Drill 2: Copy.

ظافر	عَظيم	ظا	ظ
_____	_____	_____	_____
ظاء	ظِلال	ظُنون	ظُهُور
_____	_____	_____	_____

❖

Compare the shapes and examples of the letters ط and ظ. Read aloud.

ظ	
Example	Shape
ظَاء	ظ
نَظِير	ظـ
حفيظ	ـظ
عُكاظ	ـظ

ط	
Example	Shape
طَاء	ط
لَطيف	ـطـ
ضابط	ـط
نشاط	ـط

❖

🎧 **Activity 1:** Read each word aloud then click, listen, and repeat.

13 - طريق	9 - طبيب	5 - قِطار	1 - طَـار
14 - نظير	10 - أبو ظبي	6 - ظافِر	2 - ظُنون
15 - طاهِر	11 - طلال	7 - طين	3 - طبْشور
16 - طَنْجَرة	12 - طارق	8 - شُرْطي	4 - شُروط

❖

🎧 **Activity 2:** Read out loud and contrast ط and ت. Emphatic letters like the ط change the qualities of vowels surrounding them:

ت	ط
تين	طين
بات	باط
توب	طوب

ت	ط
تار	طار
تور	طور
يتير	يطير

❖

🎧 **Activity 3:** Read out loud and contrast ظ and ذ. Again, emphatic letters like the ظ change the qualities of vowels surrounding them.

ذ	ظ
ذافر	ظافر

ذ	ظ
باذ	باظ

ذهور	ظهور	ناذور	ناظور
ذروع	ظروع	ذهران ·	ظهران

❖

🎧 **Activity 4**: Read each word aloud then click, listen, and repeat.

In the quiz

4 - ظافِر ضابط   1 - بَيْتي نظيف

5 - طبيبُ طاهِر   2 - فُطور طلال

6 - قِطار طارق   3 - رَطْلُ بَطاطا

❖

Drill 3: Join the letters into words, include all vowels, and read aloud as you write.

6 - ظ + بْ + يٌّ =   1 - ط + ب + ي + ب =

7 - ظُ + هُ + و + ر =   2 - مَ + ط + رُ + و + ب =

8 - عُ + كَ + ا + ظ =   3 - ن + ظ + ا + فَ + ة =

9 - مَ + ظ + ي + م =   4 - ط + رْ + بُ + و + ش =

10 - ط + نْ + ط + ا =   5 - ط + رْ + ش =

❖

Drill 4: Copy the handwriting style below and read aloud as you write.

نظير	لطيف	ظاء	طاء
_____	_____	_____	_____
نشاط	حفيظ	ضابط	عُكاظ
_____	_____	_____	_____

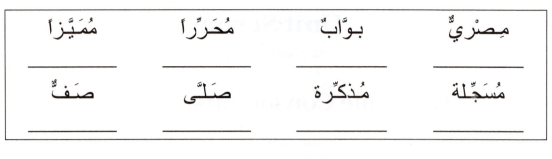

مُمَيَّزاً	مُحَرِّراً	بوَّابٌ	مِصرِيٌّ
ـــــــــ	ـــــــــ	ـــــــــ	ـــــــــ
صَفٌّ	صَلَّى	مُذكِّرة	مُسَجِّلة
ـــــــــ	ـــــــــ	ـــــــــ	ـــــــــ

❖

🎧 **Activity 1**: Read each word aloud then click, listen, and repeat.

وِدّاً	وِدٌّ
وِدٍّ	وِدِّ
بِرُّ	بِرٌّ
بِرّاً	بِرَّ
بِرِّ	بِرٍّ

❖

🎧 **Activity 2**: Read each word aloud then click, listen, and repeat.

11 - رَحَّالة	6 - رَحَّلَ	1 - رَحَلَ
12 - مُدَرِّسٌ	7 - دَرَّسَ	2 - دَرَسَ
13 - بَرَّادٌ	8 - بَرَّدَ	3 - بَرَدَ
14 - شحَّادٌ	9 - بوَّابٌ	4 - نجَّارٌ
15 - خبَّاز	10 - عَمَّان	5 - سيَّارة

❖

Drill 2: Join the letters into words, include all vowels, and read aloud as you write.

6 - سُ + و + رَ + يْ + يٌّ =	1 - ضَ + يْ + يَ + فَ =
7 - م + صْنْ + رَ + يْ + يٌّ =	2 - بَ + شْ + شَ + رَ =
8 - سَ + يْ + يَ + ا + ن =	3 - صَ + رْ + رَ + فَ =
9 - رَ + ش + شْ + بَ + مُ =	4 - ع + مْ + مَ + دَ =
10 - م + ا + سَ + سْ + رَ =	5 - دَ + رْ + رَ + سَ =

II. Hamza (ء) الهمزة

ء

The hamza ء is a glottal stop consonant that can stand alone or can be written over or under ا and over the و and ي. Each of these three long vowels can serve as the 'seat' for the hamza.

Hamza (ء) written on the line by itself in final position:

ثاء	تاء	باء

Hamza (ء) written on the line by itself in the middle:

مُروءة	مروءات	إجراءات

When the ا, و, or ي acts as the seat of the hamza, these seats are ignored in pronunciation. Only the hamza as a glottal stop consonant is pronounced.

When the *alif* (ا) serves as seat for the hamza, the hamza is written over or under the *alif*. The short vowels *damma* (ُ) and *fatha* (َ) are written on top of the hamza over the *alif*, and the *kasra* (ِ) is written below the hamza (which is already below the alif). When the hamza is under the *alif*, the kasra is pronounced whether written or not.

When the و serves as a seat for the hamza, the hamza is written over the و :

When the ي serves as a seat for the hamza, the hamza is written over the ي. The two dots under the ي are usually not used:

If the hamza comes in the middle of a word, then a 'seat' or a 'chair' is created in order to enable the hamza to connect with other letters:

To summarize, hamza is a glottal stop consonant and exists in all positions. It can be written by itself in final and medial positions. The و and ي can serve as the hamza's seat in the medial, and final positions. The ا can serve as the hamza's seat in all three positions. The seats of the hamza are ignored in pronunciation. Only the glottal stop sound of the hamza is pronounced. The hamza is not a connector letter. Thus, a 'chair' is created so that the hamza in the medial position can connect.

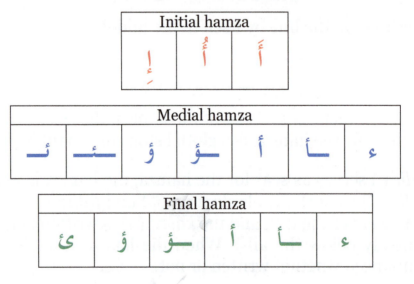

Hamza, like other consonant, takes short vowels, nunation, and sukuun:

باءٍ	باءً	باءٌ	باءٍ	باءَ	باءُ	باءْ

Hamza at the end of the word is written on the line if preceded by sukuun or a long vowel. Examples:

شَيْء	بَرِيء	بَطِيء
ضَوْء	جُزْء	سُوْء
يُسِيء	يَمُوء	سَمَاء

🎧 **Activity 1:** Read each word aloud then click, listen, and repeat.

إذا	أَوْ	أَنتِ	أَنتَ	أنا
زائِر	أُمٌّ	أُخْت	شِتاء	إناء
هَيْئَة	مِئَات	رُؤَساء	رئيس	سأَلَ
بِئْرٌ	ذِئْبٌ	شَيْءٌ	مروءة	ماء
أُستاذ	بُؤْسٌ	فُؤَاد	أنَّ	إنَّ
أَسْئِلة	رَؤُوم	رائِد	عَلاء	وَفاء
قِراءَة	قرأ	ثَأْر	بيئَة	بُؤْبُؤْ

❖

🎧 **Activity 2:** Read each word aloud then click, listen, and repeat.

إطارُ طائِرة	رئيسُ هيئة
بِئْرُ وائِل	قرأ قارِئ
رُؤُوس أموال	قالَ قائِل
أَفْهَمُ الأسئِلة	مُبْتَدَأ وخَبَر

❖

Drill 1: Join the letters into words, include all vowels, and read aloud as you write.

6 - هَ + ا + د + ئ =   1 - ب + ـئَـ + رَ + أ =

7 - شَ + يْ + ء =   2 - جُ + ز + ء =

8 - س + أ + لَ =   3 - لُ + ؤ + لُ + ؤ =

9 - ل + ا + وُ + سُ =   4 - ق + ا + ر + ئ =

10 - ل + ئِ + ا + سَ =   5 - هُ + دُ + و + ء =

69

Drill 2: Copy. Pronounce the letters and each word as you write.

قارئ	سَأَل	أوَّل	مُبْتَدَأ
ــــــــ	ــــــــ	ــــــــ	ــــــــ
بُؤْبُؤ	سَبَأ	مَلِيئَة	مَلَأ
ــــــــ	ــــــــ	ــــــــ	ــــــــ
سَماء	سائِل	سَئيل	سُؤال
ــــــــ	ــــــــ	ــــــــ	ــــــــ
أصدقائي	أصدقائِك	أصدقاءَ ك	أصدقاؤكَ
ــــــــ	ــــــــ	ــــــــ	ــــــــ

❖

Drill 3: Copy the handwriting style below and read aloud as you write.

بُؤْبُؤ	بيئَة	قِراءَة	قرأَ
ــــــــ	ــــــــ	ــــــــ	ــــــــ
ثأر	ظاء	بُؤْبُؤ	طاء
ــــــــ	ــــــــ	ــــــــ	ــــــــ

III. Madda (آ) المـدَّة

Madda is a sign (~) only written above the *alif* (١). When an *alif* with a *hamza* and a *fatha* (أ) is followed by another *alif* (١), the two *alifs* combine into one *alif* called *alif madda* (آ). Therefore, the *alif madda* sounds like an *alif* with a hamza followed by a long *alif*.

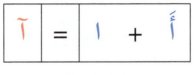

❖

🎧 **Activity 1:** Read each word aloud then click, listen, and repeat.

مَآثِر	مَآل	آمال	آداب	قرآن
آدم	الآنَ	آمين	آلات	آلة
آراء	آثار	مِرآة	آب	مآذِن

❖

Drill 1: Copy. Pronounce the letters and each word as you write.

مَآثِر	الآنَ	مَآل	مِرآة
_____	_____	_____	_____

٤

آلات	قرآن	آب	آدَم
_____	_____	_____	_____

IV. Dagger Alif الألف القصيرة

الله

The dagger *alif*, or short *alif*, is a sign that looks like a small dagger placed above a consonant as in الله. It is pronounced as a long *alif*. The dagger *alif* occurs only in a few common words. It is omitted in unvoweled texts.

Common words containing the dagger alif:

الله	إلـٰه	لله
رَحْمـٰن	هـٰذا	هـٰذه
هـٰكذا	لـٰكن	ذٰ لِك
لـذٰ لِك	كـذٰ لك	هـٰؤُلاء

V. Hamzat al-Wasl or Wasla همزة الوصل أو الوصلة

There are two kinds of hamza in Arabic. One is (همزة القطع) which is pronounced as a glottal stop consonant, as in (أَ), (أُ), or (إِ). The other hamza is (همزة الوصل) or wasla (ٱ), which is not pronounced.

Hamzat al-wasl is shown in the following examples:

هُوَ ٱلْمُدِيرُ	بابُ ٱلْبيتِ
مِنَ ٱلْمُدِيرِ	في ٱلْجَامعةِ

In Arabic, no two consonants in a row can be unvoweled. When this is the case for the start of a word, a helping vowel must be added to the alif.

اكْتُبْ = أُكْتُبْ	اذهب = إِذْهَبْ	اشْرَب = إِشْرَبْ

If a word begins with a cluster of two consonants and is preceded by a word that ends in a consonant, then the final consonant of the preceding word receives a helping vowel. The wasla indicates the two words are pronounced as one with no pause between them.

مَنِ ٱسْتَقْبَلَ	أُدْرُسْ وَٱشْرَبْ

❖

73

🎧 **Activity 1:** Read each word aloud then click, listen, and repeat.

مَا ٱسْمُها؟	مَا ٱسْمُهُ؟	مَا ٱسْمُكَ؟
اُدْرُسْ وَٱذْهَبْ	كُلْ وَٱشْرَبْ	أبو ٱلْبِنْتِ
سَيّارةُ ٱلْوَزير	شُبّاكُ ٱلْمكتبِ	ذَهَبَ إلى ٱلْجَامعة

Friendship – صداقة

Unit Eight
الوحدة الثامنة

I. The Definite Article (الـ) أداة التعريف

When ا is followed by ل, it is written الـ 'the definite article.'

الـ	=	ل	+	ا

This definite article is prefixed to nouns and adjectives to make them definite. Words either receive the definite article or nunation but cannot receive both at the same time.

اَلْجَامِعَةُ	the university
اَلذَّهَبُ	the gold

جَامِعَةٌ	university
ذَهَبٌ	gold

II. Moon Letters   الحروف القمريّة

أَلْقَمَرُ

In Arabic, there are fourteen moon letters and fourteen sun letters for a total of twenty-eight letters in the Arabic alphabet. When the definite article is prefixed to words that begin with one of the moon letters, then the definite article is pronounced ‎أَلْ. Note that ‎لْ is pronounced with sukun on it.

The fourteen 'moon letters':

أ ب ج ح خ ع غ ف ق ك م ه و ي

🎧 **Activity 1:** Read each word aloud then click, listen, and repeat.

Definite	Indefinite	Meaning	Moon Letter
الْأُسْتاذُ	أُسْتاذٌ	professor	أ
الْبَحْرُ	بَحْرٌ	sea	ب
الْجامعةُ	جامعةٌ	university	ج
الْحُبُّ	حُبٌّ	love	ح
الْخَلُّ	خَلٌّ	vinegar	خ
الْعَمَلُ	عَمَلٌ	work	ع
الْغَرْبُ	غرْبٌ	west	غ
الْفَجْرُ	فَجْرٌ	dawn	ف
الْقَهْوَةُ	قَهْوَةٌ	coffee	ق
الْكِتابُ	كِتابٌ	book	ك
المَدْرَسَةُ	مَدْرَسَةٌ	school	م
الْهَدِيَّةُ	هَدِيَّةٌ	gift	ه
الْوَزِيرُ	وَزِيرٌ	minister	و
الْيَوْمُ	يَوْمٌ	day	ي

❖

III. Sun Letters الحروف الشَّمسِيَّة

When the definite article is prefixed to words that begin with one of the sun letters, then the ل of the definite article is not pronounced because it is assimilated into the sun letter. The sun letter becomes doubled in pronunciation, and the shadda is written over the sun letter that follows the definite article. Although the ل is not pronounced, it remains written.

Example: (الرَّجل) '*al-rajul*' is pronounced '*ar-rajul.*'

The fourteen sun letters:

د ذ ت ث ر ز س ش ص ض ط ظ ل ن

The chart below shows examples of the ل assimilated into the sun letters and not assimilated into the moon letters.

ل is assimilated			ل is not assimilated		
the sun	الشَّمس	Ash-shams	the moon	الْقمر	al-qamar
the lesson	الدَّرس	Ad-dars	the house	الْبيت	al-bayt

❖

Activity 1: Read aloud. Pay attention to the assimilation of the ل and to the doubling of the sun letter that follows it.

Definite	Indefinite	Meaning	Sun Letter
التَّمْرينُ	تَمْرينٌ	drill	ت
الثَّلْجُ	ثَلْجٌ	snow	ث
الدَّرْسُ	دَرْسٌ	lesson	د
الذَّهَبُ	ذَهَبٌ	gold	ذ
الرَّبيعُ	رَبيعٌ	spring	ر
الزِّيارَةُ	زِيارَةٌ	visit	ز
السَّلامُ	سَلامٌ	peace	س
الشُّبَّاكُ	شُبَّاكٌ	window	ش
الصَّباحُ	صَباحٌ	morning	ص
الضَّبابُ	ضَبابٌ	fog	ض
الطَّويلُ	طَويلٌ	long	ط
الظُّهْرُ	ظُهْرٌ	noon	ظ
اللُّغَةُ	لُغَةٌ	language	ل
النِّمْرُ	نِمْرٌ	tiger	ن

Note that in unvoweled texts like newspapers, the shadda is not written over the sun letter, and the sukuun is not written over the ل with moon letters.

❖

Drill 1: Add the definite articles to the following words. Write shadda over the sun letters and write sukuun over the ل with the moon letters. Then, read aloud.

أَوْسَط	ذِكرى	قرآن	إسلام
_____	_____	_____	_____
كتاب	فيل	عَيْن	أب
_____	_____	_____	_____
ذِئْب	كلب	خُبْز	دَم
_____	_____	_____	_____
رَجُلٌ	وَزير	مَلِك	تَمْر
_____	_____	_____	_____
لَيْل	عَدد	جار	شرق
_____	_____	_____	_____

❖

Drill 2: Copy. Pronounce the letters and each word as you write.

الضَّبابُ	الصَّباحُ	لُغَةٌ	ظُهْرٌ
_____	_____	_____	_____
الْعَمَلُ	عَمَلٌ	دَرْسٌ	نِمْرٌ
_____	_____	_____	_____
النِّمْرُ	الذَّهَبُ	صَباحٌ	الظُّهْرُ
_____	_____	_____	_____
ذَهَبٌ	الدَّرْسُ	ضَبابٌ	اللُّغَةُ
_____	_____	_____	_____
الْفَجْرُ	الْهَدِيَّةُ	الْقَهْوَةُ	غَرْبٌ
_____	_____	_____	_____

❖

Unit Nine
الوحدة التاسعة

I. Arabic Script and Calligraphy

The Holy Qur`an

Go to the Interactive DVD to watch two students reciting *Surat al-Fatiha* (The Opening Chapter of the Qur'an). Below is the text of the same *Sura* in different styles of Arabic script. Compare the script styles and identify some letters and words.

سورة الفاتحة		سورة الفاتحة
بسم الله الرحمن الرحيم		بسم الله الرحمن الرحيم
الحمد لله رب العالمين		الحمد لله رب العالمين
الرحمن الرحيم		الرحمن الرحيم
مالك يوم الدين		مالك يوم الدين
إياك نعبد وإياك نستعين		إياك نعبد وإياك نستعين
اهدنا الصراط المستقيم		اهدنا الصراط المستقيم
صراط الذين أنعمت عليهم		صراط الذين أنعمت عليهم
غير المغضوب عليهم ولا الضالين		غير المغضوب عليهم ولا الضالين

❖

Recited by Julie McAleer and Karin Weston

II. Printed Styles of Arabic Script

Below is a paragraph from the book (نهـــج البلاغـــة) by Imam `Ali Ibn Abi Talib (الإمام علي بن أبي طالب) the fourth Islamic Caliph, in three different script styles. Compare the words and consonants in the three different scripts. Identify words that begin with sun letters and words that start with moon letters. Identify the hamza in its middle position.

مَنْ نَظَرَ فِي عَيْبٍ نَفْسِهِ اشْتَغَلَ عَنْ عَيْبِ غَيْرِه. وَمَنْ كَثُرَ كَلامُهُ كَثُرَ خَطَؤُهُ، وَمَنْ كَثُرَ خَطَؤُهُ قَلَّ حَيَاؤُهُ، وَمَنْ قَلَّ حَيَاؤُهُ قَلَّ وَرَعُهُ، وَمَنْ قَلَّ وَرَعُهُ مَاتَ قَلْبُهُ، وَمَنْ مَاتَ قَلْبُهُ دَخَلَ النَّارَ.

❖

مَــنْ نَــظَــرَ فِي عَــيْــبٍ نَــفْــسِــهِ اشْــتَــغَــلَ عَنْ عَيْبِ غَيْرِه، وَمَــنْ كَــثُــرَ كَلامُــهُ كَــثُــرَ خَطَؤُهُ، وَمَــنْ كَــثُــرَ خَطَؤُهُ قَلَّ حَــيَاؤُهُ، وَمَــنْ قَــلَّ حَيَاؤُهُ قَــلَّ وَرَعُــهُ، وَمَنْ قَلَّ وَرَعُــهُ مَاتَ قَــلْبُهُ، وَمَــنْ مَــاتَ قَــلْــبُــهُ دَخَــلَ النَّــارَ.

❖

مَــنْ نَــظَــرَ فِي عَــيْــبٍ نَــفْــسِهِ اشْتَــغَــلَ عَنْ عَيْبِ غَيْرِه، وَمَنْ كَــثُــرَ كَلَامُهُ كَــثُــرَ خَطَؤُهُ، وَمَنْ كَــثُــرَ خَطَؤُهُ قَــلَّ حَيَاؤُهُ، وَمَنْ قَــلَّ حَيَاؤُهُ قَــلَّ وَرَعُــهُ، وَمَــنْ قَــلَّ وَرَعُــهُ مَاتَ قَــلْــبُهُ، وَمَنْ مَــاتَ قَــلْــبُــهُ دَخَــلَ النَّــارَ.

* نهـــج البـلاغـــة، الإمـــام علـــي بـن أبـي طالـب، ضبـط نصّـــه صبـحي الصالح، بيـروت، دار الكتاب اللبناني، ب ت، ص 250 (بتصـرف).

III. Handwriting Samples

Individuals have their own handwriting styles in Arabic, as in other languages. Below are handwritten excerpts from several distinguished Arab writers. Look at the handwriting style of each writer and try to identify some letters and words. Underneath each excerpt is the printed form of that handwritten selection.

هشام شرابي

Hisham Sharabi – Professor of Arab Culture

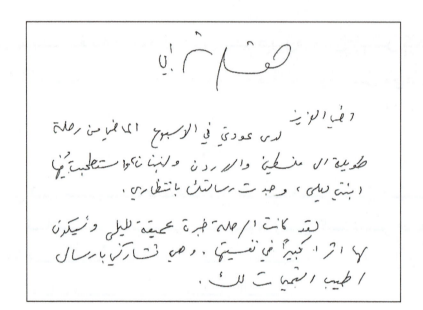

❖

أخي العزيز

لدى عودتي في الأسبوع الماضي من رحلة طويلة إلى فلسطين والأردن ولبنان، واستصحبتُ فيها ابنتي ليلى، وجدتُ رسالتك بانتظاري.

لقد كانت الرحلة خبرة عميقة لليلى وسيكون لها أثراً كبيراً في نفسيتها. وهي تشاركني بإرسال أطيب التحيات لك.

نزار قبّاني

Nizar Qabbani – Poet

❖

أنا ممتنٌّ لك جداً، جداً، لأنك حوّلتني من شاعر إلى خطّاط. فَفَجَّرْتَ بذلك بداياتي الطفولية في الرسم والخطِّ، ولعلّكَ لا تعرف أنني كنتُ بين الخامسة عشرة والتاسعة عشرة خطّاطاً، أدرس الخطَّ العربي على أصوله، ولذلك فإنَّ أقرب ديوان إلى قلبي هو (قصائد متوحشة) الذي كتبته كله بخط يدي، فاعتبر كل قارىء أنني كتبتُ الديوان له وحده، وكنتُ سعيداً بهذا الشعور الحميمي.

عبد الوهاب البيّاتي

Abdul Wahab al-Bayati – Poet

بم الله كتبـــــي

كانت أياماً رائعة ، تلك التي قضيناها في تونس وكان لي فيها شرف
تعرفي عليه .

وكم سأكون سعيداً لو التقينا ثانية في مدريد أو تونس وسواهما
من مدن هذا العالم .

وعدتني بإرسال بعض كتاباتك ، فهل أطمح بالحصول عليها
إذا كنت بحاجة إلى أي كتاب من كتبي ، فالرجاء الكتابة لي
حتى أرسله اليك .

❖

كانت أياماً رائعة، تلك التي قضيناها في تونس وكان لي فيها شرف تعرفي عليك.

وكم سأكون سعيداً لو التقينا ثانية في مدريد أو تونس وسواهما من مــدن هــذا العــالم.

وعدتني بإرسال بعض كتاباتك، فهل أطمح بالحصول عليها؟

إذا كنت بحاجة إلى أي كتاب من كتبي، فالرجاء الكتابة لي حتى أرسله إليك.

❖

84

IV. Arabic Calligraphy

Arabic calligraphy is a highly developed art form of the Arabic language. For hundreds of years, artists and calligraphers have developed new and beautiful styles and designs of Arabic calligraphy. Below are examples of Arabic calligraphy from Fayeq Oweis, a contemporary calligrapher and artist. Look at the samples and try to identify some letters and words.

الحمد لله

وقل رب زدني علماً

وجعلناكم شعوباً وقبائل لتعارفوا

مودة

لا إله إلا الله

Calligrapher Fayeq Oweis

V. Reading Practice
Voweled and Unvoweled Phrases

Below are words and sentences written both with and without vowels. Read the unvoweled text first, then compare it with the voweled text. Read aloud several times.

Hello	مَرْحَباً	مرحباً
What is your name?	ما اسْمُكَ؟	ما اسمك؟
My name is Ahmad	اِسْمِي أَحْمَد	اسمي أحمد
Where are you from?	مِنْ أَيْنَ أَنْتَ؟	من أين أنت؟
I am from Damascus	أَنَا مِنْ دِمَشْق	أنا من دمشق
Peace be upon you	السَّلامُ عَلَيْكُم	السلام عليكم
What is your name?	ما اسْمُكِ؟	ما اسمك؟
My name is Abeer	اِسْمِي عَبِير	اسمي عبير
Where are you from?	مِنْ أَيْنَ أَنْتِ؟	من أين أنت؟
I am from Baghdad	أَنَا مِنْ بَغْدَاد	أنا من بغداد
Good morning	صَبَاحَ الْخَيْر	صباح الخير
Good evening	مَسَاءَ الْخَيْر	مساء الخير

Section Two
القسم الثاني

Lessons 1 - 21
من الدرس الأول إلى الدرس الحادي والعشرين

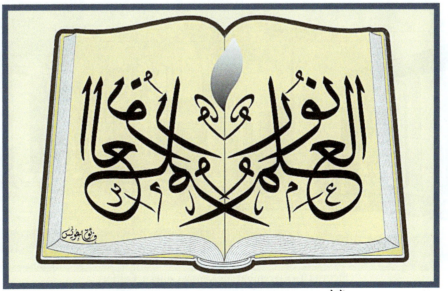

Arabic calligraphy: Knowledge is light - العلم نور

الدَّرْسُ الأوَّلُ

مِنْ أيْنَ أنت؟

Lesson One

Where Are You From?

Figure 1.1 - Claremont McKenna College, California

Lesson One Contents

🎧 Vocabulary – المفردات

🎧 Words and Expressions – كلمات وتعابير

💿 Basic Text – النص الأساسي

    ❖ Ilham and Abdulaziz – إلهام وعبد العزيز

Grammar – القواعد

    1. The Definite Article – أداة التعريف

      🎧 Activity 1

    2. Gender of Nouns – المذكر والمؤنث

      🎧 Activity 2

    3. Independent Personal Pronouns – ضمائر الرفع المنفصلة

      🎧 Activity 3

💿 Comprehension Text – الفهم والاستيعاب

    ❖ Are You a Student? – هل أنت طالب؟

🎧 Let's Speak Arabic – المحادثة

    ❖ Food – الطعام

💿 Window into Arab Culture – من الثقافة العربية

    ❖ Arabic Love Poems – قصائد حب عربية

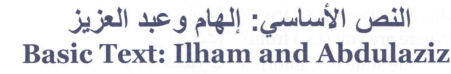

النص الأساسيِّ: إلهام وعبد العزيز
Basic Text: Ilham and Abdulaziz

إلهام: مَرْحَبَاً.

عبد العزيز: مَرْحَبَا، أهْلا وَسَهْلا.

إلهام: ما اسْمُكَ؟

عبد العزيز: أنا اسْمِي عبد العزيز. وأنتِ ما اسْمُكِ؟

إلهام: أنا اسْمِي إلهام.

عبد العزيز: تَشَرَّفْنَا، كَيْفَ الحَالُ؟

إلهام: أنا بِخَيْر، الحَمْدُ لله، وَكَيْفَ الحَالُ؟

عبد العزيز: الحَمْدُ لله، مُمْتاز، شُكْراً.

إلهام: مِنْ أيْنَ أنتَ؟

عبد العزيز: أنا مِن المَمْلَكَةِ العَرَبيَّةِ السُّعُودِيَّةِ، ومِنْ أيْنَ أنتِ؟

إلهام: أنا مِن الولايَاتِ المُتَّحِدَةِ الأمْريكِيَّةِ.

عبد العزيز: مِنْ أيِّ ولايَةٍ أنتِ؟

إلهام: أنا مِنْ ولايَةِ كاليفورنيا.

عبد العزيز: مِنْ أيِّ مَدِينَةٍ؟

إلهام: أنا مِنْ مَدينةِ سانتا مونيكا. هل أنتَ طالِبٌ؟

عبد العزيز: نَعَم، أنا طالِبٌ لكِنْ، أنا آسِفٌ، أنا عَلى عَجَلَةٍ، يَجِبُ أنْ أذهَبَ الآنَ.

إلهام: طيِّب، إلى اللقاءِ.

عبد العزيز: إلى اللقاءِ، مَعَ السَّلامَةِ.

القواعد
Grammar

1. The Definite Article - الـ: أداة التعريف

The definite article in Arabic is الـ, and it is written as the prefix of the word it modifies. For example, an indefinite word like مدينة 'a city' becomes definite المدينة 'the city' when prefixed by الـ.

All words with الـ are definite, but there are words without الـ that are also definite. These include all proper nouns, names of cities, and names of countries. For example جاسم، ريم، بيروت، مصر are all definite without the definite article. Later, we will learn that nouns without the definite article become definite in the *idafa* (الإضافة) construction.

🎧 **Activity 1:** Change all the indefinite nouns to definite by adding the definite article. Listen and speak aloud.

الطالب	=	طالب	+	الـ
الطالبة	=	طالبة	+	الـ
الاسم	=	اسم	+	الـ
الحال	=	حال	+	الـ
المدينة	=	مدينة	+	الـ
الولاية	=	ولاية	+	الـ

❖

2. Gender of Nouns - المذكر والمؤنث

Arabic nouns are either masculine or feminine. Arabic has no neutral gender. The gender of each Arabic word must be learned and memorized. In general, the feminine noun is formed from the masculine noun by adding the feminine suffix (ة) at the end of the word, such as:

كلِمات وتعابير
Words and Expressions

one thousand   ألْفٌ
I am very well   أنا بألفِ خَيْر

❖

Drill 1: Fill in the blanks with the correct words from the comprehension text.

> عادل هو ــصديــقـة عبد العزيز. هو من الكويـت أميرة هي صديقة إلـهـام
> وهي من ديـنـة عمّان في الاردن. أميرة هيَ طالبة ، وهي تدرس الـعـلاقـات
> عادل هو طـالـب كذلك وهو يدرسُ الادب في أمريكا.   الـلـر كـيـة
> الــتــعـلـيـمـيـة

❖

Drill 2: Translate into English.

١ - عادل هو من مدينة الكويت في الكويت.
٢ - عمّان هي مدينة في الأردنِّ.
٣ - عادل هو صديق عبد العزيز.
٤ - عادل هو طالب، وهو يَدْرُسُ الأدَبَ الإنكليزي.
٥ - هل أنتَ طالب؟
٦ - ماذا تدرسُ؟
٧ - مِنْ أيْنَ أنتَ؟
٨ - أنا مِن المَمْلكة العربيَّة السُّعودية.

❖

Drill 3: Translate into Arabic.

1. Ameera is Ilham's friend.
2. Ameera is a student; she studies international relations.

3. She is from the city of Amman in Jordan.
4. I am in a hurry. – على عجلة
5. I have to go now.
6. Hello, welcome.
7. What is your name?
8. I am from the Kingdom of Saudi Arabia.

❖

المحادثة
Let's Speak Arabic
الطَّعام – Food

Repeat aloud the following question:

What did you (m.s.) eat?	ماذا أَكَلْتَ؟
What did you (f.s.) eat?	ماذا أَكَلْتِ؟

Now repeat aloud the following answer:

I ate (the) hummus	أَكَلْتُ الحُمُّص

Next, repeat aloud the sentence and substitute the following words for الحُمُّص:

(the) falafel   الفَلافِل
(the) cheese   الجُبْنة
(the) chicken   الدَّجَاج
(the) cereal   الحُبُوب
(the) bread   الخُبْز

Practice the dialogue with a classmate.

Homework - الواجب

1. Listen to the vocabulary and expressions. Repeat aloud after listening to them in the basic text and the comprehension text.

2. Compose a simple dialogue between you and one of your friends. Turn it in to your teacher after you present it in class.

3. Compose five sentences using vocabulary from the lesson.

وجعلناكم شعوباً وقبائل لتعارفوا

And we made you into nations and tribes so you get to know each other

من الثقافة العربية
قصائدُ حُبٍّ عَرَبيَّة

Window into Arab Culture
Arabic Love Poems

Figure 1.4 - Nizar Qabbani

Arabic poetry is a political, social, and ethical compass in Arab culture. Poetry has represented and helped to preserve Arab identity throughout the ages. The complex and refined poetic arts eloquently express, report, and document the news, events, and wars of the Arabs, in victory or defeat, glory or decline. Above all, poetry has been a great manifestation of artistic creativity, engendering the emotional and spiritual power that unified the Arabs into a community of nations long before Islam.

Below are a few verses of modern Arabic love poetry by the Syrian poet Nizar Qabbani (1923-1998).* Identify as much of the vocabulary as you can, memorize the verses that you like most, and enjoy the reading.

Nizar Qabbani was known for the beauty of his handwriting and for his impressive calligraphy skills. In the right hand column is the handwritten version of these verses, written by the poet himself.

The verses are read by Lebanese journalist Joumana Nammour, a popular anchorwoman on Al-Jazeera Satellite Channel.

❖

Activity 2: Below are the question particles used together with a preposition. Read aloud and repeat.

Meaning	Preposition together with Particle	Preposition + Particle
From where?	مِـنْ أينَ	مِنْ + أَينَ
In which?	في أيِّ	في + أيِّ
From which?	مِنْ أيِّ	مِنْ + أيِّ
With whom?	مَعَ مَنْ	مَعَ + مَنْ
To where?	إلى أيْنَ	إلى + أيْنَ
Why? For what?	لِمَاذا	لِ + مَاذا
With what? In what?	بِمَاذا	بِ + مَاذا
To who? For whom?	لِمَنْ	لِ + مَنْ

Drill 2: Compose five sentences using the question particles with the prepositions.

❖

Drill 3: Fill in the blanks with the correct words from the comprehension text.

عادل عنده ـــــــــ ـــــــــ كثيرة. بعد المختبر سيذهب إلى ـــــــــ ـــــــــ ثم سيذهب إلى ـــــــــ

في مدينة ـــــــــ. قالت أميرة: ـــــــــ ـــــــــ الكتاب؟ قال عادل: هذا ـــــــــ ـــــــــ ـــــــــ

الكريم. وقال كذلك: ـــــــــ ـــــــــ قريباً، يا أميرة. أميرة ستذهب إلى ـــــــــ ـــــــــ وقالت: في

ـــــــــ ـــــــــ يا عادل.

❖

Drill 4: Compose six sentences using the question particles with prepositions. Also, use the question particles with prepositions in a conversation with one of your classmates.

الفهم والاستيعاب: في المكتبة
Comprehension Text: In the Library

عادل: السَّلامُ عَلَيْكُم.

أميرة: وَعَـلَـيْـكُم السَّلام، كيفَ الصِّحَّة؟

عادل: الحمدُ لله، بألفِ خَيْر، وكيفَ الحَالُ يا أميرة؟

أميرة: بخير، شُـكرا. ماذا تفعلُ الآن؟

عادل: عِندي عَمْلٌ في المُخْـتَبَر.

أميرة: ماذا سَتَفْعَلُ بَعْدَ ذلِكَ؟

عادل: سَأذهَبُ إلى المَسْجِدِ، ثم سَأذهبُ إلى البيتِ.

أميرة: المَسْـجِدُ؟ أيْنَ المَسْـجِدُ؟

عادل: المَسْـجِدُ هو في مدينةِ كليرمُونت.

أميرة: هل عِنْدَك واجباتٌ اليوم؟

عادل: نعَم، في الحقيقةِ، عِندي واجباتٌ كثيرة جداً.

أميرة: ما هذا الكتابُ؟

عادل: هذا هو القرآنُ الكريمُ. وأنتِ ماذا ستفعلينَ؟

أميرة: سَأذهبُ إلى المكتبة.

عادل: أراكِ قريباً يا أميرة، إلى اللقاء.

أميرة: في أمانِ اللهِ، يا عادل. مع السَّلامة.

🎧   كلمات وتعابير
Words and Expressions

now   الآنَ
May God protect you   في أَمَانِ اللهِ
How is your health?   كيفَ الصِّحَّة
The Holy Qur'an   القرآنُ الكريمُ

❖

Drill 5: Translate into English.

١ - السلام عليكم، يا أميرة، كيف الصِّحَّة؟.
٢ - أنا اسمي عادل. أنا بألف خير، الحمد لله.
٣ - اليوم، عندي واجبات كثيرة
٤ - أنا سأذهب إلى البيت
٥ - ثم سأذهب إلى المكتبة.
٦ - ماذا تفعلُ الآن؟
٧ - المسجدُ هو في مدينةِ كليرمونت.
٨ - ما هذا الكتابُ؟
٩ - في أمان الله يا أميرة، مع السلامة.

❖

Drill 6: Translate into Arabic.

1. This is the Holy Qur`an.
2. I will go to the mosque.
3. Then I have to work in the laboratory.
4. What will you be doing, Ameera?
5. See you soon, so long.
6. Do you have homework today?
7. Where is the mosque?
8. What is this book?

🎧

المحادثة

Let's Speak Arabic
الطَّقْس - Weather

Repeat aloud the following question:

How is the weather?	كَيْفَ الطَّقْسُ؟

Now repeat aloud the following answer:

The weather is sunny	الطَّقْسُ مُشْمِسٌ

Next, repeat aloud the sentence and substitute the following words for مُشْمِس:

hot	حَارٌّ
cold	بَارِدٌ
rainy	مُمْطِرٌ
cloudy	غَائِمٌ
humid	رَطْبٌ

Repeat this dialogue with a classmate.

෴

Homework - الواجب

1. Listen to the vocabulary and expressions. Repeat aloud after hearing them in the basic and comprehension texts.

2. Compose a dialogue between you and one of your classmates. Turn it in to your teacher after you present it in class.

3. Compose five sentences using vocabulary from the lesson.

4. Using the question particles, compose an original dialogue between you and one of your friends.

الدَّرْسُ الثَّالِثُ

إِلْهَـام

Lesson Three

Ilham

Figure 3.1 - Claremont, California

Lesson Three Contents

🎧 Vocabulary - المفردات

🎧 Words and Expressions - كلمات وتعابير

💿 Basic Text - النص الأساسي
DVD

   ❖ Ilham Abd Al-Rahman - إلهام عبد الرحمن

Grammar - القواعد

   1. The Nisba Adjective - ياء النسبة

     🎧 Activity 1

   2. Cases of the Noun - حالات الاسم

     A. The Nominative Case - حالة الرفع

     B. The Accusative Case - حالة النصب

     C. The Genitive Case - حالة الجرّ

   3. The Nominal Sentence: Subject and Predicate

     الجملة الاسمية: المبتدأ والخبر

   4. The Numbers (1-10) - الأعداد

     🎧 Activity 2

💿 Comprehension Text - الفهم والاستيعاب
DVD

   ❖ A Student from Kuwait - طالب من الكويت

🎧 Let's Speak Arabic - المحادثة

   ❖ Colors - الألْـوَان

💿 Window into Arab Culture - من الثقافة العربية
DVD

   ❖ "To My Mother" - إلى أمي

🎧

المفردات
Vocabulary

age	عُمْرٌ	Lebanon	لُبْنان
my age	عُمْري	Lebanese	لُبْنانِيٌّ - لُبْنانِيَّة
his age	عُمْرُهُ	I have	عِندي
her age	عُمْرُهَا	brother	أخٌ ج. إخْوَة
university	جامِعَة	sister	أخْتٌ ج. أخَوَاتٌ
American	أمْريكِيٌّ - أمْريكِيَّة	restaurant	مَطْعَمٌ
professor	أسْتاذٌ ج. أسَاتِذة	family	عَائِلَة
I have	لي	happy	سَعيدٌ - سَعيدة
father	أبٌ، وَالِدٌ	city	مَدينَة
my father	أبي، والِدي	year	سَنة ج. سَنَوَاتٌ
Iraq	العِراق	one	واحِدٌ - واحِدَة
Iraqi	عِراقِيٌّ - عِراقِيَّة	two (m. dual)	اِثْنانِ
Baghdad	بَغْداد	two (f. dual)	اِثْنَتَانِ
mother	أمٌّ، وَالِدَة	physician	طَبيبٌ - طَبيبة
my mother	أمِّي، والِدَتي	specialist, specialized	مُتَخَصِّصٌ - مُتَخَصِّصَة

☸

🎧

كلمات وتعابير
Words and Expressions

I was born	أنا وُلِدْتُ
studies	دِرَاسَاتٌ
The Middle East	الشَّرْقُ الأوْسَط
Arab origin	أصْلٌ عَربيٌّ
Middle Eastern Studies	دراساتُ الشَّرقِ الأوْسَطِ
he was born	وُلِدَ
she was born	وُلِدَتْ
eighteen years	ثمانية عَشَرَ عَامًا

I have two sisters لي أختان ِ اِثنتان ِ
she works هِيَ تعْمَلُ
my second sister أختي الثانية
high school مَدْرَسَة ثانويَّة
I love my family أنا أحِبُّ عائِلتي
Columbia University جامِعَة كولومبيا
Pomona College كُلِّيَّة بومونا
assistant مُسـاعِدٌ
he works يَعْمَلُ
I grew up / was raised نشأتُ
religious family عَائِلة مُتَدَيِّنَة
I pray every day أصَلِّي كُلَّ يَوْمٍ
Sunni سُـنِّيٌّ – سُـنِّـيَّة
Shi`ite شيعيٌّ – شيعيَّة
Spain إسبانيا
India الـهـند
Damascus دِمَشْـق
I love my friends أحِبُّ أصْدِقائي

Praise be to God - الحمد لله

النص الأساسي: إلهام عبد الرحمن
Basic Text: Ilham Abd Al-Rahman

أنا إلهام عبد الرحمن، عُمْري ثلاثٌ وعِشرونَ سَنةً، أنا أمريكيَّة مِنْ أصْل عربيٍّ. أنا طالبة في جامِعَةِ كليرمُونت، في ولايةِ كاليفورنيا. أنا أدرُسُ المَاجِستير ومُتَخَصِّصَة في إدارَةِ الأعْمَال، وأدْرُسُ اللغة العربية كذلِكَ. وُلِدْتُ في مدينةِ سانتا مونيكا. أبي (والدي) عِراقيٌّ، وُلِدَ في العِراق، في مدينةِ بغداد، وهو أسْتاذٌ في جامعة كولومبيا في مدينةِ نيويورك. أمِّي (والدتي) طبيبةٌ، وهي لبنانية.

لي أخٌ واحِدٌ، اسمُهُ سهيل، عُمْرُهُ ثمانية عَشَرَ عاماً، هو طالبٌ في جامعةٍ بوسطن، ومُتَخَصِّصٌ في دِراساتِ الشَّرق الأوْسَطِ. ولي أختان اِثنتانِ، واحدةٌ اسمُها عائِشة، عُمْرُها تِسْعَةَ عَشَرَ عاماً، وتَعْمَلُ في مَطْعَم الجامعةِ. أختي الثانية اسمُها سَحَر، عُمْرُها ستةَ عَشَرَ عاماً، وهي طالبةٌ في المَدْرَسَةِ الثانويَّةِ. هذهِ هي عائِلتي. أنا أحِبُّ عائِلتي.

Figure 3.2 - Northern Lebanon

القواعد
Grammar

1. The Nisba Adjective - ياء النسبة

Arabic language uses the suffixes يّ and يّة (f.) to make adjectives from nouns. This suffix is called ياء النسبة 'the *nisba* suffix.' The يّ is added to the noun to form a singular masculine adjective and the يّة is added to form a feminine singular adjective. The adjective formed by this suffix is called *nisba* adjective. Examples are:

Fem. Singular Adj.	Masc. Singular Adj.	Noun
مِصريَّة	مِصري	مِصرُ
لبنانيَّة	لبناني	لبنانُ

The *nisba* suffix is added to the noun after removing the final short vowel at the end of the noun. For example, in order to make the word دمشقُ a singular masculine adjective, we drop the *damma* and add the (يّ) to form دمشقيّ in the singular masculine. Or, we add (يّة) to form a singular feminine adjective, as in دمشقيَّة.

If the original noun has the feminine ending ة (تاء مربوطة), then we drop this feminine ending when forming a singular masculine adjective. To form the feminine adjective, simply restore the feminine ending so that the adjective looks exactly like the original noun.

Fem. Adjective	Masc. Adjective	Feminine Noun
سُعوديَّة	سُعودي	السُّعوديَّة
شيعيَّة	شيعي	شيعة
سُنّيَّة	سُنّي	سُنّة

Note that English borrows the Arabic *nisba* suffix to form some adjectives, as in Iraqi, Omani, Saudi, Kuwaiti and Bahraini.

Activity 1: Change the nouns to masculine adjectives and to feminine adjectives.

Feminine Adjective	Masculine Adjective	Nouns
أمريكيَّةٌ	أمريكيٌّ	أمريكا
أردنيَّةٌ	أردنيٌّ	الأردنُّ
إسبانيَّةٌ	إسبانيٌّ	إسبانيا
عراقيَّةٌ	عراقيٌّ	العراق
عربيَّةٌ	عربيٌّ	عربٌ
كنديَّةٌ	كنديٌّ	كندا
هنديَّةٌ	هنديٌّ	الهند

❖

Drill 1: Form adjectives from the nouns in the sentences.

Example - أنا من أمريكا ـ أنا أمريكيٌّ

١ - أستاذي من سوريا. أستاذي -

٢ - الطالبة من الجزائر. الطالبة ـ

٣ - صديقتي من ليبيا. صديقتي -

٤ - هو من الصِّين. هو ـ

٥ - أنتَ من المكسيك. أنتَ ـ

٦ - الطبيب من فرنسا. الطبيب ـ

٧ - جورج من إيطاليا. جورج -

٨ - ليلى من لبنان. ليلى ـ

٩ - أنتِ من السعودية. أنتِ ـ

❖

2. Cases of the Noun - حالات الاسم

There are three cases of nouns in Arabic. These cases are indicated by changing the vowels of the final consonant (except in the dual and the sound plural endings, which will be discussed later).

❖

A. *The nominative case* - حالة الرفع

In Arabic, the noun is in the nominative case if it ends in *damma* (ـُ) or double *damma* (ـٌ). The *damma* is the marker for a definite noun. The double *damma* (تنوين الرفع) is the marker for an indefinite noun. The noun is in the nominative case, for example, when it is the subject of a sentence.

i. When the noun ends in *damma* or double *damma* it is in the nominative case.

Meaning	Noun ends in double *damma*	Meaning	Noun ends in *damma*
a student (m.s.)	طالبٌ	the student (m.s)	الطالبُ
a student (f.s.)	طالبةٌ	the student (f.s.)	الطالبةُ

ii. Below are examples of nouns in the nominative case functioning as the subject of the sentence. The first sentence is a nominal sentence, and the second is a verbal sentence (we will study both soon). For now, just pay attention to the subject, which is in the nominative case.

Nominal Sentence: Subject and Predicate الجملة الاسمية: المبتدأ والخبر		
Meaning: المعنى	Predicate: الخبر	Subject: المبتدأ
The student is Egyptian	مِصْريٌّ	الطالبُ

Verbal Sentence: Verb and Subject الجملة الفعلية: الفعل والفاعل		
Meaning: المعنى	Subject: الفاعل	Verb: الفعل
The student studied	الطالبُ	دَرَسَ
A student studied	طالبٌ	دَرَسَ

B. *The accusative case* - حالة النصب

The noun is in the accusative case if it ends in *fatha* (ـَ) or double *fatha* (ـً) (تنوين النصب). The noun is in the accusative case, for example, when it is the direct object of a verb.

i. Examples of the noun endings in the accusative case:

Noun ends with double *fatha*	Noun ends with *fatha*
طالبًا	الطالبَ
بيتًا	البيتَ

Note: Only in the accusative case is the letter *alif* added to the singular, masculine, and indefinite nouns (as in طالبا). This extra *alif* does not lengthen the *fatha*. It is only a convention of spelling.

ii. An example of a noun in the accusative case functioning as the direct object of the verb:

Meaning	Direct object	Subject	Verb
The professor met the student	الطالبَ	الأستاذُ	قابلَ
The professor met a student	طالبًا	الأستاذُ	قابلَ

C. The genitive case - حالة الجَـرّ

A noun is in the genitive case if it ends in *kasra* (ـِ) or double *kasra* (ـٍ) (تنوين الجر). An example of the noun in the genitive case is when it is the object of a preposition in a sentence.

i. Examples of a noun ending in the genitive case:

Noun ends with double *kasra*	Noun ends with *kasra*
طالبٍ	الطالبِ
طالبةٍ	الطالبةِ

ii. Examples of the noun in the genitive case functioning as the object of the preposition:

Meaning	Object of the preposition	Preposition	Subject	Verb
The professor went with the student	الطالبِ	مَعَ	الأستاذُ	ذهبَ
The professor went with a student	طالبٍ	مَعَ	الأستاذُ	ذهبَ

Drill 2: Read the following words out loud and identify the case of each noun.

9 - أُستاذٍ	5 - اسمًا	1 - مطعمٌ
10 - البابُ	6 - درسٌ	2 - جامعةٍ
11 - بيتًا	7 - الكتابَ	3 - ولايةٍ
12 - خيرٌ	8 - لقاءٌ	4 - المدينةِ

❖

3. The Nominal Sentence: Subject and Predicate
الجملة الاسمية: المبتدأ والخبر

Arabic divides all sentences into two fundamental types: the nominal sentence and the verbal sentence. The nominal sentence simply begins with a noun. It consists of a subject and a predicate. The subject is definite and the predicate is usually indefinite, but not always. Both the subject (المبتدأ) and the predicate (الخبر) are in nominative case. (However, other rules could apply that would require different grammatical cases.)

The subject of a nominal sentence is a noun or pronoun, and the predicate could be a noun, adjective, prepositional phrase, or verb.

Examples of the basic and most common nominal sentence:

Predicate	Subject
كبيرٌ	البيتُ
لبنانيٌّ	أنا
مطعمٌ	هذا
يدرسُ في عَمَّان	هو
الطالبُ	مَنْ هذا
أمريكيٌّ	هذا الطالبُ

Sometimes, the predicate comes first, and the subject comes second. When the subject comes second it is usually indefinite. These are examples of the most common structures of this arrangement:

Meaning	Subject second	Predicate first
I have a house	بيتٌ	عِندي
There is a telephone in the house	هاتفٌ	في البيتِ
There is a man in front of you	رَجُلٌ	أمامَكَ
Who is your father?	والِدُكَ	مَنْ

❖

Drill 3: Identify the subject and predicate in the following sentences and give the English translation.

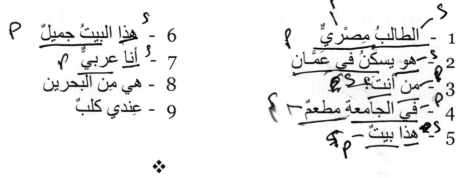

6 - هذا البيتُ جميلٌ

7 - أنا عربيٌّ

8 - هي مِن البَحرين

9 - عِندي كلبٌ

1 - الطالبُ مِصريٌّ

2 - هو يسكنُ في عمّان

3 - من أنتَ؟

4 - في الجامعةِ مطعمٌ

5 - هذا بيتٌ

❖

Drill 4: Compose and vocalize five nominal sentences, underline the subject and the predicate, then translate the sentences into English.

❖

4. The Numbers (1-10) - الأعداد

The rules governing numbers will be covered later. For now, memorize the numbers 1-10.

🎧 **Activity 2**: Repeat the cardinal numbers الأعداد الأصلية (1-10).

Meaning	Cardinal Number	Numbers
zero	صِفْر	٠
one	واحدٌ	١
two	اِثنان	٢
three	ثلاثة	٣
four	أربعة	٤

126

five	خمسة	٥
six	ستة	٦
seven	سبعة	٧
eight	ثمانية	٨
nine	تسعة	٩
ten	عَشَرَة	١٠

❖

Drill 5: Fill in the blanks with the correct words from the comprehension text.

دولَتِ

عادل جاسم الفيصل ولد ونشأ في صحيفة الكويت، عمرهُ عشرون سنة. والدهُ
يعمل في وظيفة الثقافة. وُلِدَتْ أمه في القاهرة ونشأتْ في الكويت. لهُ
ثلاثة إخوة، الأول اسمه حمد، ويعمل في شركة سياحية في. الثاني اسمه
فوّاز، وعمره تسعٌ و عشرون سنةً، وهو موظف في الحكومة. الثالث ، اسمه عبد الله،
وعمره سبع وعشرونَ سنة، ويعمل في شركة سيارات.
نشأ عادل في عائلة متدينة. هو يقرأ القرآن الكريم كل يوم. حضر عادل
إلى أمريكا قبل عامين، وهو يدرس الأدب الإنكليزي ويعمل في
المتجر.

God - الله

⊙
DVD

الفهم والاستيعاب: طالب من الكويت
Comprehension Text: A Student from Kuwait

أنا عادل جاسم الفيصل، عُمْري عِشرونَ عاماً. أنا كويتي، وُلِدْتُ ونشأتُ في مدينةِ الكويت. أبي (والدي) يَعْمَلُ في وزارةِ الثقافةِ، وهو في الحقيقةِ مُساعِدُ الوزير. أمِّي مِصْرِيَّة، وُلِدَتْ في القاهرةِ، وَنشأتْ في الكويت. لي ثلاثةُ إخوةٍ، الأوَّلُ اسمُهُ حَمَد، عُمْرُهُ خمسٌ وثلاثونَ سنةٍ، ويعملُ في شَركةٍ سِياحِيَّةٍ. أخي الثاني اسمُهُ فوَّاز، عُمْرُهُ تِسْعٌ وَعِشرونَ سنةٍ، وهو مُوَظفٌ في الحكومةِ. أخي الثالثُ، اسمُهُ عبدُ الله، عُمْرُهُ سَبْعٌ وعِشرونَ سنةٍ، ويعملُ في شركةِ سياراتٍ.

لي ثلاثُ أخواتٍ. أنا مُسْلِمٌ. نشأتُ في عائِلةٍ مُتَدَيِّنةٍ. أنا أقرأ القرآنَ الكريمَ كلَّ يوم. وأصَلِّي كلَّ يوم. حضرتُ إلى أمريكا قبلَ عامين، وأدرسُ في كليةِ بومونا في ولايةِ كاليفورنيا. أدرسُ الأدبَ الإنكليزيَ وأعْمَلُ في المُختبر. أنا أحِبُّ أمريكا، وأحِبُّ كاليفورنيا، وأحِبُّ أساتذتي، وأحِبُّ أصدقائي.

୨୦୯୪

🎧

كلمات وتعابير
Words and Expressions

Egyptian	مِصْرِيَّة
employee	مُوَظفٌ
cars	سَيَّاراتٌ
minister	وَزيرٌ
government	حُكومَة
Ministry of Culture	وزارة الثقافة
company	شـركة

المحادثة
Let's Speak Arabic
الألْـوَان - Colors

Repeat the following question out loud:

What's your (m.s.) favorite color?	ما لَوْنُكَ المُفَضَّل؟
What's your (f.s.) favorite color?	ما لَوْنُكِ المُفَضَّل؟

Now repeat aloud the following answer:

My favorite color is red	لَوْنِي المُفَضَّل هو الأحْمَر

Next, repeat the sentence and substitute the following words for الأحْمَر:

orange	البُرْتُقالي
yellow	الأصْفَر
green	الأخْضَر
blue	الأزْرَق
brown	البُنِّي
white	الأبْيَض
black	الأسْوَد

Repeat the dialogue with a classmate.

୧෧ඏ

Homework - الواجب

1. Listen to and repeat aloud all vocabulary and expressions in the basic and comprehension texts.

2. Compose a dialogue between you and one of your friends. Turn it in to your teacher after you present it in class.

3. Compose five sentences using the vocabulary from this lesson.

من الثقافة العربية
إلـى أمـــــي

Window into Arab Culture
"To My Mother"

Below and on the DVD are several verses of modern Arabic poetry by the well known Palestinian poet Mahmoud Darwish (1942-2006). The words of the poem, *Ila Ummi* (To My Mother), were put to music and performed by Marcel Khalife, the popular Lebanese composer and musician.

Try to identify as many words as you can from the vocabulary, memorize a few verses if you like, and enjoy the reading. Although this is a difficult poetic text, introduction to the complexities of Arabic early on in your studies will enhance your appreciation of the beauty of the language.

إلـــى أمِّـــــي*
محمـود درويـش

أحِنُّ إلـــى خـبـز أمِّـــــي

وقهـــــوةِ أمـــي

ولمســـــةِ أمـــي

وتكْبُـرُ فـيَّ الطفولــةُ

يومـاً على صَـدْر يـوم ِ

وأعشَـقُ عُمْري لأني

إذا مُـتُّ ،

أخجلُ من دَمْع أمي!

خذيني ، إذا عُـدْتُ يومـاً

وشاحـاً لهُـدْبِـكْ

130

وغطّي عِظامي بعُشبٍ

تعمّدَ مِن طُـهْـر كعبِك

وشُـدّي وثاقي

بخُصْلةِ شَعْـر

بخيطٍ يُلَـوِّحُ في ذيل ثوبِك

عَسانِـي أصيرُ إلهــاً

إلهــاً أصيـــــرُ

إذا ما لمَسْتُ قرارةَ قلبِك!

ضَعيني إذا ما رجَعْتُ

وَقوداً بتنور نـارك

وَحَبْلَ غسيلٍ على سَطْحِ دارك

لأني فقدْتُ الوقوفَ

بدونِ صَلاةِ نهارك

هَرمْتُ، فرُدّي نجومَ الطفولـةِ

حتى أشارك صغارَ العصافير

دربَ الرجوع لِعُش انتظارك

* Bassam K. Frangieh, *Anthology of Arabic Literature, Culture, and Thought from Pre-Islamic Times to the Present.* Yale University Press, New Haven and London, 2005, pp 368-372.

الدَّرْسُ الرَّابِعُ

طالِبٌ مِنْ نَجْران

Lesson Four

A Student from Najran

Figure 4.1 - Najran, Saudi Arabia

Lesson Four Contents

🎧 Vocabulary - المفردات

🎧 Words and Expressions - كلمات وتعابير

💿 Basic Text - النص الأساسي

   ❖ From Saudi Arabia to America - من السُّعودية إلى أمريكا

Grammar - القواعد

   1. The Attached Pronoun - الضمائر المتصلة

     🎧 Activity 1

   2. The *Idafa* Construction - الإضافة

💿 Comprehension Text - الفهم والاستيعاب

   ❖ At Claremont McKenna College - في كلية كليرمونت مكينا

     🎧 Activity 2

   3. The Numbers (11-19) - الأعداد

🎧 Let's Speak Arabic - المحادثة

   ❖ Are You Happy? - هل أنت سعيد؟

💿 Window into Arab Culture - من الثقافة العربية

   ❖ Arabic Music - الموسيقى العربية

المفردات
Vocabulary

manager, director	مُديرٌ - مُديرة
house, home	بَيْتٌ ج. بُيُوتٌ
work, job	عَمَلٌ ج. أعْمَالٌ
health	صِحَّة
ministry	وزارة ج. وزارات
small, little	صَغيرٌ
his name	اسْمُهُ
I study	أدْرُسُ
he studies	يَدْرُسُ
she studies	تدْرُسُ
of course	طبْعًا
I love	أحِبُّ
much, many	كثيرٌ ج. كثيرونَ
I grew up	نشأتُ
company	شركةٌ ج. شركاتٌ
oil	نفْطٌ، زَيْتٌ
no, does not	لا
he works	يَعْمَلُ
she works	تـعْمَلُ
big, older	كبيرٌ
before, ago	قَبْلَ
year	سَنـةٌ ج. سَنواتٌ
friend	صَديقٌ ج. أصْدِقاءُ
among them	مِنْهُم
here	هُنا
twenty	عِشْـرُونَ

134

كلمات وتعابير
Words and Expressions

في الحقيقة	in fact, in reality
الأدَبُ الإنكليزيُّ	English literature
العَلاقاتُ الدُّوَلِيَّة	international relations
لِلدِّراسةِ	to study (literally 'for studying')
ثماني عَشْرَةَ	eighteen (m.)
ثمانية عَشَرَ	eighteen (f.)
تسعَ عَشْرَةَ	nineteen (m.)
تِسْعَةَ عَشَرَ	nineteen (f.)
واحِدٌ وعِشْرونَ	twenty-one
رَبَّةُ بَيْتٍ	housewife
صِحَافة	journalism
رَجُلُ أَعْمَالٍ	businessman
إدارَةُ أَعْمَالٍ	business administration
سَكَنُ الطُّلابِ	dormitory, students' residence
مـادَّةٌ ج. مَـوَادُّ	course, school subject
رياضِيَّات	mathematics, calculus
الحُكومَة الأمريكيةُ	the American government
تاريخٌ	history
زميلٌ ج. زُمَلاءُ	colleague, classmate

Figure 4.2 - Claremont McKenna College, California

النص الأساسي: من السُّعوديَّة إلى أمريكا
Basic Text: From Saudi Arabia to America

أنا عبدُ العزيز أبو ساق، مِنْ مدينةِ نَجران، في المملكةِ العربيةِ السُّعوديةِ. عُمْري أرْبَعٌ وعِشرونَ سَنةً. وُلِدْتُ ونشأتُ في مدينةِ نجران. أنا سُعُوديٌّ طَبْعَاً. أبي (والدي) هو رجُلُ أعْمَال. أمي لا تعمل. هي ربَّةُ بيتٍ. وهذا عَمَلٌ كبيرٌ في الحقيقةِ. أخي الكبيرُ اسمُهُ حَسَنٌ، يَعْمَلُ في وزارةِ الصِّحَّةِ السُّعوديَّةِ، عُمْرُهُ اثنان وثلاثونَ عاماً، ولَهُ ثلاثةُ أبناءٍ، وبنتان اثنتان. أخي الثاني اِسمُهُ مُحَمَّدٌ، عُمْرُهُ ثلاثونَ عاماً ويَعْمَلُ في الصِّحَافةِ. أخي الثالثُ اسمُهُ حُسَيْنٌ، عُمْرُهُ واحدٌ وعِشرونَ عاماً ويعملُ في شركةِ نَفْطٍ. أخي الصغيرُ اسمُهُ عَلِيٌّ، عُمْرُهُ سَبْعَ عَشْرَةَ سنة، وهو طالبٌ في المَدْرَسَةِ الثانويَّةِ.

حضرتُ مِن المملكةِ العربيةِ السعودية إلى الولاياتِ المتحدةِ الأمريكية قبلَ سنةٍ للدِّراسةِ في جامعةِ كليرمونت. أنا أدْرُسُ الدكتوراه في الاقتصادِ. لي أصْدِقاءُ كثيرونَ هُنا، مِنْهُم ريم، وهي متخصصة في دراساتِ الشرقِ الأوسطِ، وعادل وهو يدْرُسُ الأدبَ الإنكليزي، وأميرة وهي متخصصة في العَلاقاتِ الدُّوَلِيَّةِ، وإلهامُ وهي تَدْرُسُ الماجستير في إدارةِ الأعْمَال. أنا أحِبُّ كاليفورنيا، أنا سعيدٌ جداً هنا.

Figure 4.3 - Dohan Hamad Al-Salem and Fahd Soman Al-Salem in Najran

القواعد
Grammar

1. The Attached Pronoun - الضمائر المتصلة

In addition to the independent nominative subject pronouns you have already studied, such as هو 'he,' هي 'she,' and أنت 'you,' there are suffixes to denote possession. For example, in اسمي 'my name,' the ي expresses possession and serves as a possessive pronoun. When the suffixes are added to verbs, they serve as direct objects, as in دَرَسَهُ 'he studied it.' You can also attach the suffixes to prepositions to serve as the object of the preposition, as in مِنهُ 'from him.'

There is a pronoun suffix corresponding to each of the independent pronouns, as shown in the chart below.

🎧 **Activity 1:** Listen and repeat.

Meaning	Noun with attached pronouns	Attached pronoun	Meaning	Independent Pronoun
his house	بَيْتُهُ	هُ	He	هُوَ
her house	بَيْتُها	ها	She	هِيَ
their house (m. dual)	بَيْتُهُما	هُما	They (m. dual)	هُمَا
their house (f. dual)	بَيْتُهُما	هُما	They (f. dual)	هُمَا
their house (m. plural)	بَيْتُهُم	هُم	They (m. plural)	هُم
their house (f. plural)	بَيْتُهُنَّ	هُنَّ	They (f. plural)	هُنَّ
your house (m.s.)	بَيْتُكَ	كَ	You (m.s.)	أنتَ
your house (f.s.)	بَيْتُكِ	كِ	You (f.s.)	أنتِ
your house (m. dual)	بَيْتُكُما	كُمَا	You (m. dual)	أنتُما
your house (f. dual)	بَيْتُكُما	كُمَا	You (f. dual)	أنتُما
your house (m. plural)	بَيْتُكُم	كُمْ	You (m. plural)	أنتُم
your house (f. plural)	بَيْتُكُنَّ	كُنَّ	You (f. plural)	أنتُنَّ
my house	بَيْتِي	ي	I	أنا
our house	بَيْتُنا	نا	We	نَحْنُ

When the pronoun suffix is added to the noun, the noun becomes definite. For example, the noun بيتٌ 'house' becomes definite بيتي 'my house.' Because the noun has become definite, it does not take the definite article or nunation. Example:

Definite noun with pronoun suffix	Definite noun with الـ	Indefinite noun
بيتي	البيتُ	بيتٌ

Also, note that the pronoun suffixes are added to nouns after the case ending. Example:

Gen.	Acc.	Nom.
كتابِكَ	كتابَكَ	كتابُكَ

For phonological reasons, the first person singular suffix ي is added directly to the stem of the word without the case ending. Example:

Gen.	Acc.	Nom.
كتابي	كتابي	كتابي

Also for phonological reasons, the pronoun suffixes (ـهُ), (ـهُما), (ـهُم), and (ـهُنَّ) have vowel changes to (ـهِ), (ـهِما), (ـهِم), and (ـهِنَّ) when preceded by كسرة (ـِ). Example:

Gen.	Acc.	Nom.
كتابِهِ	كتابَهُ	كتابُهُ
كتابِهِمَا	كتابَهُما	كتابُهُما
كتابِهِم	كتابَهُم	كتابُهُم
كتابِهِنَّ	كتابَهُنَّ	كتابُهُنَّ

Drill 1: Write the independent pronoun (هو، أنتَ، هي etc.) that corresponds to the attached pronoun suffix in each word.

Example - بيتُكَ - أنتَ

7 - كِتابي -		1 - أبي -
8 - دَرسُهَا -		2 - لغتُنا -
9 - أستاذكُنَّ -		3 - صديقهُنَّ -
10 - مَدينتُكَ -		4 - اسمُهُ -
11 - ولايتُهُم -		5 - مادَّتكُم -
12 - جامِعتُكِ -		6 - وزارتُهُمَا -

❖

Drill 2: Add pronoun suffixes.

Example - *My house is beautiful.* بيت + (ي) جميلٌ - بيتـي جميلٌ

I studied his book.	1 - درست كتاب + ( )
I love your (f.s.) house!	2 - أحبُّ بيت + ( )
My father and her father are friends.	3 - والد + ( ) ووالد + ( ) أصدقاء
Our university is big.	4 - جامعة + ( ) كبيرة
Your college (m.s.) is beautiful.	5 - كلية +( ) جميلة
Their (m. pl.) father is famous.	6 - والد + ( ) مشهور
There is a library in my city.	7 - في مدينة + ( ) مكتبة
His sister is a doctor.	8 - أخت + ( ) طبيبة

❖

2. The *Idafa* Construction - الإضافة

The *idafa* is a phrase made up of two nouns. The first noun is called the first term of *idafa* (مُضاف) and the second noun is the second term of *idafa* (مُضاف إليه). The second noun follows the first noun immediately, as in:

the door of the house	بابُ البيتِ
the city of Kuwait	مدينـةُ الكويتِ

The first term of the *idafa* is indefinite and can be in any of the three grammatical cases, depending on its position in the sentence. The second term is always in the genitive case and can be definite or indefinite.

The *idafa* expresses the relationship of possession: the first term is the possessed and the second term is the possessor. Example:

Meaning	Second term of *idafa*	First term of *idafa*
the door of the house	البيتِ	بابُ
a door of a house	بيتٍ	بابُ

Here are examples of different versions of the *idafa*:

the director of the office/ the office director	مديرُ المكتبِ
the city of Kuwait	مدينةُ الكويتِ
the Studies of the Middle East/ Middle Eastern Studies	دراساتُ الشرقِ الأوسطِ
the college of Pomona/Pomona College	كليَّةُ بومونا
the house of my father/my father's house	بيتُ والدي

There are two types of *idafa*: definite *idafa* (الإضافة المُعَرَّفة) and indefinite *idafa* (الإضافة غير المعرفة). The second term determines the definiteness or the indefiniteness of the *idafa* structure:

Meaning	Indefinite *idafa*	Meaning	Definite *idafa*
a director of an office	مديرُ مكتبٍ	the director of the office	مديرُ المكتبِ
a manager of a house	مديرةُ بيتٍ	the manager of the house	مديرةُ البيتِ

There is also a complex *idafa* (الإضافة المركَّبة) made up of a string of several nouns. The first noun in the *idafa* may be in any case, but all following nouns must be in the genitive case. All nouns except the last one must be indefinite.

❖

Examples of the complex *idafa*:

a director of an office of a company	مديرُ مكتبٍ شركةٍ
the director of the office of the company	مديرُ مكتبِ الشركةِ
the director of the office of the oil company	مديرُ مكتبِ شركةِ النفطِ
the director of the office of the oil company of Kuwait	مديرُ مكتبِ شركةِ نفطِ الكويتِ

❖

Drill 3: Form *idafa* phrases from the isolated words, then translate them.
Example: *The director of the company.* مدير. شركة - مديرُ الشركة

6 - بيت. أستاذ -	1 - باب. بيت -
7 - مفتاح. باب. بيت -	2 - شركة. نفط -
8 - مطعم. جامعة -	3 - مديرة. متحف -
9 - مدير. مكتب. شركة	4 - كتاب. طالب -
10 - سيارة. مدير -	5 - باب. بيت. والدي -

❖

Drill 4: Translate the following *idafa* constructions.

1. the restaurant of the university
2. the book of the professor
3. the table of the library
4. the language of the text
5. the director of the office of the oil company of Iraq
6. the car of my father
7. the city of New York
8. the professor of the Arabic language class
9. the mother of the father of my father

الفهم والاستيعاب: في كلية كليرمونت مكينا
Comprehension Text: At Claremont McKenna College

أنا أميرة عبد المجيدِ. أبي (والدي) اسمُهُ مروان عبد المجيدِ. والدي أردنيٌّ، حَضَرَ إلى أمريكا من الأردنِّ قبلَ خمسةٍ وعِشرينَ عاماً، ودَرَسَ في جامعةِ واشنطن في مدينةِ سياتل. هو أستاذ متخصِّصٌ في التاريخ. أمي (والدتي) أمريكية، اسْمُهَا روز، وهي مديرة شركةٍ. أنا أدرسُ في كليةِ كليرمونت مكينا في ولايةِ كاليفورنيا.

أنا أسكنُ في سَكَنِ الطلابِ في الكليةِ. كليةُ كليرمونت مكينا هي كلية صغيرة وجميلة وهادئة. أنا متخصصةٌ في العَلاقاتِ الدُّوَلِيَّةِ. أدرسُ أربعَ موادَ دراسية هذه السنة. أدرس مادة الرياضياتِ ومادة التاريخ ومادة الحكومةِ الأمريكية. كما أدرسُ مادة الأدبِ الإنكليزي في كليةِ قريبةٍ أخْرَى، اسْمُهَا كلية بتزر. أنا أحِبُّ زُمَلائِي وزَمِيلاتِي وأحِبُّ أساتِذتي.

৪৩৫

كلمات وتعابير
Words and Expressions

subjects, courses	مَوادُّ دِرَاسِـيَّةٌ
beautiful	جَميلةٌ
near, close	قـريبـةٌ
also, as well	كَمَا
specializing in	متخصِّصَة في
quiet	هَادِئَة
this year	هذه السَّنة
another, other (f.s.)	أخْـرَى

3. The Numbers (11-19) - الأعداد

We will study the grammatical rules governing the numbers later in the book. For now, please memorize the following numbers.

🎧 **Activity 2**: Repeat the cardinal numbers 11-19.

With feminine noun	With masculine noun	Numbers	Numbers
إحدى عَشْرةَ سنةً	أحَدَ عَشَرَ عاماً	١١	11
اِثْنَتا عَشْرةَ سنةً	اِثْنا عَشَرَ عاماً	١٢	12
ثلاثَ عَشْرةَ سنةً	ثلاثةَ عَشَرَ عاماً	١٣	13
أربعَ عَشْرةَ سنةً	أربعةَ عَشَرَ عاماً	١٤	14
خمسَ عَشْرةَ سنةً	خَمْسةَ عَشَرَ عاماً	١٥	15
سِتَّ عَشْرةَ سنةً	سِتَّةَ عَشَرَ عاماً	١٦	16
سَبعَ عَشْرةَ سنةً	سَبعةَ عَشَرَ عاماً	١٧	17
ثماني عَشْرةَ سنةً	ثمانيةَ عَشَرَ عاماً	١٨	18
تِسْعَ عَشْرةَ سنةً	تِسْعةَ عَشَرَ عاماً	١٩	19

❖

Drill 5: Fill in the blanks with the correct words from the comprehension text.

والدُ أميرة اسمُهُ _____ عبد المجيد، وهو من _____، حضر إلى أمريكا قبل خمسة

و _____ عاماً، ودرس في _____ واشنطن في _____ سياتل. هو أستاذ

_____ في التاريخ. والدة أميرة اسمها _____ وهي أمريكية وهي _____

_____ .

أميرة تدرس في _____ كليرمونت مكينا وهي تدرس أربع _____ دراسية. أميرة

متخصصة في _____ _____ . وهي تدرس كذلك مادة _____ الإنكليزي في

كلية أخرى، اسمها _____ .

❖

🎧

المحَادثة

Let's Speak Arabic

هَلْ أنتَ سَعِيد؟ - Are You Happy?

Repeat the following question out loud:

Are you (m.s.) happy?	هَلْ أنتَ سَعِيدٌ؟
Are you (f.s.) happy?	هَلْ أنتِ سَعِيدة؟

Now repeat aloud the following answer:

I am happy	أنا سَعِيدٌ - أنا سَعِيدة

Next, repeat the sentence and substitute the following words for سَعِيد:

tired   أنا تَعْبَان - أنا تَعْبَـانة

hungry   أنا جُـوعَـان - أنا جُـوعَـانة

thirsty   أنا عَطْشَـان - أنا عَطْشَـانة

sad   أنا حَـزين - أنا حَـزينَـة

afraid, scared   أنا خَائِـف - أنا خَائِـفة

Repeat the dialogue with a classmate.

❧❧❧

الواجب - Homework

1. Listen to the vocabulary and expressions. Say them aloud after hearing them in the basic and comprehension texts.

2. Compose a dialogue between you and one of your friends and present it in class. Turn it in to your teacher.

3. Compose five sentences using vocabulary from the lesson.

من الثقافة العربية
الموسيقى العربية

Window into Arab Culture
Arabic Music

Figure 4.4 - Shams Ismael

Shams Ismael (شمس اسماعيل) is a rising star and singer of classical Arabic music. She was born in 1982 in Lattakia, Syria, and has received a degree in English literature and a diploma in translation from Tishreen University in Syria. She has already performed in several Arab cities including Cairo, Alexandria, Beirut, Damascus, Amman, and Tunis.

The song selected is إسهار *Is-haar* (Stay Longer into the Night). The verses in this song are performed in colloquial Lebanese Arabic. Enjoy the music and memorize a few verses. Also, identify words you know and put them into sentences.

إسهار بعد إسهار
كلمات الأخوين رحباني

إسهار بعد إسهار
تايحرز المشوار
كتار هو زوار

شوي وبيفلوا

وعنا الحلا كلوا

وعنا القمر بالدار

ورد، حكي، وأشعار

بس إسهار

بيتك بعيد، وليل

ما بخليك ترجع

أحق الناس نحنا فيك

رح فتِّح بوابي

وانده على اصحابي

قلون: قمرنا زار

وتتلج الدنيي قمار

بس إسهار

وننام

مين بينام غير الأولاد

بيغفوا، بيروحوا، ويلملموا أعياد

مادام إنك هون

يا حلم ملوا الكون

شو هم ليل وطال

ويبنقص العمر نهار

بس إسهار

إسهار

الدَّرْسُ الخَامِسُ

أُستاذٌ مِنَ العِراق

Lesson Five

A Professor from Iraq

Figure 5.1 - Imam Ali Shrine in Iraq

Lesson Five Contents

🎧 Vocabulary - المفردات

🎧 Words and Expressions - كلمات وتعابير

💿 Basic Text - النص الأساسي

   ❖ Ahmad Abd Al-Rahman - أحمد عبد الرحمن

Grammar - القواعد

   1. The Verbal Sentence - الجملة الفعلية

   2. The Perfect Tense - الفعل الماضي

      🎧 Activity 1

   3. Expressing Possession with (عند) and (لـ)

      🎧 Activity 2

💿 Comprehension Text - الفهم والاستيعاب

   ❖ A Physician in New York - طبيبة في نيويورك

      🎧 Activity 3

      🎧 Activity 4

🎧 Let's Speak Arabic - المحادثة

   ❖ Places - أماكن

💿 Window into Arab Culture - من الثقافة العربية

   ❖ Arabic Satellite Television Channels - الفضائيات العربية

🎧

المفردات
Vocabulary

I arrived	وَصَلْتُ	I worked	عَمِلْتُ
a period of time	فترة ج. فترات	before (prep.)	قَبْلَ
son	إبْنٌ	class	صَفٌّ ج. صُفوفٌ
daughter	إبْنَةٌ	I studied	دَرَسْتُ
today	اليَوْم	my wife	زَوْجَتي
Sunday	الأَحْد	I traveled	سَافَرْتُ
I lived, I resided	سَكَنْتُ	doctor	طبيبٌ ج. أطبّاءُ
very well	جَيِّداً	eye	عَيْنٌ ج. عُيُونٌ
I work	أعْمَلُ	I moved, transfered	إنْتَقَلْتُ
before that (prep.)	قَبْلَهَا	after that (prep.)	بَعْدَهَا
I know	أعْرِفُ	conference	مُؤْتَمَرٌ
first, at first	أوَّلاً	I live, I reside	أسْكُنُ

☸

🎧

كلمات وتعابير
Words and Expressions

earlier, before	مِنْ قَبْلُ - مِنْ قَبْلِ
she was born and raised	وُلِدَتْ وَنَشَأَتْ
thirty years ago	قَبْلَ ثلاثينَ عاماً
during my university study	أثناءَ دراسَتي الجَامِعِيَّة
I met my wife	تَعَرَّفْتُ على زوجتي
I fell in love with her at first sight	أحْبَبْتُهَا مِن النظرةِ الأولى
I fell in love with her	وَقَعْتُ في حُبِّهَا
I love her so much	أنا أحِبُّهَا كثيراً
my first and last love	حُبِّي الأوَّلُ والأخِيرُ
I met (for the first time)	تَعَرَّفْتُ
I married her quickly	تَزَوَّجْتُهَا بِسُرْعَة
I spent one night	أمْضَيْتُ لَيْلَة واحِدَة
to meet with, in order that I meet with	لألتقي مَعَ
I will go to, head for	سَأتَوَجَّهُ إلى
a long period of time	فترة طويلة

النص الأساسي: أحمد عبد الرحمن
Basic Text: Ahmad Abd Al-Rahman

أنا أحمد عبد الرحمن، والِدُ إلهام. وصلتُ مِنْ مدينةِ نيويورك هذا اليومَ، الأحد، إلى كاليفورنيا لزيارةِ ابنتي إلهام. أنا في الحقيقةِ أعـرفُ كاليفورنيا جَيِّداً. أنا سكنتُ فيها فترة طويلة مِنْ قبلُ وعِندي بَيْتٌ فيها. وابْنتي إلهام وُلِدَتْ وَنشَأَتْ فيها. أنا أسكنُ، الآنَ، في مدينةِ نيويورك، وأعْمَلُ في جامعةِ كولومبيا. أنا أستاذٌ في العلومِ السياسيةِ. قبلَ هذا، عَمِلتُ في جامعةِ ستانفورد، وقَبْلَهَا عَمِلتُ في جامعةِ كاليفورنيا في لوس أنجلوس.

حَضَرْتُ مـن العِراق قبلَ ثلاثينَ عامـاً للدراسةِ في أمريكا. دَرَسْتُ أوَّلاً في جامعةِ بوسطن ثم انتقلتُ بَعْدَهَا إلـى جامعةِ هارفارد. أثنـاءَ دراستي الجامعِيَّةِ تعَرَّفتُ على زوجتي عبير. كانت عبير قَدْ حَضَرَتْ مِنْ لبنانَ إلى بوسطن للدراسةِ أيْضَـاً. أحْبَبْتُـها مـن النظرةِ الأولـى، وَوَقَعْتُ في حُبِّهَا. وتزَوَّجْتُـها بسُرْعَةٍ. عبير هي حُبِّي الأوَّلُ والأخيرُ، وأنـا أحِبُّهَا كَثيراً. لَـنَا ابنٌ واحِدٌ، اسْمُهُ سُهَيْل. ولنا ثلاثُ بناتٍ، هُنَّ إلهامُ وَعائِشة وَسَحَرَ. نحنُ عَائِلة سعيدة جدّاً.

Figure 5.2 - Narrated by Dany Doueiri

القواعد
Grammar

1. The Verbal Sentence: Verb, Subject, and Object
الجملة الفعلية: الفعل والفاعل والمفعول به

The verbal sentence in Arabic begins with a verb followed by a subject. In a verbal sentence the subject is always in the nominative case (مرفوع) and the verb must agree with the subject in gender.

We use the term "verbal sentence" differently in Arabic than in English. In English the term "verbal sentence" signifies any sentence with a verb in it, while in Arabic a verbal sentence means that the first word of the sentence must be a verb, not a noun or pronoun. Example of a verbal sentence:

Subject	Verb
الطالبُ	دَرَسَ
الطالبةُ	دَرَسَتْ

The verbal sentence includes an object *if* the verb is transitive. The object of the verb is always in the accusative case (منصوب). The usual order of the verbal sentence is that the verb must come first, then the subject, then the object. Example:

III. Object	II. Subject	I. Verb
الدرسَ	الطالبُ	دَرَسَ
الدرسَ	الطالبةُ	دَرَسَتْ

The subject of the verbal sentence can be expressed or hidden (مُسْتَتِر). When not expressed, it still exists in the verb. The hidden subject is in the verb's conjugation. For example, the subject of دَرَسَ is hidden as دَرَسَ indicates '*he* studied.'

Example of the expressed subject:

III. Object	II. Subject	I. Verb
الدرسَ	الطالبُ	دَرَسَ

151

Example of the hidden (مُسْتَتِر) subject:

Object	Verb
الدَّرْسَ	دَرَسَ

The verbal sentence that includes a transitive verb consists of at least three elements: verb, subject, and object. It can be a two-element sentence if the subject is contained in the verb مُسْتَتِر. Also, if the subject and object are pronouns, then the sentence has only one word. Example:

Meaning	Object	Subject	Verb	Sentence
I saw her.	ـها	تُ	شاهَدَ	شاهَدْتُها
He saw her.	ـها	Hidden مُسْتَتِر	شاهَدَ	شاهَدَها

Simply, a verbal sentence starts with a verb, while a nominal sentence starts with a noun. The main difference is the word order. A verbal sentence and a nominal sentence can convey the same meaning. There is a slight difference in emphasis between the verbal sentence and the equivalent nominal sentence. Example:

Verbal sentence
دَرَسَ الطالبُ

=

Nominal sentence
الطالبُ دَرَسَ

Also, if a sentence has a compound subject, then the verb must agree with the first member of the compound subject:

Compound subject	Verb
جاسمٌ وريمُ	دَرَسَ
ريمُ وجاسمٌ	دَرَسَتْ

If a feminine subject is separated from the verb by a phrase or a word, then the verb can be either feminine *or* masculine. Example:

Subject	(Separator)	Verb
أسْتاذةٌ مِصريةٌ	إلى الجامعةِ	حَضَرَتْ
أسْتاذةٌ مِصريةٌ	إلى الجامعةِ	حَضَرَ

A (female) Egyptian professor came to the university

Drill 1: Compose six sentences: three with transitive verbs and three with intransitive verbs (note that intransitive verbs do not require an object).

❖

Drill 2: Translate the following into Arabic using verbal sentences.

1. He wrote a letter to his father.
2. She went to the university with him.
3. You (m.s.) traveled with your father.
4. I studied the Arabic language, and she studied Spanish.
5. The (female) professor and the (male) professor came to the class.
6. He worked at Washington University.

❖

Drill 3: Change the verbal sentences to nominal sentences. Start the sentences with a noun or an independent pronoun.

Example - درسَ في بيروت *سَليمٌ* — درسَ *سَليمٌ* في بيروت

6 - أحببتها كثيراً -	1 - حضر من الكويت قبل سنة -
7 - تعرّفتْ مريم على خالد في بيروت -	2 - عمل أحمد في شركة نفط -
8 - ذهبوا الى صف اللغة العربية -	3 - كتب والدي رسالة إلى أمي -
9 - فعلا واجبهما -	4 - درس في جامعة القاهرة -
10 - شاهدتُ مدينة مدريد -	5 - سكنت أختي في بوسطن -

❖

2. The Perfect Tense - الفعل الماضي

The past (perfect) tense in Arabic signifies that the action of a given verb has occurred and been completed. This is in contrast to the present tense (imperfect), which means that the event or the action of the verb has not been completed.

The third-person masculine singular perfect tense (هُوَ) in Arabic carries the root of the verb. It is the source from which all other forms of Arabic words are derived. Therefore, all derived forms have a specific relationship to a verb's simple past tense. This is the key to using an Arabic dictionary. Arabic verbs are listed in the third-person masculine singular perfect form. Then, the derived forms follow in a systematic order. Vocabulary lists usually introduce words in the same manner.

The past tense consists of a stem and a subject marker: the stem indicates the basic meaning of the verb, while the subject marker indicates the gender, person, and number of the subject. The subject markers are called pronoun suffixes in Arabic (ضمائر رفع متصلة) (only used with verbs) and act as the subject of the verb. In other words, the stem denotes a completed action/event and the subject marker denotes who or what (including person, number, and gender) has done the action.

Below is a complete conjugation of the perfect tense دَرَسَ 'he studied' (stem is دَرَس), along with the corresponding independent pronouns and subject markers.

Activity 1: Listen to the verb conjugations and repeat.

Subject Marker	Meaning	Verb Conjugation	Independent Pronoun
ـَ	he studied	دَرَسَ	هُوَ
ـَتْ	she studied	دَرَسَتْ	هِيَ
ـَا	they studied (m. dual)	دَرَسَا	هُمَا
ـَتَا	they studied (f. dual)	دَرَسَتَا	هُمَا
ـوا	they studied (m. plural)	دَرَسُوا	هُم
ـنَ	they studied (f. plural)	دَرَسْنَ	هُنَّ
ـتَ	you studied (m.s.)	دَرَسْتَ	أنتَ
ـتِ	you studied (f.s.)	دَرَسْتِ	أنتِ
ـتُمَا	you studied (m. dual)	دَرَسْتُمَا	أنتما
ـتُمَا	you studied (f. dual)	دَرَسْتُمَا	أنتما
ـتُم	you studied (m. plural)	دَرَسْتُم	أنتم
ـتُنَّ	you (f. plural)	دَرَسْتُنَّ	أنتُنَّ
ـتُ	I studied	دَرَسْتُ	أنا
ـنا	we studied	دَرَسْنا	نحْنُ

Drill 4: Write the independent pronoun that corresponds to the following verb forms.

5 – ذَهَبُوا   1 – حَضَرْنَ

6 – رَجَعَ   2 – عَمِلْتَ

7 – أَحْبَبْتُ   3 – تَعَلَّمْنا

8 – كَتَبْتُمَا   4 – سَافرْتُنَّ

❖

Drill 5: Conjugate the following verbs.

3 – رَجَعَ   1 – عَرَفَ

4 – عَمِلَ   2 – سَمِعَ

❖

3. Expressing possession with عِند and لِـ

عِند and لِـ are prepositions. Each has several connotations, which depend upon the context. Both are introduced here to express possession. Both mean 'to have' but are not expressed with a verb in Arabic. When expressing possession, both عِند and لِـ are used by many in spoken Arabic almost interchangeably. Formally, عِند conveys the idea of simple possession:

| عِندي بيتٌ | I have a house |

And لِـ is mostly used to describe human relationship or to convey a concrete or abstract concept of possession.

الحرية لـها ثَمَنُها	Freedom has a price
لـلبيتِ شباكٌ	The house has a window
لِـي ابْنٌ	I have a son

You can see in the chart below all the suffix pronouns of عِند and لِـ along with their corresponding independent pronouns.

Activity 2: Listen to the possessive nouns with their attached pronoun suffixes and repeat aloud.

Meaning	لِ with Attached Pronouns	عِنْدَ with Attached Pronouns	Attached Pronoun	Independent Pronoun
he has	لَـهُ	عِندَهُ	هُ	هو
she has	لَـهَا	عِندَهَا	هَا	هي
they have (m. dual)	لَـهُمَا	عِندَهُمَا	هُمَا	هُمَا
they have (f. dual)	لَـهُمَا	عِندَهُمَا	هُمَا	هُمَا
they have (m. plural)	لَـهُمْ	عِندَهُمْ	هُمْ	هُمْ
they have (f. plural)	لَـهُنَّ	عِندَهُنَّ	هُنَّ	هُنَّ
you have (m.s.)	لَـكَ	عِندَكَ	كَ	أنتَ
you have (f.s.)	لَـكِ	عِندَكِ	كِ	أنتِ
you have (m. dual)	لَـكُمَا	عِندَكُمَا	كُمَا	أنتما
you have (f. dual)	لَـكُمَا	عِندَكُمَا	كُمَا	أنتما
you have (m. plural)	لَـكُمْ	عِندَكُمْ	كُمْ	أنتم
you have (f. plural)	لَـكُنَّ	عِندَكُنَّ	كُنَّ	أنتنَّ
I have	لِي	عِندِي	ي	أنا
we have	لَـنَا	عِندَنَا	نَا	نحنُ

Note: The vowel at the end of the prepositions عند and لـ is *fatha* (فتحة) when attached to the pronoun suffixes. When attached to ي, the vowel changes to *kasra* (كسرة) for phonological reasons.

❖

Drill 6: Translate into Arabic.

    1. Do you (f.s.) have a car?
    2. I have a house. My house has a big door.
    3. Do you (m.p.) have a question?
    4. I have a friend in Spain.
    5. The Arabic language has difficult grammar.
    6. I have a brother and two sisters.
    7. I have two eyes.
    8. He has my book.

Drill 7: Combine the prepositions with the correct attached pronouns.

7 - علي _____ أخ يعمل في شركة نفط   1 - _____ واجبات كثيرة جداً اليوم (عند + أنا)

(لـ + هو)   2 - _____ بيت في كاليفورنيا (عند + هو)

8 - أنتما _____ عمل في المختبر (عند + أنتما)   3 - الأستاذ أحمد وزوجته _____ ثلاثة أولاد

9 - هي _____ سيارة جميلة (عند + هي)   (لـ + هما)

10- الصين _____ تاريخ طويل من الحضارة   4 - هل _____ سؤال؟ (عند + أنت)

(لـ + هي)   5 - مكتب المدير _____ شباك كبير (لـ + هو)

                                             6 - _____ أصدقاء في بيروت (لـ + نحن)

❖

Drill 8: Fill in the blanks with the correct words from the comprehension text.

وصلت عبير جواد محمد من نيويورك إلى لوس أنجلوس أول _____ الجمعة، وأمضت

فيها _____ واحدة، سافرت بعدها _____ مؤتمر الأطباء. عبير هي _____

عيون وتعمل في _____ خاصة.

حضرت عبير من _____ إلى أمريكا لدراسة _____ في جامعة هارفارد حيثُ

_____ على زوجها أحمد. ستمضي عبير مع إلهام _____ أيام تتعرف فيها على

بعض _____ وتحضر بعض الصفوف.   ثم ترجع _____ إلى بيتها في

_____ نيويورك.

❖

الفهم والاستيعاب: طبيبة في نيويورك
Comprehension Text: A Physician in New York

أنا عبير جـواد محمد، والدةُ إلهام. وَصَلْتُ من نيويورك إلى لوس أنجلوس أوّلَ أمس، الجمعة، وأمضيتُ فيها ليلة ًواحدة، سَافَرْتُ بَعْدَهَا إلى مدينةِ سان فرانسيسكو لِحُضُور مُؤْتـَمَر الأطِبَّاء فيها. بَعْدَ المُؤْتَمَر، سَأتوَجَّهُ إلى مدينةِ كليرمونت لألتقي مَعَ زوجي أحمد الذي وَصَلَ إليها يَوْمَ الأحد ولألتقي مَعَ ابنتي إلهام التي تدْرُسُ هناك. أنا طبيبة عيون وأَعْمَلُ في عيادةٍ خاصةٍ في مدينةِ نيويورك. أنا أحِبُّ عَمَلي كثيراً.

حضرتُ مِنْ لبنانَ إلى أمريكا لدراسةِ الطِّبِّ في جامعةِ هارفارد وأثناءَ دِرَاسَتِي الجامِعِيَّة تعَرَّفْتُ على زَوْجي أحمد. أحمد هو رَجُلٌ مُمْتازٌ. أنا فِعْلاً أحِبُّهُ مِنْ كُلِّ قلبي، وأنا سعيدة جداً مَعَهُ. سَعَادَتُنَا الآنَ هِيَ في أوْلادِنا. نحنُ نُحِبُّهُم جداً. سَنُمْضِي مَعَ إلهامَ ثلاثة أيّام نتعرَّفُ فيها على بَعْض أسَاتِذتِهَا ونحْضُرُ بعضَ الصُّفوفِ في كُلِّيَّتِهَا ثُـمَّ نرجعُ بَعْدَهَا إلى بَيْتِنَا في مَدينةِ نيويورك.

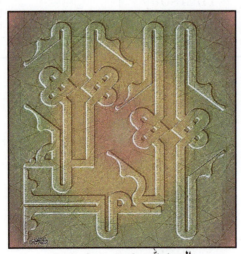

الحمد لله - Praise be to God

🎧

كلمات وتعابير
Words and Expressions

I traveled	سَافَرْتُ	conference	مُؤتمر
we will spend	سَنُمْضِي	medicine	طِبٌّ
clinic, practice	عِيَادة	my husband	زوْجِي
during	أثناءَ	in order that I meet	لألتقي
my university study	دِراستي الجَامِعيَّة	I indeed love him	أنا فِعلاً أحِبُّهُ
my heart	قلبي	all	كلٌّ
our children	أوْلادُنَا	happy	سَعِيدة
we attend	نَحْضُرُ	some	بَعْض

❖

🎧 **Activity 3:** Below are the days of the week. Please repeat out loud.

أيَّام الأسْبُوع

Sunday	الأحَد
Monday	الإثنين
Tuesday	الثَّلاثاء
Wednesday	الأرْبِعَاء
Thursday	الخَميس
Friday	الجُمُعة
Saturday	السَّبْت

🎧 **Activity 4:** Below are the seasons of the year. Please repeat out loud.

فُصُول السَّنة

Spring	الرَّبِيع
Summer	الصَّيْف
Fall	الخَريف
Winter	الشِّتَاء

الدَّرْسُ السَّادِسُ

شَاعِرٌ مِنْ دِمَشْقَ

Lesson Six

A Poet from Damascus

Figure 6.1 - Damascus, Syria

Lesson Six Contents

🎧 Vocabulary - المفردات

🎧 Words and Expressions - كلمات وتعابير

💿 Basic Text - النص الأساسي

    ❖ A Poet from Damascus - شاعر من دمشق

Grammar - القواعد

    1. The Demonstrative Pronouns - أسماء الإشارة

       🎧 Activity 1

       🎧 Activity 2

    2. The Relative Pronouns - الأسماء الموصولة

       🎧 Activity 3

    3. The Present Tense (Imperfect) - الفعل المضارع

       🎧 Activity 4

    4. The Future Tense - المستقبل

💿 Comprehension Text - الفهم والاستيعاب

    ❖ A Writer from Damascus - كاتبة من دمشق

🎧 Let's Speak Arabic - المحادثة

    ❖ Studying - الدراسة

💿 Window into Arab Culture - من الثقافة العربية

    ❖ Sadness in the Moonlight - حزن في ضوء القمر

المفردات
Vocabulary

child, baby	طِفْلٌ ج. أطْفالٌ
soil, dust	تُرَابٌ
rain	مَطَرٌ ج. أمْطارٌ
old, ancient	قديمٌ
they died (m. pl.)	مَاتوا
they departed (m. pl.)	رَحَلوا
I love, I like	أحِبُّ
who, which (m.s.)	الذي
who, which (f.s.)	التي
poet	شاعِرٌ ج. شُـعَرَاءُ
poetry	شِـعْر
street	شارعٌ ج. شوارعُ
market	سُوق ج. أسْواقٌ
district, quarter	حيٌّ ج. أحْيَاءٌ
simple, modest	بَسيطٌ ج. بُسطاءُ
grandfather, forefather	جَدٌّ ج. أجْـدادٌ
man	رَجُلٌ ج. رجَالٌ
woman	اِمْرأة ج. نِسَاءٌ

كلمات وتعابير
Words and Expressions

history	تاريخٌ ج. تواريخُ
civilization	حَضَارَةٌ ج. حَضَارَاتٌ
I remember	أتَذكَّرُ
her men, people, folk	ناسُهَا
I love passionately	أعْشقُ
my life	حَياتي
my love, beloved (f. s.)	حَبيبتي

النص الأساسي: شَاعِرٌ مِنْ دِمَشْقَ
Basic Text: A Poet from Damascus

أنا شاعِرٌ دِمَشْقِيٌّ. أنا أعْشَقُ دِمَشْـقَ، وأعْشَقُ شوارعَهَا وأسْوَاقَهَا وأحْيَاءَهَا. أنا أعْشَقُ نِسَاءَهَا ورجَالَهَا وأطْفـالَهَا. أنا أعْشـقُ دمشقَ، وأعْشقُ ترابَهَا وشتاءَهَا وأمْطارَهَا. أنا ابْنُ دمشقَ وأعشقُ فيها تِلكَ الحَضَارَة القديمـة وذاكَ التاريخَ القديمَ. وأعشقُ فيها هؤلاءِ الناسَ البسطاءَ.

دمشـقُ هي المدينة التي وُلِـدْتُ فيها، وهي المدينة التي أعيشُ فيها. هي المدينة التي تَعَرَّفتُ فيها على حَبيبَتي الأولى، وكتبتُ الشِّعْرَ فيها عَن الحُبِّ وعن النِّساء اللواتي أحْبَبْتُهُنَّ في حَياتي. فيها أتذكَّرُ أجْدادي الذين مَاتوا ورَحَلوا. أنا أعشقُ هَذِهِ المدينة، وأعشقُ هَذا الوطنَ.

Figure 6.2 - Narrated by Ayman Ramadan

القواعد
Grammar

1. The Demonstrative Pronouns – أسماء الإشارة

A. Demonstrative pronouns denoting nearness

🎧 **Activity 1:** Listen and repeat. These are the most common and frequently used demonstratives.

Example	Case	Meaning	Demonstrative
هذا جميل	all cases	this (m. s.)	هَذا
هذِهِ جميلة	all cases	this (f. s.)	هَذِهِ
هذان ِ جميلان	nominative	these (m. dual)	هَذان ِ
هاتان ِ جميلتان	nominative	these (f. dual)	هـاتان ِ
هؤلاء جميلون/جميلات	all cases	these (m. and f. plural)	هَؤُلاء

Note: The accusative and genitive case of the masculine dual هَذان is هَذين. The accusative and genitive case of the feminine dual هاتان is هاتين. Also, note that هَذا، هَذِهِ and هَؤُلاء all have a long vowel after the هاء but that it is not ordinarily written. (Same for ذلك on the next page.)

If a demonstrative is immediately followed by a noun with the definite article, then this definite article binds the noun to the demonstrative. This makes it a phrase that functions as a single word. The demonstrative pronoun must have the same gender as the noun with which it forms a phrase. Example:

This poetry is beautiful	هذا الشِعْرُ جميلٌ
This city is beautiful	هذه المدينةُ جميلةٌ

If the predicate of a demonstrative pronoun begins with a definite article, then we must insert the appropriate corresponding independent pronoun between the two.

This is the house	هذا هو البيتُ
This is the city	هذه هي المدينة

166

B. Demonstrative pronouns denoting distance

🎧 **Activity 2:** Listen and repeat. These are the most common and frequently used demonstratives.

Example	Case	Meaning	Demonstrative
ذاكَ/ذلكَ الطالبُ	all cases	that (m.s.)	ذاكَ/ذلكَ
تلكَ الطالبةُ	all cases	that (f.s.)	تلكَ
ذانِكَ الطالبانِ	Nominative (rarely used)	those (dual m.)	ذانِكَ
تانِكَ الطالبتانِ	Nominative (rarely used)	those (dual f.)	تانِكَ
أولئكَ الطلابُ–الطالباتُ	all cases	those (plural m. & f.)	أولئكَ

Note: The accusative and genitive case of ذانِكَ is ذَيْنِكَ and of تانِكَ is تَيْنِكَ (both are rarely used).

Drill 1: Fill each blank with one of the following demonstratives.

هَذا، هَذِهِ، هَذانِ، هَاتانِ، هَؤُلاءِ

1 - _____ الطالبتانِ جميلتان.
2 - _____ الرجلُ من ليبيا.
3 - _____ المرأةُ حَضَرَتْ من لبنان.
4 - _____ الرجالُ والنساءُ رحلوا إلى أمريكا.
5 - درسَ _____ الطالبان في لبنان
6 - _____ الطاولةُ كبيرة.
7 - _____ البنتانِ فرنسيتان.

❖

Drill 2: Translate into Arabic.

1. That woman is pretty.
2. Those men are Egyptians.
3. Those two female students are from Iraq.
4. Those two men are from Bahrain.
5. Those female students studied in New York.
6. That house is big.

Drill 3: Translate into English.

4 – ذلك بيتٌ

5 – ذلك بيتٌ كبيرٌ

6 – ذلك هو البيتُ الكبيرُ

1 – هذا كتابٌ

2 – هذا الكتابُ جديدٌ

3 – هذا هو الكتابُ الجديدُ

❖

2. The Relative Pronouns - الأسماء الموصولة

The relative pronouns refer to preceding nouns. The nouns preceding them must be definite. The relative pronouns mean who, which, or that.

🎧 **Activity 3**: Repeat.

Case Appropriate	Gender	Relative Pronoun
all cases	m.s.	الذي
all cases	f.s.	التي
nominative	m. dual	اللذانِ
nominative	f. dual	اللتانِ
all cases	m. plural	الذينَ
all cases	f. plural	اللاتِي/اللواتِي/اللائِي

Note: The accusative and genitive cases of اللذان is اللذينِ and of اللتان is اللتينِ.

❖

Other pronouns that are used as relatives pronouns: مَنْ and مَا.

Meaning	Example	Meaning	Pronoun
I like who came	أحِبُّ مَنْ حَضَرَ	Who (refers to people)	مَنْ
I studied what you studied	دَرَسْتُ ما دَرَسْتَـهُ (ما دَرَسْتَ)	which, what (refers to objects)	مَا

❖

168

Drill 4: Fill the blank with the correct relative pronoun.

١ - الكتابُ ــــــ قرأتُهُ أمس ممتع.

٢ - النساءُ ــــــ سافرن إلى الشرق الأوسط أمريكيات.

٣ - الأستاذُ ــــــ دَرَّسَني هو من سوريا.

٤ - الطالبةُ اليابانية ــــــ تَدْرُسُ اللغة العربية ممتازة.

٥ - البيتُ ــــــ أسْكُنُهُ كبير.

٦ - البنتُ ــــــ حَضَرَتْ اليوم مغربية.

٧ - الطالبتانِ ــــــ ذهَبَتا إلى الجامعة اليوم مِصريَّتان.

٨ - الرجلانِ ــــــ وصلا أمس سُعوديان.

❖

Drill 5: Translate into Arabic.

1. The girl with whom I went to the city returned.
2. The man whom they (f.) loved arrived.
3. The students (m.) with whom I studied left.
4. He is the only man whom I have ever loved in my life.
5. The women who came yesterday are Tunisian.
6. The boy who lived here went to the university.
7. The homework that I did was long.
8. The poetry that I read is beautiful.
9. The books that arrived today are old.

❖

3. The Present Tense (Imperfect) - الفعل المضارع

The imperfect tense الفعل المضارع expresses an unfinished action or state taking place in the present time. It may express a habitual action as in يَدْرُسُ كُلَّ يَوْم 'he studies every day' or a progressive action as in يَدْرُسُ الآن 'he is studying now.' It may express future meaning as in يَدْرُسُ غداً 'he will study tomorrow.' The imperfect tense is conjugated by adding prefixes and suffixes, whereas the perfect verb is conjugated by adding only suffixes.

The conjugation of imperfect verbs is regular except for the vowel over the second radical of Form I. Form I means that the perfect tense is in its simplest form ('he' and its simple past), as in دَرَسَ 'he studied' or كَتَبَ 'he wrote.'

After the prefix, the first radical (or consonant) of the imperfect verb must have سكون ﹾ, but the vowel of the second radical in the imperfect (as well as in the perfect) could be *fatha* (ﹷ), *damma* (ﹹ), or *kasra* (ﹻ).

The dictionary shows you which vowel the second consonant must take in any particular verb. The chart below shows the prefix of the third person masculine singular, the first radical, which must have *sukun* (ﹾ), and the vowels of the second radical, which vary from one verb to another:

Vowel of 2nd Radical of the Imperfect	Vowel of 1st Radical of the Imperfect	Prefix	Imperfect	Perfect
رُ	دْ	يَـ	يَدْرُس	دَرَسَ
رَ	شْ	يَـ	يَشْرَب	شرِبَ
جِ	رْ	يَـ	يَرْجِع	رجَعَ

On the next page is a complete conjugation of the imperfect tense in the indicative mood (المضارع المرفوع), along with the corresponding independent pronouns, subject markers, and mood markers.

God - الله

🎧   **Activity 4:** Listen and repeat.

Mood Marker	Subject Marker	Meaning	Verb Conjugation	Independent Pronoun
ـُ	يَـ	he studies	يَدْرُسُ	هو
ـُ	تَـ	she studies	تَدْرُسُ	هي
ـ ن	يَـ + ا	they study (m. dual)	يَدْرُسَانِ	هما
ـ ن	تَـ + ا	they study (f. dual)	تَدْرُسَانِ	هما
نَ	يَـ + و	they study (m. plural)	يَدْرُسُونَ	هـم
none	يَـ + نَ	they study (f. plural)	يَدْرُسْنَ	هنَّ
ـُ	تَـ	you study (m.s.)	تَدْرُسُ	أنتَ
نَ	تَـ + يـ	you study (f.s.)	تَدْرُسِينَ	أنتِ
ـ ن	تَـ + ا	you study (m. dual)	تَدْرُسَانِ	أنتما
ـ ن	تَـ + ا	you study (f. dual)	تَدْرُسَانِ	أنتما
نَ	تَـ + و	you study (m. plural)	تَدْرُسُونَ	أنتم
none	تَـ + نَ	you study (f. plural)	تَدْرُسْنَ	أنتنَّ
ـُ	أ	I study	أَدْرُسُ	أنا
ـُ	نَـ	we	نَدْرُسُ	نحنُ

Note: The last radical of the indicative imperfect verbs corresponding with the pronouns نحن، أنا ،أنتَ،هي،هو always is *damma* (ـُ). The indicative imperfect المضارع المرفوع and other moods of the imperfect tense will be discussed later.

❖

4. The Future Tense - المستقبل

Putting the independent particle سَوْفَ or its abridged form ـسَ as a prefix before the imperfect tense indicates the future tense:

he studies	يَدْرُسُ
he will study	سَوْفَ يَدْرُسُ
he will study	سَيَدْرُسُ

Drill 6: Change the perfect tense to the imperfect in these sentences.

١ - <u>عَمِلَ</u> والد حسين في شركة نفط.

٢ - أمي <u>ذهبتْ</u> إلى الشرق الأوسط.

٣ - نحن <u>أحْبَبْنا</u> اللغة العربية كثيراً.

٤ - الشاعر السوري الذي درسناه <u>عَشِقَ</u> دمشق.

٥ - هم <u>عَمِلُوا</u> في جريدة الجامعة كل يوم.

٦ - أنت <u>عَرَفْتَ</u> كلَّ الطلاب في الصف.

٧ - سمير وسليم <u>دَرَسا</u> الكتابَ.

٨ - أمُّ مريمَ <u>طبخَتْ</u> في المطبخ.

٩ - <u>دَرَسَتْ</u> سميرة في جامعة أوهايو.

❖

Drill 7: Conjugate the following verbs.

Example - دَرَسَ – **هُم**: يَدْرُسُونَ

٦ - شــاهَدَ – **هُنَّ**:   ١ - رَحَلَ – **أنا**:

٧ - كَتَبَ – **هو**:   ٢ - سَافَرَ – **أنتنَّ**:

٨ - ذهَبَ – **أنت**:   ٣ - سكَنَ – **أنتم**:

٩ - عَمِلَ – **هم**:   ٤ - تذكرُ – **هي**:

١٠ - طبَخَ – **هما**:   ٥ - جلَسَ – **نحن**:

❖

Drill 8: Translate into English.

١ - الأستاذ الذي يُدَرِّسُ اللغة العربية مصريٌّ.

٢ - الفيلمُ الذي سنشاهدُهُ اليومَ حصلَ على جائزة.

٣ - الشاعرة التي سنستمعُ إلى شِعرِهَا هذا المساء عراقيةٌ.

٤ - الطلابُ الذين يحضرونَ اليوم هم من المغرب.

٥ - المرأة التي يُحِبُّهَا أخي هي شاعرة فرنسية.

٦ - الكتابُ الذي سأقرأُهُ غداً طويل.

٧ - الواجبُ الذي سيَكتبُهُ الطلابُ هذا المساء سَهْلٌ.

❖

Drill 9: Translate into Arabic.

1. I am writing to my friend who lives in Jordan.
2. I go to the university every day.
3. I love you.
4. I will study Arabic in Lebanon.
5. I live in Boston.
6. The book they (f.) wrote last year is excellent.
7. I left the university that I loved after four years.
8. I will write the vocabulary.

❖

Drill 10: Conjugate the following verbs in the past and present tenses.

١ - تَكَلَّمَ
٢ - شَاهَدَ
٣ - حَضَرَ

❖

Drill 11: Fill in the blanks with the correct words from the comprehension text.

في دمشق أبواب قديمة منها _____ _____ توما. في مدينة _____ _____ تسكن الكاتبة السورية وفيها _____ عائلتها وفيها _____ _____ الحب الأول وفيها _____ _____.

الكاتبة السورية نشأت في _____ دمشق، وترعرعت في _____ _____ القديمة. دمشق كانت _____ حضارات سابقة. فيها _____ _____ قاسيون وفيها أسواق _____ منها _____ الحميدية.

❖

الفهم والاستيعاب: كاتبة من دمشق
Comprehension Text: A Writer From Damascus

وُلِدْتُ في دِمَشْقَ، وفيها نشأتُ، وفي أحْيائِهَا القديمةِ تَرَعْرَعْتُ. في دمشقَ، عَرَفتُ الحُبَّ الأوَّلَ الذي أعيشُهُ كلَّ يوم، وفيها عَرَفتُ ذلكَ الرَّجُلَ الرائِعَ الذي أصْبَحَ زَوْجِي.

دِمَشقُ مدينةٌ عريقة. كانتْ عَاصمةَ حضاراتٍ كثيرةٍ سابقةٍ. فيها جَبَلُ قاسِيُون الذي يَزيدُ المدينة جَمَالاً. وفيها المدينة القديمة التي تزيدُ دمشقَ سِحْراً. في دمشقَ أسواقٌ جميلة ساحرة، منها سوقُ الحميديةِ. وفي دمشقَ أبـوابٌ قديمة مشهورة رائعة، منها بابُ تومـا.

في هذِهِ المدينةِ تاريخٌ وحضارة وثقافة. في هذِهِ المدينةِ أسْكُنُ وأعيش، وفيها تَسْكُنُ عَائلِتِي وتعيشُ. فيها أهْلي وزَوْجي وأوْلادِي. وفيها أعْمَلُ وأكْـتُبُ وأحِبُّ.

ജ

كلمات وتعابير
Words and Expressions

markets	أسْواقٌ	became	أصْبَحَ
old, ancient	عَريقة ، قديمة	I grew up, was raised	تـرَعْرَعْتُ
wonderful	رائِع	every day	كلَّ يوم
it was	كانت	capital	عَاصِمَة
civilizations	حضارات	previous	سَابقة
Qasyun Mountain	جَبَل قاسيون	it (m.s.) increases	يَزيد
culture	ثقافة	gates, doors	أبْـوابٌ
many	كثيرة	parents, family	أهْـلي

المحادثة

Let's Speak Arabic
Studying - الدراسة

Repeat the following question out loud:

What will you (m.s.) study tonight?	ماذا سَتَدْرُسُ الليلة؟
What will you (f.s.) study tonight?	ماذا سَتدرسينَ الليلة؟

Now repeat aloud the following answer:

I will study the Arabic language	سَأَدْرُسُ اللغة العربية

Next, repeat the sentence and substitute the following words for
اللغة العربية:

science	العُلـُوم
literature	الأدب
history	التَّاريـخ
philosophy	الفَلْسَفة
medicine	الطِّبّ

Repeat the dialogue with a classmate.

Homework - الواجب

1. Listen to the comprehension text again. Identify five verbs in the present. Change them to the past and future.

2. Write a short composition on a day in your life. Turn it in to your teacher after you present your composition in class.

الدَّرْسُ السَّابِعُ

يَوْمٌ في حَيَاتي

Lesson Seven

A Day in My Life

Figure 7.1 - Damascus, Syria

Lesson Seven Contents

🎧 Vocabulary - المفردات

🎧 Words and Expressions - كلمات وتعابير

💿 Basic Text - النص الأساسي

   ❖ Music and Literature - الموسيقى والأدب

Grammar - القواعد

   1. Negating the Perfect - نفي الفعل الماضي

   2. Negating the Present - نفي الفعل المضارع

   3. Negating the Future - نفي المستقبل

   4. The Adjective - النَّعْت (الصِّفة)

   5. Colors and Defects- الألوان والعيوب

   🎧 Activity 1

💿 Comprehension Text - الفهم والاستيعاب

   ❖ A Day in the Life of a Friend - يوم في حياة صديق

🎧 Let's Speak Arabic - المحادثة

   ❖ Clothes - الملابـس

💿 Window into Arab Culture - من الثقافة العربية

   ❖ Poetry Reading - قراءة في الشعر

المفردات
Vocabulary

bread	خُبْزٌ
cheese	جُبْنٌ - جُبْنة
white	أَبْيَضُ
olive	زَيْتُونٌ
green	أَخْضَرُ
newspaper	جَريدةٌ ج. جَرائِدُ
in the evening (adv.)	مَسَاءً
boring (adj.)	مُمِلٌ - مُمِلَّة
to eat	أَكَلَ، يَأْكُلُ
to sit	جَلَسَ، يَجْلِسُ
market, bazaar	سُوقٌ ج. أَسْواقٌ
to tell, speak, talk	حَدَّثَ، يُحدِّثُ
to drink	شربَ، يشرَبُ
usually (adv.)	عَادةً
simple (adj.)	بَسِيطٌ
to make	صنعَ، يَصْنعُ
to bathe, shower	اِستَحَمَّ، يَسْتَحِمُّ
cold (adj.)	بَارِدٌ
kitchen	مَطْبَخٌ ج. مَطابخُ
breakfast	فَطُورٌ - فُطورٌ
lunch	غَدَاءٌ
dinner	عَشَاءٌ
normal, usual (adj.)	عَادِيٌّ

🎧

كلمات وتعابير
Words and Expressions

a day in my life	يَوْمٌ في حَيَاتي
to wake up (from sleep)	اِسْتَيْقَظَ، يَسْتَيْقِظ
I don't watch television	لا أشَاهِدُ التِلفَازَ
fruits	فاكِهةٌ ج. فواكِـهُ
vegetables, greens	خُضَارٌ - خُضْرَوَاتٌ
to buy, purchase	اِشْتَرَى، يَشْتَري
meat, flesh	لَحْمٌ ج. لُحُومٌ
midnight	مُنْتَصَف اللَّيْل
I am vegetarian	أنا نباتِيَّة
at noon (adv.)	ظُهْراً
never (adv.)	أبَداً
color	لَوْنٌ ج. ألْوَانٌ
I don't go anywhere	لا أذهبُ إلى أيِّ مكان

الله - God

النص الأساسي: الموسيقى والأدب
Basic Text: Music and Literature

سَأُحَدِّثُكُم عَنْ يَوْم في حَيَاتِي، عَنْ يَوْمٍ عَادِيٍّ بَسِيطٍ من أيَّامِ حَيَاتِي. أَسْتَيقظُ عادةً في السَّاعَةِ الخَامِسَةِ والنِّصْفِ صَبَاحاً. أَصْنَعُ القهوة العَرَبِيَّة، ثُمَّ أَسْتَحِمُّ بالماء البارِدِ، بَعْدَهَا أذهَبُ إلى المطبخ وأَحَضِّرُ الفطُورَ. فطُوري عادة بَسيط، أنا آكُلُ الخُبْزَ العربيَّ والجُبْنَ الأبيضَ.

أنا لا أُحِبُّ الجرائدَ ولا أشاهدُ التِلفازَ، بل أسْتَمِعُ إلى الموسيقى وأقرأ الأدبَ حتى الساعةِ الحادية عَشْرة. أنا ما قرأتُ جريدة في حياتي، ولَنْ أقرأ الجرائدَ. فالجرائدُ مُمِلَّةٌ جدًّا.

أذهبُ إلى السوق ظُهراً، أشتري الخضرواتِ والفواكِهَ ثم أرْجِعُ إلى البيتِ. أنا لا آكُلُ اللُّحُومَ. ما أكلتُ اللحومَ في حياتي، ولن آكُلَ اللحومَ أبداً. أنا نباتيَّة. في الغداء آكُلُ السَّلطة والزيتونَ الأخضرَ وأشربُ الشايَ.

مساءً، بعد العَشاءِ، أنا لا أذهبُ إلى أيِّ مكان، بَلْ أجْلِسُ في البيتِ، أقرأ وأكتبُ حتى مُنْتَصَفِ الليل.

Figure 7.2 - Narrated by Majida Hourani

ഓ‌ൽ

القواعد
Grammar

1. Negating the Perfect – نفي الفعل الماضي

A. The particle ما in negating the perfect tense

One way to negate the past tense is to place the particle ما before the verb. The particle ما does not affect the verb form. Example:

he studied	دَرَسَ
he did not study	ما دَرَسَ

B. The particle ما in negating the present

The particle ما is also used to negate the present tense. As with the past tense, it does not affect the form of the present tense. Example:

he knows	يَعْرِفُ
he does not know	ما يَعْرِفُ

In the Qur`an, the present tense is negated with both ما and لا.

C. Alternate negation of the past tense

There is another way to negate the past tense: using the present tense form of the verb with لَمْ, forming a past tense negative, as in لَمْ يَدْرُسْ 'he did not study.' Using لَمْ affects the verb form of the present and changes it from indicative (مَرْفوع) to jussive (مَجْزوم). We will learn about the jussive later.

❖

2. Negating the Present - نفي الفعل المضارع

A. The particle ما

We negate the present tense, as mentioned, by placing ما before the present tense. Example:

he studies	يَدْرُسُ
he does not study	ما يَدْرُسُ

B. The particle لا

Another way to negate the present is to place the particle لا before the present tense in the same way we place the particle ما. Neither particle affects the verb form. The present tense still remains in the indicative case (مضارع مرفوع), as it was before we added the negative particle. Example:

he studies	يَدْرُسُ
he does not study	ما يَدْرُسُ
he does not study	لا يَدْرُسُ

❖

3. Negating the Future - نفي المستقبل

To negate the future, the particle لن is placed before a verb in the future tense. Using the particle لن changes the form of the verb that comes after it. The verb's mood changes and becomes subjunctive (منصوب). When using لن to negate the future we must drop the particles ـسَ and سَوْفَ that precede the verb. Example:

he will go	سَيذهبُ - سوفَ يذهبُ
he will not go	لن يذهبَ

❖

Drill 1: Negate the following sentences using the correct particles. If needed, make changes to the verbs.

١ - سافرتَ إلى السودان.

٢ - أعملُ في الجامعة.

٣ - درستُ اللغة الفرنسية.

٤ - سوفَ أرْحَلُ من هنا.

٥ - أنا آكلُ الخبز العربيَ مع فطوري.

٦ - يذهبُ الطلابُ إلى الدَّرْس في الساعةِ الثامنة.

٧ - ماتَ الرَّجلُ أمس وماتتْ زوجتُهُ اليومَ.

٨ - تحْضُرُ الأستاذة إلى عَمَلِهَا بالسيارة.

٩ - سأشْرَبُ القهوة بعدَ الصَّفِ.

❖

Drill 2: Translate into Arabic.

1. I did not go to the university with him.
2. I shall not live in Canada.
3. She does not know Arabic.
4. You will not read that book.
5. They did not study at Columbia University.
6. He does not usually eat dinner.
7. Those two men will not drink coffee.
8. I do not like the color green.

❖

Drill 3: Translate into English.

١ - ما شاهَدْتُ الفيلمَ أمسِ.

٢ - لا أعْرفُ أيْنَ تسكُنينَ.

٣ - ما تَعَرَّفْتُ عليها عِنْدَمَا حَضَرَتْ.

٤ - لن أتحدَّثَ معكَ في هذا الموضوع.

٥ - ما يدري أيْنَ يذهبُ.

٦ - لا يَعْرفُ ماذا يقولُ.

٧ - لَنْ أذهبَ الى أيٍّ مَكان.

٨ - لَنْ تأكُلَ الزيتونَ.

٩ - لا أذهَبُ إلى السُّوق عادةً.

❖

4. The Adjective - (النَّعْت) الصِّفة

In Arabic the adjective follows the noun that it modifies, and agrees with it in definiteness, case, gender, and number. For example: If the noun is definite, masculine, singular, and nominative, then the adjective modifying that noun must also be definite, masculine, singular, and nominative:

Noun + Adjective	اسم + صفة
the house + the beautiful = the beautiful house	البيتُ الجميلُ

Therefore, if the noun is feminine then the adjective is feminine; if it is dual then the adjective is dual; if it is plural then the adjective is plural, and so forth:

the (m. s.) Egyptian student	الطالبُ المِصريُّ
the (m. d.) Egyptian students	الطالبانِ المِصريانِ
the (m. pl.) Egyptian students	الطلابُ المِصريونَ
the (f. s.) Egyptian student	الطالبةُ المِصريَّةُ
the (f. d.) Egyptian students	الطالبتانِ المِصريتانِ
the (f. pl.) Egyptian students	الطالباتُ المِصرياتُ

There is one exception to the above rule: if the noun is plural and does not refer to human beings, then the noun takes a singular feminine adjective. All non human plurals are modified by a singular feminine adjective. Example:

the beautiful houses	البُيُوتُ الجَميلةُ
the Egyptian universities	الجامِعَاتُ المِصريةُ

One major difference between noun-adjective phrases (a noun followed by an adjective) and the nominal sentence (usually a subject followed by a predicate) is the presence or the absence of the definite article الـ. Example:

Noun + Adj	Noun + Adj	Subject + Predicate
بيتٌ جميلٌ	البيتُ الجميلُ	البيتُ جميلٌ
a beautiful house	the beautiful house	The house is beautiful.

Possessive suffixes naturally make nouns definite (we must use *either* the
definite article *or* a possessive suffix to make nouns definite but cannot use
them together). Example:

the beautiful house	البيتُ الجميلُ
my beautiful house	بيتي الجميلُ
our beautiful houses	بيوتُنا الجميلةُ

❖

Drill 4: Change the following from nominal sentences (subject+ predicate)
to noun-adjective phrases (noun + adjective):

6 - النساءُ جميلاتٌ.

7 - الطاولاتُ كبيرةٌ.

8 - المطاراتُ صغيرةٌ.

9 - الكتبُ هامّةٌ.

10 - زوجتُهُ فرنسِيَّةٌ.

1 - الطالبُ أمريكيٌّ.

2 - الأستاذةُ ممتازةٌ.

3 - سيارتي جميلةٌ.

4 - جامِعَتُنا جَديدةٌ.

5 - الرِّجالُ مِصريُّونَ.

❖

Drill 5: Change the following definite noun-adjective phrases to indefinite
noun adjective phrases. Example: الطالبُ السعيدُ - طالبٌ سعيدٌ

1 - الشبّاكُ الكبيرُ-

2 - الجامعةُ الجميلة -

3 - صديقي المغربيُّ -

4 - صديقاتي الأردنياتُ -

5 - بَيْتُها الجميلُ -

6 - مدينتُنا الرائعة -

7 - إسْمُكَ العربيُّ -

8 - ابنُهُم الكبيرُ -

9 - أستاذهُنَّ الأمريكيُّ -

❖

5. Colors and Defects - الألـوان والعُيوب

Colors and physical defects are a separate category of adjectives. This type of adjective is known as the أفْعَلُ form adjective and is used only for colors and defects. The masculine singular form أَفْعَلُ and the feminine singular form فَعْلاءُ are used. One plural form فُعْلٌ is used for both genders.

🎧 **Activity 1:** Colors and defects. Repeat aloud.

Meaning	Plural	Sing. Femin.	Sing. Masc
black	سُـودٌ	سَوْداءُ	أسْـوَدُ
red	حُمْرٌ	حَمْراءُ	أحْمَرُ
blue	زُرْقٌ	زَرْقاءُ	أزْرَقُ
green	خُضْرٌ	خَضْراءُ	أخْضَرُ
yellow	صُفْرٌ	صَفْراءُ	أصْفَرُ
white	بِيضٌ	بَيْضاءُ	أبْيَضُ
deaf	طُرْشٌ	طَرْشاءُ	أطْرَشُ
lame	عُرْجٌ	عَرْجاءُ	أعْرَجُ
blind	عُمْيٌ	عَمْياءُ	أعْمَى
mute	خُرْسٌ	خَرْساءُ	أخْرَسُ

❖

Drill 6: Translate into English.

1 - الزيتونُ الأخضرُ لذيذٌ.

2 - اللونُ الأزرقُ جميلٌ.

3 - البيتُ الأبيضُ هو في واشنطن.

4 - الدارُ البيضاءُ هي في المغرب.

5 - أخي الكبيرُ ذهبَ إلى أوروبا.

6 - أختي الصغيرة تدرسُ في كندا.

7 - أصدقائي السعوديون يعملون في التجارة.

Drill 7: Translate into Arabic.

1. The Algerian man is very well liked.
2. The Chinese woman has arrived.
3. Tunis is green.
4. Green Tunis is beautiful.
5. The color of the professor's car is beautiful.
6. The door of the house is large.
7. The large door of the house is black.

❖

Drill 8: Fill in the blanks with the correct words from the comprehension text.

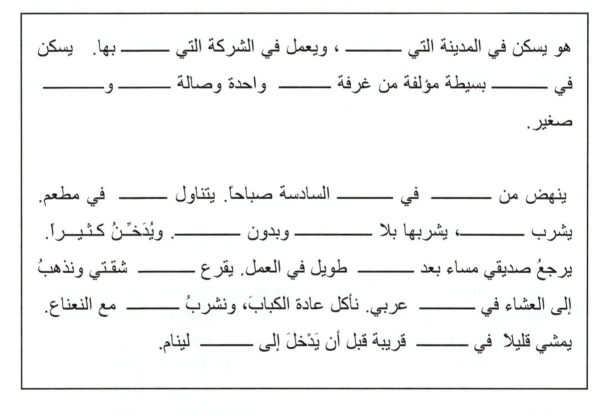

هو يسكن في المدينة التي ـــــــ ، ويعمل في الشركة التي ـــــــ بها. يسكن في ـــــــ بسيطة مؤلفة من غرفة ـــــــ واحدة وصالة ـــــــ وـــــــ صغير.

ينهض من ـــــــ ـــــــ في ـــــــ السادسة صباحاً. يتناول ـــــــ ـــــــ في مطعم. يشرب ـــــــ ، يشربها بلا ـــــــ وبدون ـــــــ ـــــــ. ويُدَخِّنُ كثيــراً. يرجعُ صديقي مساء بعد ـــــــ طويل في العمل. يقرع ـــــــ شقتي ونذهبُ إلى العشاء في ـــــــ عربي. نأكل عادة الكبابَ، ونشربُ ـــــــ مع النعناع. يمشي قليلاً في ـــــــ قريبة قبل أن يَدْخلَ إلى ـــــــ لينام.

❖

189

🔘
DVD

الفهم والاستيعاب: يوم في حياة صديق
Comprehension: A Day in the Life of a Friend

أَعْرِفُهُ مُنْذ سَنَوَاتٍ طويلةٍ، هو يَسْكُنُ في المدينةِ التي أَسْكُنُهَا، ويَعْمَلُ في الشركةِ التي أَعْمَلُ بها. هو صَديقي المُخلِصُ، وزميلي في العَمَلِ، وجاري في السَّكَن. يَسْكُنُ في شقةٍ بَسيطةٍ مُؤَلَّفةٍ مِنْ غُرْفةِ نَوْم واحِدَةٍ وصَالَةٍ صغيرةٍ ومَطْبَخٍ صغير. يَنْهَضُ مِنَ النَّوْم في الساعةِ السادسةِ صباحاً كلَّ يوم. يتناولُ فطورَهُ في مَطْعَم قريبٍ من الشَّركَةِ. يَشربُ القهوة كثيراً، يَشْرَبُهَا بلا سُكَّر وبدون حَليبٍ. يشْرَبُهَا سَوْداء. ويُدَخِّنُ كثيراً. ولكِنَّ صِحَّتَهُ ممتازة.

يَرْجِعُ إلى شَـقَّـتِهِ مَسَاءً بَعْدَ يوم طويلٍ. يَقْرَعُ بابَ شقَّتي ونذهَبُ معاً إلى العَشاء في مَطعم عربيٍّ. نأكلُ عادة الكبابَ والحُمُّصَ والتبولة، ونشربُ بَعْدَهَا الشايَ مَعَ النَّعْناع. هو يَمْشي عادة في حديقةٍ عامَّةٍ قريبةٍ من المنزل قَبْلَ أنْ يَرْجِعَ إلى شَقَّتِهِ.

৪০৫৪

🎧

كلمات وتعابير
Words and Expressions

since	مُنذ	my sincere friend	صَديقي المُخلِصُ
my neighbor	جاري	long years	سنواتٌ طويلة
composed, made of	مُؤَلفة مِن	simple	بَسيطة
his apartment	شقَّتُهُ	bedroom	غرْفة نوْم
kitchen	مَطبخ	hall	صَالة
he eats his breakfast	يتناولُ فطورَهُ	he wakes up	يَنهَضُ من النوم
he drinks	يَشرَبُ	restaurant	مَطعَم
without sugar	بلا سُكَّر	coffee	قهوة
he knocks	يَقرَع	without milk	بدون حَليب
mint	نَعْناع	together	مَعَاً
home	مَنزل	park	حَديقة عَامَّة

190

🎧

المحادثة

Let's Speak Arabic
Clothes - الملابـس

Repeat aloud the following question:

What are you (m.s.) going to wear?	ماذا ستلبَسُ؟
What are you (f.s.) going to wear?	ماذا ستلبَسينَ؟

Now repeat the following answer out loud:

I am going to wear a suit	سَألبَسُ بَذلَـة

Repeat the sentence and substitute the words below for بَذلَـة. Note that the direct object must be in the accusative case.

فُستان dress
قَميص shirt
بُلوزة blouse
بَنطلون pants
تَنـُّورة skirt

Repeat the dialogue with a classmate.

ৡৡৡ

Homework - الواجب

1. Listen to the comprehension text again. Identify four verbs in the present. Change them to the past and the future. Then, negate them all.

2. Write a short composition on a day in your life or on a day in the life of one of your friends. Turn in the composition to your teacher after you present it in class.

من الثقافة العربية
قراءة في الشِـــعر

Window into Arab Culture
Poetry Reading

Figure 7.3 - Joumana Haddad

Joumana Haddad was born in 1970 in Beirut, Lebanon. A poet and translator, Joumana is the chief editor of the cultural pages of the Lebanese daily newspaper *An-Nahar* (النهار). She has published five collections of poetry and translated several works of poetry and prose.

Listen to the poetry reading, and try to understand as much as you can. Identify five words you know and put them into sentences. Identify five words you do not know. Research 'Lilith' and write five sentences on the subject.

عَــوْدَة ليليت*
جُمَانة حَدَّاد

أنا ليليت المرأة القدَرُ. لا يَتَمَلَّصُ ذكَرٌ مِنْ قَدَري ولا يُريدُ ذكَرٌ أنْ يَتَمَلَّصَ.أنا المـرأةُ القمَـران، ليليت. لا يَكْـتَمِلُ أسْوَدُهُمَا إلا بأبْيَضِهِمَا، لأنَّ طهارتي شـرارةُ

المُجُــون وتمنـُّعي أوَّلُ الاحتمـال. أنـا المـرأة الجَنَّـة التي سَـقطتْ مِـنَ الجَنَّـة، وأنـا السُّـقوط الجَنَّة. أنا المرأة المائدةُ وأنا المدعوونَ إليْهَا.

جاءَ في تفسيرِ الكتابِ الأوَّل أنِّي مِنْ تُرابٍ خُـلِقتْ، وجُعِلـتْ زوجةَ آدَمَ الأولى فَلَمْ أخْضَعْ. أنا الأولى التي لَمْ تَكْتَفِ لأنَّهَا الوصَالُ الكامِلُ، الفِعْلُ والتَّلَـقِّي، المرأة التَّمَرُّدُ لا المرأة النَّعَمُ. سَئِمْتُ آدَمَ الرَّجُلَ وَسَئِمْتُ آدَمَ الجَنَّة. سئمتُ ورفضتُ وخرجتُ على الطَّاعَة.

أنا ليليت المرأة الأولى، شريكة آدَمَ في الخَـلْـقِ، لا ضِلْـعَ الخُضُـوعِ. مِنَ التُّرابِ خَلَقَني إلهي لأكُونَ الأصْلَ، ومِنْ ضِلْـعِ آدَمَ خلقَ حَوَّاءَ لِتَكُونَ الظِّـلَّ.

❖

* جمانة حداد، عودة ليليت، دار النهار، 2004، ص 13-11، بتصرف.

الدَّرْسُ الثَّامِنُ

الجامِعُ الأُمَوِيُّ

Lesson Eight

The Umayyad Mosque

Figure 8.1 - The Umayyad Mosque in Damascus, Syria

Lesson Eight Contents

🎧 Vocabulary - المفردات

🎧 Words and Expressions - كلمات وتعابير

💿 Basic Text - النص الأساسي
DVD

    ❖ The Umayyad Mosque - الجامع الأموي

Grammar - القواعد

    1. The Three Moods of the Imperfect Verb

    المضارع المرفوع والمنصوب والمجزوم

       A. The Indicative - المضارع المرفوع

       B. The Subjunctive - المضارع المنصوب

       C. The Jussive - المضارع المجزوم

      🎧 Activity 1

    2. The Negative Command - المضارع المجزوم بـ (لا) الناهية

💿 Comprehension Text - الفهم والاستيعاب
DVD

    ❖ Souq al-Hamidiyyah - سوق الحميدية

🎧 Let's Speak Arabic - المحادثة

    ❖ Evening Activities - نشاطات مسائية

💿 Window into Arab Culture - من الثقافة العربية
DVD

    ❖ Fairuz - فيروز

المفردات
Vocabulary

end	نِهايَة ج. نِهايَاتٌ	wish, desire	أُمْنِية
to build	بَنَى، يَبْنِي	of course	طَبْعَاً
caliph	خَليفةٌ ج. خُلَفاءُ	then, therefore	إذنْ
capital	عاصِمَةٌ ج. عَواصِمُ	history	تاريخٌ ج. تواريخُ
empire	إمْبَراطوريَّة	historical	تاريخِيٌّ
famous	شَهيرٌ - شَهيرة	to listen, hear	سَمِعَ، يَسْمَعُ
to meet	التقى، يلتقي	to be located, to lie	وَقَعَ، يَقَعُ
to tour, walk around	تَجَوَّلَ، يَتَجَوَّلُ	heart	قَلْبٌ ج. قُلُوبٌ
to visit	زارَ، يَزورُ	big, large	كَبيرٌ

كلمات وتعابير
Words and Expressions

the Umayyad Mosque	المَسْجِدُ الأمَوِيُّ / الجَامِعُ الأمَوِيُّ
clear idea	فِكْرَة واضِحَة
my wish is to go with you	أُمْنِيَتي أنْ أذهبَ مَعَكِ
anywhere (to any place)	إلى أيِّ مَكان
it is a deal (we have agreed)	اتَّفَقْنا
could you tell me?	هَلْ لكَ أنْ تُحَدِّثَني
Who built it?	مَنْ بَناهُ
In what year was it built?	في أيِّ عَام بُنِيَ
Al-Walid ibn Abdul Malek	الوليد بن عبد الملك
Souq al-Hamidiyyah	سُوقُ الحَميدِيَّة
because you are coming with me	لأنَّكِ سَتَأتِينَ مَعي
among the most beautiful mosques of the world	مِنْ أجْمَل مَساجِدِ العَالَم

النص الأساسي: الجَامِعُ الأمَويُّ
Basic Text: The Umayyad Mosque

Figure 8.2 - The Umayyad Mosque

جُمان: أتذهبُ مَعِي إلى الجَامِعِ الأمويِّ يا منير؟

منير: طبعاً، طبعاً، يا جُمان، أمنيتي أن أذهبَ مَعَكِ إلى أيِّ مَكان.

جُمان: إذنْ نلتقِي غَداً في التاسِعَةِ صباحاً، ونتجَوَّلُ قليلاً قبلَ أنْ نذهبَ إلى المسجدِ.

منير: اِتفقنا، أراكِ غداً في التاسعةِ صباحاً يا جُمان.

جُمان: هل لكَ أن تحدثني قليلاً عن المسجدِ؟

منير: طبعاً. طبعاً. المسجدُ الأموي يَقَعُ في قَلبِ مدينةِ دمشق القديمة، وهو مِنْ أجْمَلِ مساجدِ العَالم. والمسجدُ كبيرٌ وتاريخِيٌّ وهَـامٌّ ، ويقعُ في نِهايةِ سوقِ الحميديةِ الشهيرِ.

جُمان: مَنْ بناهُ؟ وفي أيِّ عَام بُنيَ؟

منير: بَنَاهُ الخَليفة الأمويُّ الوليد بن عبدِ الملكِ في عام 705 م عندما كانتْ دِمشقُ عاصمةَ الإمبراطوريةِ العربيةِ الإسلاميةِ.

جُمان: لمْ أعْرفْ هذِه المَعْلومَاتِ مِنْ قَبْل. الآنَ لَدَيَّ فكرةٌ واضحةٌ . شُكْراً لكَ.

منير: الشُّكْرُ لكِ يا جُمان لأنَّكِ سَتأتينَ مَعِي.

القواعد
Grammar

1. The Moods of the Imperfect Verb - المضارع المرفوع والمنصوب والمجزوم

There are three moods of the imperfect: the indicative (المضارع المرفوع), the subjunctive (المضارع المنصوب), and the jussive (المضارع المجزوم).

A. The indicative - المضارع المرفوع

A verb in the imperfect (present) tense is normally in the indicative mood, unless certain particles precede it to cause it to be in a different mood.

You have learned how to conjugate the present (imperfect) tense in the indicative mood. For example, the imperfect verb يَدْرُسُ is in the indicative mood; it looks just like the regular present tense conjugation. The mood markers in the third column (seen in red) show what puts this verb in the indicative mood. These are the same mood markers that you learned in Chapter 6.

Mood Marker	Imperfect Indicative	Independent Pronoun
ـُ	يَدْرُسُ	هو
ـُ	تدْرُسُ	هي
نِ	يَدْرُسَانِ	هما
نِ	تدْرُسَانِ	هما
نَ	يَدْرُسونَ	هـم
none	يَدْرُسْـنَ	هنَّ
ـُ	تدْرُسُ	أنتَ
نَ	تدْرُسينَ	أنتِ
نِ	تدْرُسَانِ	أنتما
نِ	تدْرُسَانِ	أنتما
نَ	تدْرُسُونَ	أنتم
none	تدْرُسْـنَ	أنتنَّ
ـُ	أدْرُسُ	أنا
ـُ	ندْرُسُ	نحنُ

The imperfect is in the indicative mood when the vowel of the last consonant of the verb is ضمة (ـُ) in the singular form, ـنِ in the dual form, نَ in the plural form أنتم and هم, and نَ in the feminine singular form أنتِ. However, the imperfect ends in نَ in the feminine plural أنتنَّ and هنَّ in all moods.

i. Examples of the imperfect indicative ending in (ـُ) in the singular verb forms correspond to the independent pronouns: هو، هي، أنتَ، أنا ، نحن:

يدرُسُ	هو
تدرُسُ	هي
تدرُسُ	أنتَ
أدرُسُ	أنا
ندرُسُ	نحنُ

ii. Example of the imperfect indicative ending in ـنِ in the dual verb forms corresponding to the independent pronouns هما and أنتما:

يدرُسانِ	هما
تدرُسانِ	هما
تدرُسانِ	أنتما
تدرُسانِ	أنتما

iii. Example of the imperfect indicative ending in نَ corresponding to the feminine singular independent pronoun أنتِ and to the plural masculine forms أنتم and هم:

تدرسيـنَ	أنتِ
تدرسونَ	أنتم
يدرسونَ	هم

iv. Example of the imperfect indicative ending in نَ corresponding to the feminine plural forms of the independent pronouns أنتنَّ and هنَّ. This نَ is called نون النِسْوة 'the *nun* of feminine plural.'

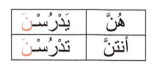

يَدرُسْنَ	هُنَّ
تَدْرُسْنَ	أنتنَّ

The feminine plurals of the imperfect verbs always end in نْ in all moods: indicative, subjunctive, and jussive (as we will see).

❖

B. The subjunctive - المضارع المنصوب

The imperfect indicative, which expresses a statement in the present or the future, changes slightly when in the subjunctive or jussive moods. The slight changes that make the indicative become subjunctive:

i. The ضمة changes to فتحة for the last radical in the singular imperfect verbs of the independent pronouns نحن ، أنا ، أنتَ ، هي ، هو .
    Example:

Imperfect Subjunctive Singular	Imperfect Indicative Singular
يدرسَ	يدرسُ

ii. The نْ is dropped from the imperfect indicative for the verb forms of the feminine singular أنتِ, masculine plural هم, and masculine plural أنتم. So, when the verb يدرسُونَ loses its نْ, it is no longer in the indicative mood. It becomes subjunctive. Example:

Imperfect Subjunctive	Imperfect Indicative
يدرسُوا	يدرسُونَ
تدرسي	تدرسينَ

The final alif (ا) at the end of the subjunctive يدرسُوا is merely a spelling convention that is a remnant from early classical Arabic.

iii. The نْ is dropped from the dual second person masculine and feminine أنتما and the dual third person masculine and feminine هما:

Imperfect Subjunctive Dual	Imperfect Indicative Dual
يَدْرُسا	يَدْرُسانِ
تدْرُسا	تدْرُسانِ

iv. When to use the subjunctive?

A verb becomes subjunctive when it is preceded by certain particles. Each particle has a particular meaning. The subjunctive particle لَنْ negates the future, as in لَنْ أذهبَ 'I will not go.' This particle has caused the indicative to become subjunctive. Also, in the sentence أريدُ أنْ أذهبَ 'I want to go,' the subjunctive particle أنْ has caused the second verb to become subjunctive. Here are the most common subjunctive particles:

Meaning	Subjunctive	Meaning	Particle
I want to study.	أريدُ أنْ أدْرُسَ	that	أنْ
I want (not to) study.	أريد ألاَّ أدرسَ	that not	أنْ+لا = ألاَّ
He came in order to study.	حضر لِيَدْرُسَ	in order to	لِ
I shall not study.	لَنْ أدْرُسَ	shall not	لَنْ
He came to study (he came so that he might study).	حَضَرَ حتى يَدْرُسَ	so that	حَتَّى
He came in order to study.	حضر كَيْ يَدْرُسَ	in order to	كي
He slept in order not to study.	نامَ كَيْلا يَدْرُسَ	in order not to	كي+أنْ+لا = كيلا

v. Below is a complete conjugation of the imperfect verb in the subjunctive mood (المضارع المنصوب), along with the corresponding independent pronouns:

Changes	Imperfect Subjunctive	Imperfect Indicative	Independent Pronoun
Damma became *fatha*	يَدْرُسَ	يَدْرُسُ	هو
Damma became *fatha*	تدْرُسَ	تدْرُسُ	هي
(ن) was deleted	يَدْرُسا	يَدْرُسانِ	هما
(ن) was deleted	تَدْرُسا	تدرسانِ	هما
(ن) was deleted Silent (ا) was added	يَدْرُسوا	يَدْرُسونَ	هـم

Changes	Imperfect Subjunctive	Imperfect Indicative	Independent Pronoun
No change	يَدْرُسْنَ	يَدْرُسْنَ	هُنَّ
Damma became *fatha*	تَدْرُسَ	تَدْرُسُ	أنتَ
(ن) was deleted	تَدْرُسِي	تَدْرُسِينَ	أنتِ
(ن) was deleted	تَدْرُسا	تَدْرُسانِ	أنتما
(ن) was deleted	تَدْرُسا	تَدْرُسانِ	أنتما
(ن) was deleted, Silent (ا) was added	تَدْرُسوا	تَدْرُسونَ	أنتم
No change	تَدْرُسْنَ	تَدْرُسْنَ	أنتنَّ
Damma became *fatha*	أدْرُسَ	أدْرُسُ	أنا
Damma became *fatha*	ندْرُسَ	ندْرُسُ	نحنُ

❖

C. The jussive - المضارع المجزوم

i. The imperfect jussive verb (المضارع المجزوم) has almost the same forms as the subjunctive. The only difference is the vowel on the last radical of the singular imperfect verbs: It becomes سكون in the jussive (it is فتحة in the subjunctive). These singular imperfect verbs correspond to the independent pronouns نحن ، أنا ،أنتَ، هي ، هو.

Imperfect Jussive	Imperfect Subjunctive	Imperfect Indicative
يدرسْ	يدرسَ	يدرسُ

ii. Exactly as in the subjunctive, the نَ is dropped from the imperfect jussive in the second feminine singular (أنتِ), third masculine plural (هم), and second masculine plural forms (أنتم). As in the subjunctive, in the verb يدرسُونَ, for example, the نَ is dropped in the jussive and a silent *alif* (ا) is added after the deleted نَ.

Imperfect Jussive	Imperfect Subjunctive	Imperfect Indicative
يدرسُوا	يدرسُوا	يدرسُونَ

iii. When to use the jussive?

The indicative verb becomes jussive when it is preceded by certain particles. Each particle has a certain meaning. The most common jussive particles are:

Meaning	Example	Meaning	Jussive Particle
he did not study	لـم يدرسْ	did not	لمْ
he has not yet studied	لـمَّا يدرسْ	has not	لمَّا
let him study	لِـيدرسْ	indirect command	لِـ

iv. Below is a complete conjugation of the imperfect verb يَدْرُس in the jussive mood (المضارع المجزوم), along with the corresponding independent pronouns:

Imperfect Jussive	Independent Pronoun
يَدْرُسْ	هو
تَدْرُسْ	هي
يَدْرُسا	هما
تَدْرُسا	هما
يَدْرُسوا	هـم
يَدْرُسْنَ	هنَّ
تَدْرُسْ	أنتَ
تَدْرُسي	أنتِ
تَدْرُسا	أنتما
تَدْرُسا	أنتما
تَدْرُسُوا	أنتم
تَدْرُسْنَ	أنتنَّ
أَدْرُسْ	أنا
نَدْرُسْ	نحنُ

❖

🎧 **Activity 1:** Below is a complete conjugation of the imperfect verb in the indicative, subjunctive, and jussive moods, along with the corresponding independent pronouns. Repeat aloud.

Imperfect Jussive	Imperfect Subjunctive	Imperfect Indicative	Independent Pronoun
يَدْرُسْ	يَدْرُسَ	يَدْرُسُ	هو
تَدْرُسْ	تَدْرُسَ	تَدْرُسُ	هي
يَدْرُسا	يَدْرُسا	يَدْرُسانِ	هما
تَدْرُسا	تَدْرُسا	تَدْرُسانِ	هما
يَدْرُسوا	يَدْرُسوا	يَدْرُسونَ	هـم
يَدْرُسْنَ	يَدْرُسْنَ	يَدْرُسْنَ	هنَّ
تَدْرُسْ	تَدْرُسَ	تَدْرُسُ	أنتَ
تَدْرُسي	تَدْرُسي	تَدْرُسينَ	أنتِ
تَدْرُسا	تَدْرُسا	تَدْرُسانِ	أنتما
تَدْرُسا	تَدْرُسا	تَدْرُسانِ	أنتما
تَدْرُسُوا	تَدْرُسُوا	تَدْرُسُونَ	أنتم
تَدْرُسْنَ	تَدْرُسْنَ	تَدْرُسْنَ	أنتنَّ
أدْرُسْ	أدْرُسَ	أدْرُسُ	أنا
نَدْرُسْ	نَدْرُسَ	نَدْرُسُ	نحنُ

❖

2. The Negative Command - المضارع المجزوم بـ (لا) الناهية

The imperfect takes the jussive form when it is preceded by the negative particle لا. When this negative particle precedes the imperfect, it changes the imperfect to a negative imperfect or a negative command (to command someone not to do something). The verb then becomes jussive.

do not write (you, s. m.)	لا تكْتُبْ

The negative particle لا only comes with imperfect verbs of the second-person pronouns أنتَ، أنتِ، أنتما، أنتم، أنتنَّ.

Examples:

لا + Imperfect = Negative Command	Independent Pronoun
لا تدرُسْ	أنتَ
لا تدرُسي	أنتِ
لا تدرُسا	أنتما
لا تدرُسوا	أنتم
لا تدرُسْنَ	أنتنَّ

❖

Drill 1: Change the verb in the following sentences from the indicative mood to the subjunctive and then to the jussive.

Example - لَم أشربْ القهوة - أريد أن أشربَ القهوة - أشربُ القهوةَ كُلَّ يَوْم

5 - تشاهدون الفيلم في يوم الجمعة .
حضرتم لـ ــــ ــــ الفيلم في يوم الجمعة .
لم ــــ الفيلم في يوم الجمعة .

1 - علي يدرسُ في مِصر .
علي لن ــــ في مصر .
علي لم ــــ في مصر .

6 - الطالبات الأمريكيات يسافرنَ إلى المغرب .
الطالبات الأمريكيات لن ــــ إلى المغرب .
الطالبات الأمريكيات لم ــــ إلى المغرب .

2 - نذهبُ إلى الجامعةِ يومَ الأحدِ .
لن ــــ إلى الجامعة يوم الأحد .
لم ــــ إلى الجامعة يوم الأحد .

7 - أنتِ تأكلين في السابعة مساء .
تعالي في السابعة مساء كي ــــ معي .
لم ــــ اليوم .

3 - تكتبونَ الواجبَ كل أسبوع .
تريدون أن ــــ الواجب كل أسبوع .
لم ــــ الواجب كل أسبوع .

8 - يغادرالأستاذ الجامعة .
يريدُ الأستاذ أن ــــ الجامعة .
لِـ ــــ الأستاذُ الجامعة .

4 - تبحثين عن عمل كل شهر .
لن ــــ عن عمل كل شهر .
لم ــــ عن عمل كل شهر .

❖

الفهم والاستيعاب: سُوقُ الحَميديَّة
Comprehension Text: Souq al-Hamidiyyeh

Figure 8.3 - Souq al-Hamidiyyeh, Damascus

يَقُولُ الدِّمَشْقِيُّونَ: مَنْ زارَ دِمَشقَ، ولم يَزُرْ سوقَ الحميديةِ، كأنَّهُ لمْ يَزُرْها. سوقُ
الحميديةِ هو سوقٌ تقليديٌّ قديمٌ ومشهورٌ، يقعُ سوقُ الحميديةِ الدمشقي العريق، أشهرُ أسواقِ
الدنيا، وأكثرُها جمالاً، في قلبِ مدينةِ دمشق القديمة. وسوقُ الحميديةِ هو في الحقيقة مركزٌ
تِجاريٌّ و سِيَاحِيٌّ، يحضُرُ الناسُ لِزيارتِهِ من كلِّ مكان. وسوقُ الحميديةِ قديمٌ جداً، بُنِيَ
قبْلَ مِئاتِ السنين، وقد بُنِيَ في شَكْلِهِ الجديدِ في عام 1780 م.

تَتَفَرَّعُ عَنْ سوق الحميدية أسواقٌ كثيرة أخرى وكلُّ سُوق لَهُ مِهْنةٌ خاصّةٌ به، مِن هذِهِ
الأسواق، سوقُ الخياطينَ وسوقُ الذهبِ وسوقُ الحرير. في سوق الحميديةِ مَحَلاتٌ
وصَالوناتٌ كثيرة لبيع الحُلْوِيَّاتِ والبُوظةِ. وَيُوجَدُ في السوق كذلك مئاتٌ من الدكاكين
والمحلاتِ الصغيرةِ والكبيرةِ، وفيه بيوتٌ ومساجدُ وآثارٌ تاريخية هامة.

🎧

كلمات وتعابير
Words and Expressions

to say	قَالَ، يقولُ
as if he	كَأنَّهُ
traditional	تَقليدي
to fall, to be located	وَقَعَ، يَقعُ
center	مَركز
touristic	سِيَاحِيٌّ
hundreds of years	مِئاتُ السِّنين
to branch out	تـتـفرع
special, peculiar	خاصة
tailors	خيَّاطين
to sell pastries	لبيع الحُلْويَّات
there is, there are	يُوجَدُ
he visited	زارَ
he did not visit	لم يَزُرْ
famous	مَشْـهُور
the world	الدُّنيا
commercial	تِجاريٌّ
place	مَكانٌ
its appearance	شكله
vocation, profession	مِهْنة
gold	ذهَبٌ
silk	حَرير
shops, places	دَكاكين / مَحَلات
historic ruins	آثار تاريخية

🎧

المحادثة
Let's Speak Arabic
Evening Activities – نشاطات مسائيَّة

Repeat the following question out loud:

What do you (m.s.) want to do tonight?	ماذا تريدُ أن تفْعَلَ الليلةَ؟
What do you (f.s.) want to do tonight?	ماذا تريدينَ أن تفْعَلي الليلةَ؟

Now repeat the following answer out loud:

I want to watch the movie	أريدُ أن أشاهِدَ الفيلم

Repeat the sentence and substitute the following for أشاهِدَ الفيلم:

go out to dinner	أذهبَ إلى العَشاء
listen to music	أستمعَ إلى الموسيقى
dance	أرقصَ
go out to the party	أذهبَ إلى الحَفْلة
go to church	أذهبَ إلى الكنيسة

Repeat the dialogue with a classmate.

෴

Homework – الواجب

1. Listen to the vocabulary and expressions. Read and recite the basic and comprehension texts after listening to them.

2. Write a composition about a place you have visited. Present it in class, and then turn it in to your teacher.

3. Conjugate three verbs aloud in all moods of the imperfect, then write them down.

من الثقافة العربية
فيروز

Window into Arab Culture
Fairuz

Figure 8.4 - Fairuz

Fairuz is an Arab superstar and a modern cultural phenomenon who has performed all over the world, including at the Kennedy Center in Washington, D.C. Born in 1935 in Lebanon, Fairuz is known to the Arabs as 'Our Ambassador to the Stars.' She developed a unique school of music that mixes music and singing with folklore traditions, dance, and poetry.

The song "Give Me the Flute and Sing" (أعطني النايَ وغنِّ) is among her most celebrated classical songs. The words of the song come from a poem written by the Lebanese-American poet Jubran Khalil Jubran (d. 1931).

Enjoy watching the video. Listen to the song and write down five words you know. Use each one of these words in a sentence. Also write down five words you do not know and see if you can understand their meanings from the context. Try to memorize a few verses of the song.

أعْطِني النَّايَ وَغنِّ

شِعْر جبران خليل جبران

أعطني الناي وغن فالغنا سرُّ الخلود

وأنين الناي يبقى بعد أن يفنى الوجود

هل اِتخذت الغاب مثلي منزلاً دون القصور

فتتبعتَ السواقي وتسلقتَ الصخور

هل تحممتَ بعطر وتنشفت بنور

وشربتَ الفجرَ خمراً في كؤوس من أثير

أعطني الناي وغنِّ فالغنا خير الصلاة

وأنينُ الناي يبقى بعد أن تفنى الحياة

هل جلستَ العصرَ مثلي بين جَفناتِ العنب

والعناقيدُ تدلَّت كثريات الذهب

هل فرشتَ العشبَ ليلاً و تلحفتَ الفضا

زاهداً في ما سيأتي ناسياً ما قد مضى

أعطني الناي وغن فالغنا عدلُ القلوب

وأنينُ الناي يبقى بعد أن تفنى الذنوب

أعطني الناي وغنِّ وانسَ داءً ودواء

إنما الناسُ سطورٌ كُتبت لكن بماء

* جبران خليل جبران، المجموعة الكاملة، دار بيروت، 1961، بتصرف.

الدَّرْسُ التَّاسِعُ

جمَـال عبد النَّاصِرِ

Lesson Nine
Gamal Abd Al-Nasser

Figure 9.1 – Cairo, Egypt

Lesson Nine Contents

🎧 Vocabulary - المفردات

🎧 Words and Expressions - كلمات وتعابير

💿 Basic Text - النص الأساسي

    ❖ A Nationalist Leader - قائد قومي

Grammar - القواعد

    1. The Patterns of the Verbs: Forms 1-10 أوزان الفعل

      🎧 Activity 1

    2. Using the Arabic Dictionary - إستعمال القاموس

💿 Comprehension Text - الفهم والاستيعاب

    ❖ Excerpts from Nasser's Speech - من خطاب جمال عبد الناصر

🎧 Let's Speak Arabic - المحادثة

    ❖ Activities - نشاطات

💿 Window into Arab Culture - من الثقافة العربية

    ❖ Gamal Abd Al-Nasser - جمال عبد الناصر

🎧

المفردات
Vocabulary

leader, chief	قائِدٌ ج. قُوّاد، قادَة
president	رَئيسٌ ج. رُؤَساءُ
to be (Form I)	كانَ، يَكُونُ
to continue, remain	ظَلَّ
to love (Form IV)	أَحَبَّ، يُحِبُّ
to encourage (Form II)	شَجَّعَ، يُشَجِّعُ
to call (Form III)	نادَى، يُنادِي
to be unified (Form V)	تَوَحَّدَ، يَتَوَحَّدُ
to continue, go on (Form X)	اِسْتَمَرَّ، يَسْتَمِرُّ
to be separated (Form VII)	اِنْفَصَلَ، يَنْفَصِلُ
to cancel (Form IV)	أَلْغَى، يُلْغِي
to recognize (Form VIII)	اِعْتَرَفَ، يَعْتَرِفُ
to name (Form II)	سَمَّى، يُسَمِّي
most of, the majority	مُعْظَم

🎧

كلمات وتعابير
Words and Expressions

suddenly	فَجْأَةً
unification	تَوْحِيدٌ
political and popular leader	قائِدٌ سِياسِيٌّ وشَعْبِيٌّ
hero of the Arab nation	بَطَلُ الأُمَّةِ العَرَبِيَّة
during his time, era, reign	في عَهْدِهِ
Arab unity	الوَحْدَة العَرَبِيَّة
the idea of Arab nationalism	فِكْرَة القَوْمِيَّة العربِيَّة
modern times	العَصْرُ الحَدِيثُ
indeed, in reality	فِعْلاً
one state	دَوْلَة واحِدَة
United Arab Republic	الجُمْهُورِيَّة العَرَبِية المُتَّحِدَة
until he died	حَتَّى ماتَ
for escaping from, to get rid of	لِلتَّخَلُّص = لِ + الـ + تَخَلُّص
unity, union	اِتِّحادٌ
independence	اِسْتِقْلالٌ

215

النص الأساسي: قائِدٌ قَـوْمِيّ
Basic Text: A Nationalist Leader

Figure 9.2 - Gamal Abd Al-Nasser

كانَ الرئيسُ المِصريُّ جمال عبد الناصر قائداً سياسياً وشعبياً. أَحَبَّهُ العربُ كثيراً. شجَّعَ عبدُ الناصر العربَ على الوَحْدَةِ العربيةِ ونادَى بفكرةِ القوميةِ العربيةِ. وفِعْلاً تَوَحَّدَتْ مِصرُ وسُوريا في دولةٍ واحدة في عَهْدِهِ، وصَارَ اسْمُ الدَّولةِ الجَديدةِ، الجُمْهُورية العربية المتحدة. اِستمرت الوَحْدة بَيْنَ سوريا ومِصرَ ثلاثَ سنواتٍ ونِصْف.

اِنْفَصَلَتْ سوريا عن مِصرَ في سنة ١٩٦١ وألْغَتْ الوَحْدة. لكِنَّ جمالَ عبدَ الناصر لم يَعْتَرِفْ بهذا الانْفِصَال وظلَّ يُسمِّي مِصرَ باسْم الجمهوريةِ العربيةِ المتحدةِ حتى ماتَ. يقولُ معظمُ العربِ إنَّ الرئيسَ جمالَ عبد الناصر كانَ بطلَ الأمَّةِ العربيَّةِ، وبطلَ القوميَّةِ العربيَّةِ في العصر الحديثِ.

ෂ෪ශ

القواعد
Grammar

1. The Patterns of the Verbs: Forms 1-10 أوزان الفعل

A. Arabic is rich in form derivations, which are derived from the three original radicals of the verb. Every word in Arabic has a root (جَذر). All verb derivations are meant to expand on the meaning of the root verb. This root verb is the basic verb form known as فِعْل مُجَرَّد, the 'naked' or 'stripped' verb, because it consists of only the three radicals. It is also the simplest form that refers to the masculine singular third person. Thus, it is called Form I.

All patterns of verbs and nouns alike are derived from this root form. For example, the verb كَتَبَ 'he wrote' is the basic verb (Form I) that consists of three radicals ك ت ب. From these radicals we can create any word related to the root verb's meaning. For example, the verbs كَتَّبَ 'to make someone write', كَاتَبَ 'to write to someone' and تَكَاتَبَ 'to write to each other' are all derived from the same radicals ك ت ب . Similarly, the nouns كِتاب 'a book,' مَكْتَب 'an office,' مَكْتَبَة 'a library' and كاتِب 'a writer' are all derived from the same basic verb كَتَبَ 'he wrote,' which carries the three-consonant root form ك ت ب.

B. The derived forms are known as أوْزان 'patterns.' These patterns (or forms) modify and expand upon the meaning of the root.

These derived patterns are formed by adding letters before or between the three radicals of the root or by doubling one of the radicals by adding شَدَّة *shadda*. Doubling the second radical of Form I كَتَبَ 'to write' gives us a new pattern كَتَّبَ 'to make someone write' (this is called Form II). By adding ا *alif* after the first radical, the pattern becomes كَاتَبَ 'to write to someone' (Form III). If we add the prefix تَ at the beginning and add ا *alif* after the first radical, the pattern becomes تَكَاتَبَ 'to write to each other' (Form VI). And so forth.

217

C. Because we add letters or double a letter in the root verb in order to derive patterns, we call the derived verb pattern (فِعْل مَزيد) 'an increased verb,' in contrast to the basic 'naked' verb (فِعْل مُجَرَّد), or Form I.

These derived patterns are numbered from Form II upwards. Form I is always the root form with three radicals. There are approximately fifteen derived verb patterns of the triliteral verb. Only ten of these forms are commonly used. The remaining patterns are rarely used.

D. Here are the ten patterns (or forms) of the triliteral verb in the perfect and imperfect. The vowel of the medial radical varies only in Form I (both in the perfect as well as the imperfect). The vowel of the medial vowel of Form I could be *fatha*, *damma*, or *kasra*, as in the perfect (يَفْـعَـلُ، يَفْـعُـلُ، يَفْـعِـلُ) and (فَعَـلَ، فَعُـلَ، فَعِـلَ) in the imperfect. You need to consult the dictionary to know the medial vowel of Form I in both the perfect and imperfect. The medial vowel of Forms II-X follows a fixed vowel system as shown in the chart below.

Activity 1: Forms II-X (patterns)

Imperfect	Perfect	Form
يفعل	فعل	I
يُـفَـعِّـلُ	فَعَّلَ	II
يُـفَـاعِلُ	فَاعَلَ	III
يُـفْـعِـلُ	أفْعَلَ	IV
يَتَفَعَّلُ	تفَعَّلَ	V
يَتَفاعَلُ	تفاعَلَ	VI
يَنْـفَـعِلُ	انْـفَعَلَ	VII
يَفْـتَـعِلُ	إفْتَعَلَ	VIII
يَفْـعَـلُّ	إفْعَلَّ	IX
يَسْتَـفْعِلُ	اسْتَـفْعَلَ	X

Note: The majority of Arabic verbs have roots with three radicals, and they are called triliteral verbs. However, Arabic also has a few derived forms from quadriliteral verbs, such as تَرْجَمَ "to translate." In this lesson, we only cover the triliteral verbs.

E. We can systematically derive all the patterns of any given root verb. However, not all of these derived patterns are in actual use for every verb.

For example, we can derive Form IX (اِكْتَبَّ) from the root verb كتب but this derived form number IX (اِكْتَبَّ) has no meaning in the language.

F. There is a great number of meanings that overlap between the derived verb patterns. As you progress in your Arabic studies, you will get a better sense of when to use which form. Also, sometimes the root form of the verb is not used, but the patterns derived from it are.

G. Native Arabic speakers do not use Roman numerals to represent these ten verb patterns. Instead, they know the patterns by their original forms. Arabs use الْمِيزان الصَّرْفِي 'the morphological scale' as a check on the added letters and vowels in each derived form. Whenever letters or vowels are added to the root form, then the same letters or vowels are added to the pattern(s), and vice versa.

All patterns are created and classified through this precise morphological process. The Arabs selected the three letters ف . ع . ل to represent the original radicals of the triliteral verb; these three radicals combine with short vowels to make up the basic verb form فَعَلَ 'to do.' Arab grammarians decided to use the verb form فَعَلَ as the model on which the entire Arabic morphological pattern system is centered.

H. The letters of the root form فعل represent all patterns for all triliteral verbs. The first letter ف represents the first radical, the second letter ع represents the second radical, and the third letter ل represents the third radical of any verb or pattern.

For example, the pattern of the verb كَتَبَ is represented by the root form فَعَلَ. Not only do the letters of فعل parallel the letters of كَتَبَ, but the vowels of each letter correspond, as well as the prefixes, suffixes, and infixes. So the pattern of the verb كَتَبَ is فَعَلَ, the pattern of كَتَّبَ is فَعَّلَ, and the pattern of اِسْتَكْتَبَ is اِسْتَفْعَلَ and so forth. The root and pattern system applies to nouns and adjectives as well.

I. Western grammarians and students of Arabic know the verb كَتَبَ as

Form II, but Arabs know it as Form فَعَّلَ. Similarly, the verb تكاتَبَ is known as Form VI, but it is known to Arabs as Form تفاعَلَ.

❖

2. Using the Arabic Dictionary

Arabic dictionaries list words alphabetically according to the root verb form. After learning the patterns, it becomes easy to identify the root form. To use the dictionary you must know the root form of any given word in order to be able to look it up. Using the dictionary will take some practice, but the more Arabic you learn, the easier it becomes.

In order to find the meaning of a pattern, you must eliminate the prefix, suffix, and infix of the pattern so you can identify its root form. If you want to find the meanings of a pattern, you must follow the process of elimination in order to identify the root form. For example, under the root form عَلِمَ 'to know' you will find the following derived patterns:

- أعْلَمَ 'to inform' (Form IV). Its prefix is أ .

- تَعَلَّمَ 'to learn' (Form V). It has a prefix تَ and an infix شدَّة added on its second radical.

- اِسْتَعْلَمَ 'to inquire' (Form X). Its prefix is اِسْتَ .

- عَالِمٌ 'a scholar.' This is the active participle of Form I. It has one infix ا after the first radical.

- عُلُومٌ 'sciences.' This is the plural of the singular noun عِلْمٌ . It has an infix و after the second radical.

- تَعْليمٌ 'teaching.' This is the verbal noun of Form II. It has the prefix تَ and the infix ـلـ.

Studying the verbal nouns, plurals, and active and passive participles will further help you identify the root form of the words. For example, if you want to look up the meaning of the word المَدْرَسَة you must delete the definite article الـ, the م, and the feminine ة from the word, then look it up under the root form دَرَسَ 'to study.' Under this root form you will find the derived word مدرسة which means 'a school.'

Not only verbs but every word in Arabic fits into a pattern. Whether a noun, verb, adjective, or adverb, every word is interrelated and part of a family. Once you find the root, you can find the meaning and function of the word. Particles and prepositions such as حتى and إلى do not fit into patterns.

Words can be singular, dual, plural, masculine, or feminine. For example, the pattern of مُدَرِّسُونَ 'teachers' is مُفَعِّلُونَ, which is the masculine sound plural of the singular noun مُدَرِّس. After eliminating the added letters and the shadda, we are left with the original radical letters دَرَسَ. It corresponds and rhymes with فَعَلَ.

Drill 1: Give the pattern, meaning, and Form I of each word.

Meaning	Form I	Pattern	Word
Muslims (f.pl.)	سَلِمَ	مُفْعِلات	مُسْلِمات
			الجَامِع
			المَسْجِد
			الخليفة
			الشَّهير
			نَتجوَّل
			جَميلة
			المَعْلومات
			أكْرَمَ
			سَفارَة
			حُكُومَة
			تَراسَلَ
			إسْتَغْفَرَ

Drill 2: Give the derived verb patterns from Form I.

Form X	Form VIII	Form V	Form IV	Form III	Form II	Form I
–	–	–	–			دَرَسَ
–			–	–		عَرَفَ
						جَمَعَ
	–	–				رَجَعَ
	–					قَبِلَ
–		–	–	–		شَغَلَ
–			–	–		هَرَبَ
	–		–	–		وَحَدَ
			–			فَتَحَ
	–	–	–			حَلَفَ

❖

Drill 3: Give the meaning and root of the following words.

Root	Meaning	Word
ط . ع . م	restaurants	مَطاعِمُ
		شاعِرٌ
		حَدَّثَ
		قُلُوبٌ
		أَسْلَمَ
		اِنْتَحَرَ
		مَشاهِيرُ
		واجِبَاتٌ
		مُفَكِّرٌ
		اِسْتِعْلامَاتٌ

❖

Drill 4: Translate into English.

١ - احتفلَ الشاعرُ بصدور كتابه الجديد.

٢ - اشتغلتُ في الجامعة الأردنية في الصيف الماضي.

٣ - حدَّث الأستاذ الطلابَ عن رحلته الممتعة إلى القاهرة.

٤ - حَثَّ الرئيسُ جمال عبد الناصر العربَ على الوحدة.

٥ - سَجَنَ رجالُ الشرطةِ رجلاً بريئًا .

٦ - أكرمَ الطالبُ أستاذه .

❖

Drill 5: Translate into Arabic.

1. The woman believed the man when he said he loved her.
2. The woman and the man exchanged love letters.
3. The professor lectured at Tunis University.
4. The president met with the students yesterday.
5. The physician corresponded with the patient.
6. The Frenchman found Arabic to be a difficult language.
7. He married her in the city of Damascus.
8. The president canceled the meeting.
9. He read the letter of his friend.
10. She loved the popular leader.

❖

Drill 6: Listen to the comprehension text several times. Try to understand as much as you can. Write down the words you understand and the words you do not know, then look them up in the dictionary. Translate some parts of the text at home. Turn in the translation to your teacher.

❖

الشَّعْبُ العَرَبِيُّ شَعْبٌ واحِدٌ

والجيشُ العربيُّ جيشٌ واحِد

ولنْ يُفَرِّقَ بيننا الاستعمارُ أو أعْوانُ الاستعمار

لقد خُلِقَتْ هذِهِ الأمة

أمـة عربيـة واحدة

وستبقى هذه الأمة أمـة عربية واحدة

لقد أرادَ الاستعمارُ أنْ يُفَرِّقَ هذه الأمة وأن يقيمَ الحدود

وأن يَبْذرَ في النفوس الشكوك

لقد حَاوَلَ أيها الإخوة

الاستعمارُ معنا هذا في مصر طوالَ الاعوام الماضيةِ

الاستعمارُ يُحَاوِلُ أنْ يُفتتَ ثورتنا ويحاولُ أن يقيمَ الفرقة بيننا

ولكنْ تكاتفَ الشعبِ العربي في مِصر اِستطاعَ أنْ يقضي على مُحَاولاتِ الاستعمار

واستطاعَ أنْ يسيرَ في طريقِهِ

وهو يرفعُ رايةَ العروبةِ ورايةَ الوحدة

وعليكم أنتم أيها الإخوة

يا ليبيـا الثورة

أيتها الجماهيرُ الثائرة

أن تأخذوا من عِبْرَتِـنا هذِهِ الدروس.

الدَّرْسُ العَاشِرُ

جَامِعة دِمَشق

Lesson Ten

Damascus University

Figure 10.1 - Damascus, Syria

Lesson Ten Contents

🎧 Vocabulary – المفردات

🎧 Words and Expressions – كلمات وتعابير

💿 Basic Text – النص الأساسي

    ❖ Conversation at the University – حديث في الجامعة

Grammar – القواعد

    The Imperative Mood

        A. Forming the Imperative in Form I

        B. Forming the Imperative in Forms II, III, V, VI

        C. Forming the Imperative in Form IV

        D. Forming the Imperative in Forms VII, VIII, IX, X

        🎧 Activity 1

💿 Comprehension Text – الفهم والاستيعاب

    ❖ A Letter from Damascus – رسالة من دمشـق

🎧 Let's Speak Arabic – المحادثة

    ❖ In the Restaurant – في المطعم

💿 Window into Arab Culture – من الثقافة العربية

    ❖ Modern Arabic Poetry – الشعرالعربي الحديث

🎧

المفردات

appointment	مُوْعِدٌ ج. مَواعِدُ / مَواعِيدُ
dean	عَمِيدٌ ج. عُمَداءُ
you (f.s.) go (imperative Form I)	إذهَبِي
library	مَكْتَبَة ج. مَكْتَبَاتٌ
you. (f.s.) wait for me (imp. VIII)	إنْتَظِرِينِي
to come back, return	عَادَ، يَعُودُ
cafeteria, snack room, buffet	مَقْصَفٌ ج. مَقَاصِفُ
hungry (adj.)	جَائِعٌ ـ جَائِعَة
you (m.s.) meet (imp. VIII)	إجْتَمِعْ
you (m.s.) talk (imp. V)	تَحَدَّثْ
you (m.s.) meet me (imp. III)	قابِلْـنِي
I will try	سَأُحَاوِلُ
you (m.s.) complete (imp. IV)	أكْمِلْ
job, work, business	عَمَلٌ ج. أعْمَالٌ

☸

🎧

كلمات وتعابير

I would like (love) to see	أحِبُّ أنْ أشاهِدَ
please (you, f. s.) come with me	تَفَضَّلِي مَعِي
I am on my way to	أنا في طريقي إلى
take me with you (m.s.)	خُذْنِي مَعَكَ
I will try not to be late for you	سَأُحَاوِل ألاَّ أتَأخَّرَ عَلَيْكِ
take your time (m.s.)	خُذْ وقْتَكَ
please do not rush (you, m.s.)	لا تُسْرعْ رَجَاءً
I will be waiting for you (m.s.)	سَأكُونُ في إنْتِظارِكَ
Always be happy!	كُنْ سَعِيداً دائِماً
I do not know	لا أعْرفُ
let me think (you, m.s.)	دَعْنِي أفَكِّر
You (f.s.) are the most beautiful friend in the world (existence)	أنتِ أجْمَلُ صَدِيقَةٍ في الوُجُودِ
I love you (f.s.) so much (Oh, how much I love you!)	كَمْ أحِبُّكِ

231

prefix *alif* must take *kasra* in both cases as in إشرَبْ 'ishrab' "you (m.s.) drink" and إصْبِرْ 'isbir' "you (m.s.) be patient."

Examples: Form I, Pronoun - أنتَ

Meaning	Changes	Imperative	Medial Vowel	Imperfect Jussive	Imperfect Indicative
write	The prefix of the verb changes	أكْتُبْ	ـُ	تَكْتُبْ	تَكْتُبُ
go	The prefix of the verb changes	إذهَبْ	ـَ	تَذهَبْ	تَذهَبُ
return	The prefix of the verb changes	إرْجِعْ	ـِ	تَرْجِعْ	تَرْجِعُ

❖

B. Forming the imperative in Forms II, III, V, VI

The imperative is formed from the second person of the imperfect jussive. In Forms II, III, V, and VI, we cut off the prefix تَ and its vowel (the subject marker of the imperfect jussive verb). Since the verbs in Forms II, III, V, and VI still begin with voweled consonants even after cutting off the prefix, there are no further modifications required (meaning there is no need to add the hamza in order to carry the vowel). For example, to form the imperative in the second person singular masculine verb تُدَرِّسْ 'tudarris,' we simply remove the prefix تُ 'tu.' By doing so, the verb becomes دَرِّسْ 'darris' "you (m.s.) study." Examples:

Meaning	Changes	Imperative	Imperfect Jussive	Imperfect Nominative	Pronoun	Form
teach	Prefix تُ deleted	دَرِّسْ	تُدَرِّسْ	تُدَرِّسُ	أنتَ	II
help	Prefix تُ deleted	سَاعِدِي	تُسَاعِدِي	تُسَاعِدِينَ	أنتِ	III
speak	Prefix تَ deleted	تَكَلَّمُوا	تَتَكَلَّمُوا	تَتَكَلَّمُونَ	أنتم	V
cooperate	Prefix تَ deleted	تَعَاوَنَا	تَتَعَاوَنَا	تَتَعَاوَنَانِ	أنتما	VI

Notice that النون in the second person plural feminine remains as is. But the subject marker (prefix) of the imperfect jussive is removed:

Imperative	Imperfect Jussive	Imperfect Nom.	Pronoun
دَرِّسْنَ	تُدَرِّسْنَ	تُدَرِّسْنَ	أنْتُنَّ

❖

C. Forming the imperative in Form IV

The imperative verbs in Form IV are formed by removing the prefix تُ and its vowel (the subject marker) from the imperfect jussive verb and adding another prefix that is همزة القطع 'hamzat al qat', which is an *alif* with a hamza on the top of it plus a *fatha* on top of the hamza (أَ). For example, the verb تُكْرِمْ 'tukrim' becomes أكْرِمْ 'akrim' 'you (m.s.) honor'. Other examples are:

Meaning	Changes	Imperative	Imperfect Jussive	Imperfect Indicative	Pronoun	Form
honor	The prefix of the verb changes	أكْرِمْ	تُكْرِمْ	تُكْرِمُ	أنتَ	IV
send	The prefix of the verb changes	أرْسِلِي	تُرْسِلِي	تُرْسِلِينَ	أنتِ	IV
bring	The prefix of the verb changes	أحْضِرا	تُحْضِرا	تُحْضِران	أنتما	IV
tell	The prefix of the verb changes	أخْبِروا	تُخْبِروا	تُخْبِرونَ	أنتم	IV
contribute	The prefix of the verb changes	أسْهِمْنَ	تُسْهِمْنَ	تُسْهِمْنَ	أنتنَّ	IV

❖

D. Forming the imperative in Forms VII, VIII, IX, X

In Forms VII, VIII, IX, and X, the imperative is also formed by omitting the prefix that is the subject marker. But, the omitted prefix is replaced by همزة الوصل 'hamzat al-Wasl' which is an *alif* written with no hamza. This *alif* must take the كسرة 'kasra' as a vowel. The *kasra* is placed under the *alif* (إ).

Examples:

Meaning	Changes	Imperative	Imperfect Jussive	Imperfect Indicative	Pronoun	Form
go away	The prefix of the verb changes	اِنْصَرِفْ	تَنْصَرِفْ	تَنْصَرِفُ	أنتَ	VII
listen	The prefix of the verb changes	اِسْتَمِعي	تَسْتَمِعي	تَسْتَمِعينَ	أنتِ	VIII
meet	The prefix of the verb changes	اِسْتَقْبِلوا	تَسْتَقْبِلوا	تَسْتَقْبِلونَ	أنتم	X

❖

🎧 **Activity 1:** Below are imperatives of some useful verbs that have not been covered. Review.

أنتنَّ You	أنتم You	أنتما You	أنتِ You	أنتَ You	المعنى Meaning	الفعل Verb
كُنَّ	كُونوا	كُونا	كُوني	كُنْ	to be	كانَ، يَكُونُ
كُلْنَ	كُلوا	كُلا	كُلي	كُلْ	to eat	أكَلَ، يأكُلُ
خُذْنَ	خُذوا	خُذا	خُذي	خُذْ	to take	أخَذَ، يأخُذُ
تَرْجِمْنَ	تَرْجِمُوا	تَرْجِمَا	تَرْجِمي	تَرْجِمْ	to translate	تَرْجَمَ، يُتَرْجِمُ
اِسْألْنَ	اِسْألوا	اِسْألا	اِسْألي	اِسْألْ	to ask	سَألَ، يَسْألُ

❖

Drill 1: Change the verb in each sentence from the imperfect to the imperative. Vocalize the verb.

Example - اِذَهَبْ إلى الجامعة اليوم – تَذهَبُ إلى الجامعة اليوم

1 - تذهبينَ إلى البيتِ في الساعة السابعة.

2 - تطبخونَ الدجاجَ مساءً.

3 - تعملان في المصنع.

4 - تسافِرْنَ إلى القاهرة.

5 - أنت ترجعُ إلى المكتبةِ بعد ساعة.

6 - تُكْرِمُونَ الأستاذ.

7 - تَتَزَوَّجِينَ الرجلَ الذي يُحِبُّكِ.

8 - تستقبلونَ المدير.

9 - أنتَ تأكُلُ البطيخ كلَّ يوم.

10 - تَدْرُسَان في البيت.

❖

Drill 2: Change the imperative to the perfect, then to the imperfect.
Example: اِذهَبُوا - ذَهَبُوا - يَذهَبُونَ

6 - اِحْتَرَمَا الكبير.	1 - اِشربي القهوة.
7 - اِبْحَثوا عَنْ عمل جديد.	2 - تكَلَّمَا مع الطالب الجديد.
8 - اِنْصَرِفْ من وجهي.	3 - دَرِّسْ الدرسَ الجديد.
9 - خُذْ السيارة الحمراء.	4 - اِسْتمِعْنَ جيِّداً.
10 - اُكْتُبوا الدرسَ التاسع.	5 - أخْبِرْ عائلتكَ عن الموضوع.

❖

Drill 3: Translate into Arabic.

1. Ask (f.s.) the professor about the exam.
2. Help (m.s.) your father in the house.
3. Thank (m. pl.) God for your good health.
4. Go (f. pl.) to the market today.
5. Be (f.s.) a good student of Arabic.
6. Eat (dual) in that restaurant.
7. Listen (m.s.) to what I say to you.
8. Get away (m. pl.) from here.
9. Tell me (f.s.) about the new professor.

DVD

الفهم والاستيعاب: رسالة من دمشق

دِمَشْقُ في 27 أيلول، 2011
صديقتي العزيزة مَنال،

تَحِيّة طَيِّبة أرْسِلُهَا لكِ من دِمَشْق. وصلتُ إلى سوريا قَبْلَ شَهْر وأنا سعيدة جدّاً هُنا. الطَّقْسُ جَميلٌ والنَّاسُ طَيِّبُونَ والطَّعَامُ لذيذ. كلُّ شيءٍ في دمشقَ رائعٌ. أسْكُنُ في شَقّةٍ صغيرةٍ في مِنْطقةِ باب توما وهي مِنْ أجْمَل المَناطِق في دمشق القديمة.

والشقة التي أسكنها تَمْلِكُهَا عائلةُ العظم وهي عَائِلة سوريّة مَعروفة. تسكنُ عائلة العظم في الطابق الأوّل مِن البناء الذي أسكنُ فيه. وأسكنُ أنا في الطابق الثاني. لِي أصدقاءُ كَثيرونَ هنا، منهم مَريم وهي ابنة صَاحبِ الشَّقة التي أسكنها. أذهبُ مَعَ مريمَ إلى السوق والمَكتَبَاتِ أثناءَ النَّهار، وفي المساء نَطبُخُ مَعَاً طَعَامَ العَشَاء.

لي صديقٌ آخَرُ اسمُهُ مُنير، هو طالبٌ في جامعةِ دمشقَ ويَدْرُسُ اللغة الإنكليزية ويَنْوي الدراسة في الولاياتِ المتحدةِ الأمريكية. ذهبتُ مع منير إلى أمْكِنَةٍ كثيرةٍ، وشاهَدْتُ مَعَهُ الجامعَ الأمويَّ والمتحفَ الوطنيَّ وسوقَ الحميدية.

سأكون في عَمَّان بَعْدَ أسبوع لزيارةِ صديقتي عفاف. سأكتُبُ لكِ ثانية مِنْ هناك. اكْتُبي لي. سَلامي وقُبْلاتي إليكِ وإلى والدِكِ الحبيب.

المُخلِصَة
جُمان

ৱ৩ও

🎧

كلمات وتعابير

good greetings	تحية طيبة	my dear friend	صَدِيقتي العَزيزة
the weather	الطَّقَس	I send	أرْسِلُ
district of Baab Touma	مِنطقة باب توما	delicious	لَذيذ
well-known	مَعْروفة	Al-Azm family	عَائلة العَظم
we cook	نَطبخُ	floor, flat	الطابق
The National Museum	المَتحَفُ الوَطني	he intends	يَنوي
write to me	أكْتبي لـي	I will be	سَأكونُ
sincerely	المُخْلِصَة	my kisses	قُبُلاتي

❖

Drill 4: Translate into English.

6 - أُطلُبوا العلمَ ولو في الصين.

7 - اِحْتَرِمي مَنْ هو أكبرُ منكِ.

8 - اِذهَبْ إلى الصف في الثامنة صباحاً.

9 - اُشْكُرا الله على هذه النعمة.

10 - دَعِيني أفكِّر.

1 - تكَلَّمْ اللغة العربية مع زملائك.

2 - تعلَّموا العربية وعلِّموها للناس.

3 - شاهدي الفيلمَ الجديدَ عن أم كلثوم.

4 - عامِلوا الخيرَ بالخير.

5 - اِعْملي واجبكِ كلَّ يوم.

❖

Drill 5: Read the letter from Damascus several times. Try to understand as much as you can. Look up the words you do not know in the dictionary. Translate the letter and hand in your translation to your teacher.

❖

Drill 6: Write a letter to a friend. Hand in your letter to your teacher.

239

🎧   المحادثة
In the Restaurant - في المطعم

Repeat the following question:

| What would you (m.s.) like to order? | ما طَلَبُكَ؟ |
| What would you (f.s.) like to order? | ما طَلَبُكِ؟ |

Now repeat the following answer:

| I would like a plate of salad | أريدُ صَحْن سَلطة |

Next, repeat the sentence and substitute the words below for صَحْن سَلطة:

grilled beef	لَحْم بَقَر مَشوي
a plate of kabaab	صَحْن كَباب
a cup of coffee	فِنجان قهوة
grilled chicken	فَرُّوج مَشوي
fish and rice	سَمَك وَرُزّ (أَرُزّ)

Repeat the dialogue with a classmate.

৶৶৶

Homework - الواجب

Read the words of the following poem along with the video. The poem contains the imperative and imperfect tenses in different moods. Make a list of the vocabulary you know and use the dictionary to find the meanings of other words you do not know. Translate a few verses and hand in the translation to your teacher. Finally, memorize some of the verses.

من الثقافة العربية
الشعر العربي الحديث

Figure 10.3 - Nizar Qabbani

أحِبِّينـي

نزار قباني

Love Me

أحبينـي بلا عُـقَـدِ

وضيعي في خُطُوطِ يدي

أحبينـي لأُسْبوعٍ، لأيامٍ، لساعاتٍ

فلستُ أنا الذي يهتمُّ بالأَبَدِ

❖

أنا تشرين شَهْرُ الرِّيـــح

والأمطارِ والْـبَرَدِ

أنا تشرين فانْسَحِقِي

كصَاعِقةٍ على جَسَــدِي

أحبينـي

بكُلِّ توَحُّشِ التَّـــتَر

بكُلِّ حَرارةِ الأَدْغَالِ

كُلِّ شراسةِ الْـمَـطَر

ولا تُبقي ولا تَذَري

ولا تَتَحَضَّري أبداً

فَقَدْ سَقَطَتْ على شَفَتَيْكِ

كُلُّ حَضَارَةِ الْحَـضَر

أحبيـنـي

كَزَلْزَالٍ كَمَوْتٍ غيرِ مُنتظَر

وخَلِّي عِطْرَكِ المعجون

بالكِبْريتِ والشَّرَر

يُهَاجِمُنـي كَذِئْبٍ جَائِعٍ خَطِـرٍ

وينهشُنـي ويضربنـي

كما الأمطارُ تضربُ ساحِلَ الجُزُر

❖

أنا رَجُلٌ بِلا قَــدَرٍ

فكُوني أنتِ لي قَدَري

وأبقينـي على شفتيكِ

مِثْلَ النقشِ في الحجرِ

❖

* نزار قباني، الأعمال الشعرية الكاملة، منشورات نزار قباني، بيروت، 2000.

الدَّرس الحادي عشر

عبد الرحمن الكواكبي

Lesson Eleven
Abd Al-Rahman Al-Kawakibi

Figure 11.1 - Castle of Aleppo, Syria

Lesson Eleven Contents

🎧 Vocabulary - المفردات

🎧 Words and Expressions - كلمات وتعابير

💿 Basic Text - النص الأساسي
DVD

    ❖ A Pioneer in the Arab Renaissance - رائد في النهضة العربية

Grammar - القواعد

    Kana and Its Sisters - كانَ وأخواتها

        A. كان in the Nominal Sentence - كان في الجملة الاسمية

        B. كان in the Verbal Sentence - كان في الجملة الفعلية

        🎧 Activity 1

        🎧 Activity 2

💿 Comprehension Text - الفهم والاستيعاب
DVD

    ❖ Personalities and Celebrities - أعلام ومشاهير

🎧 Let's Speak Arabic - المحادثة

    ❖ Traveling - السفر

💿 Window into Arab Culture - من الثقافة العربية
DVD

    ❖ Traditional Singing - الغِناء التقليدي

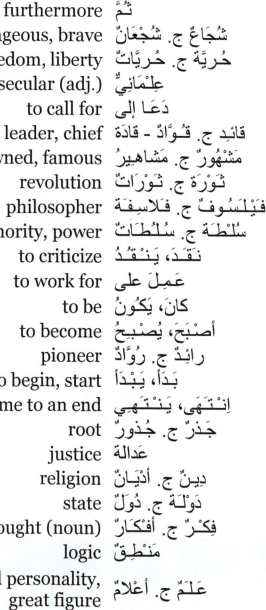

المفردات

then, furthermore	ثُمَّ
courageous, brave	شُجَاعٌ ج. شُجْعَانٌ
freedom, liberty	حُرِّيَّةٌ ج. حُرِّيَّاتٌ
secular (adj.)	عِلْمَانِيٌّ
to call for	دَعَا إلى
leader, chief	قائِد ج. قُوَّادٌ – قادَة
renowned, famous	مَشْهُورٌ ج. مَشاهِيرُ
revolution	ثَوْرَة ج. ثَوْرَاتٌ
philosopher	فَيْلَسُوفٌ ج. فَلاسِفَة
authority, power	سُلْطَةٌ ج. سُلْطَاتٌ
to criticize	نَقَدَ، يَنْقُدُ
to work for	عَمِلَ على
to be	كانَ، يَكُونُ
to become	أصْبَحَ، يُصْبِحُ
pioneer	رائِدٌ ج. رُوَّادٌ
to begin, start	بَدَأ، يَبْدَأ
to come to an end	اِنْتَهَى، يَنْتَهِي
root	جَذرٌ ج. جُذورٌ
justice	عَدالة
religion	دِينٌ ج. أَدْيَانٌ
state	دَوْلَة ج. دُوَلٌ
thought (noun)	فِكْرٌ ج. أفْكَارٌ
logic	مَنْطِقٌ
distinguished personality, great figure	عَلَمٌ ج. أعْلامٌ

كلمات وتعابير

the Arabic Renaissance	النَّهْضَة العَرَبِيَّة
the nineteenth century	القَرْنُ التاسِعَ عَشَرَ
the midpoint of the twentieth century	مُنتصَف القَرْن العِشْرين
the fourth Islamic caliph	الخَليفة الإسلامي الرَّابِع
prominent personality	بَارِزٌ ج. بارزونَ
the nature of despotism	طَبَائِعُ الاسْتِبْدَاد
at the beginning of his life	بِدَايَة حَيَاتِه
principle	مَبْدأ ج. مَبَادِئ
one nation	أُمَّة واحِدَة
Islamic law	الشَّريعة الإسْلامِيَّة
modern Arab history	تاريخُ العربِ الحَديث
Islamic history	التاريخُ الإسْلامِيُّ
he died poisoned (through poisoning)	مَاتَ مَسْمُوماً
Arab nationalism	القَوْمِيَّة العَرَبِيَّة
unification	تَوْحِيدٌ
the religious sects	الطَّوائِفُ الدِّينِيَّة
Ottoman	عُثْمانيٌّ - عُثْمانيَّة
against (prep.)	ضِدَّ
corruption	فَسَادٌ
ruler, governor	الوالي ج. الوُلاة

Figure 11.2 - Aleppo, Syria

النص الأساسي: رائِدٌ في النهضة العربية

Figure 11.3 - Abd Al-Rahman Al-Kawakibi

عبدُ الرحمن الكواكبي

كانَ عبدُ الرحمن الكواكبي رائداً من رُوَادِ النهضةِ العربيةِ في القَرْنِ التاسِعَ عَشَرَ. وكانَ عَالِمَاً مَشْهُوراً، وفَيْلَسُوفاً. وُلِدَ عبدُ الرحمن الكواكبي في عام 1854 في مَدينةِ حَلَب في سوريا. دَرَسَ اللغة العربية والشريعة الإسلامية والتاريخَ والفَلْسَفة والمَنْطِقَ.

اِشْتَغَلَ الكواكبي في بدايةِ حياتِهِ بالصِّحافة، ثُمَّ عَمِلَ مُدَرِّساً وكانَ عُمْرُهُ عِشرين سنة، ثُمَّ أصبحَ قائداً اِجْتِمَاعِيَّاً. كان رَجُلاً شُجَاعَاً، فَقَدْ نَقَدَ السُّلْطة العثمانية وفَضَحَ فَسَادَ الوُلاةِ، ونَقَدَ الظُّلمَ المَوْجُودَ في المُجْتَمَع، وَدَعَا إلى الثورة. كَمَا عَمِلَ على تسهيل تَدْريس اللغةِ العربيةِ والعلوم الدينية. كَتَبَ الكواكبي كُتُبَاً كثيرة، منها (طبَائِعُ الاسْتِبْدَاد) و(أمُّ القُرَى). هاجرَ إلى مِصْرَ. وماتَ فيها مَسْمُومَاً.

القواعد

Kana and Its Sisters - كان وأخواتها

The verb كَانَ means 'to be.' كَانَ is the perfect form of the third-person masculine singular which means literally 'he was.' Its imperfect tense form is يَكُونُ, which means 'he usually is.' كَانَ and its sisters (see the list below) are a small group of linking verbs that take their subjects in the nominative case and their predicates in the accusative. The verb كَانَ is used widely in both nominal and verbal sentences, so it is important to understand the rules below. كَانَ is also one of the hollow verbs, which will be discussed in Lesson Nineteen.

❖

A. كَانَ *in the nominal sentence*

We have learned that the nominal sentence (الجُمْلة الاسْمِيَّة) begins with a noun and consists of a subject and a predicate (المبتدأ والخبر). We also learned that both the subject (المُبْتَدَأ) and the predicate (الخَبَر) are in the nominative case in their usual, simple arrangements as in the following sentence:

the house is big	البيتُ كبيرٌ

When the perfect form of verb كَانَ is used with nominal sentences, three things must be noted: The sentence is then in the past tense; the subject of the nominal sentence must remain in a nominative case; and the predicate of the nominal sentence must change from the nominative case to the accusative case:

the house is big	البيتُ كبيرٌ
the house was big	كانَ البيتُ كبيراً

In the sentence 'كانَ البيتُ كبيراً' the word البَيْتُ is the subject of *kana* (اسـم كان) and nominative (مَرْفُوع). The word كبيراً is the predicate of *kana* (خبر كان) and accusative (مَنْصُوب).

All the sisters of كَانَ change the meaning of the sentence, keep the subject in the nominative case, and cause the predicate to change from the nominative case to the accusative case. All the sisters of kana (كَانَ وأخَوَاتُهَا) function in the same grammatical manner. While كَانَ means 'to be,' its sisters generally have the meaning of 'to continue,' or 'to become,' or 'to remain,' except for the sister لَيْسَ, which means 'not to be.' Example:

| the house is not big | لَيْسَ البيتُ كبيراً |

The most frequently used sisters of كَانَ are:

to remain	بَقِيَ
to keep on, continue	ظَلَّ
not to cease (still)	ما زَالَ
to become	صَارَ
to become	أصْبَحَ
to become	أمْسَى
to become	بَاتَ

كان وأخواتها 'Kana and its sisters' are conjugated in the perfect, imperfect, and imperative, except for لَيْسَ, which is conjugated only in the perfect.

The verb كَانَ is conjugated fully. The imperfect tense يَكُونُ is used infrequently. The perfect and future tenses are used most often. Examples:

I was at home yesterday	كُنْتُ في البيتِ أمْس
I am usually at home at 7:00 in the evening	أكُونُ في البيتِ في السابعةِ مَساءً
I will be in the house tomorrow	سَأكُونُ في البيتِ غَدَاً

❖

i. Negating كَانَ

كَانَ is negated by placing the particle ما before the perfect form, as in:

He was not at home	مَا كَانَ في البيتِ

Or, كَانَ is negated by using لَمْ before the imperfect tense.
(لَمْ) + *the imperfect tense = negation in the jussive mood:*

He was not at home	لَمْ يَكُنْ في البيتِ

ii. One may express the past continuous and the past habitual by using the perfect of كَانَ followed by the imperfect of the verb concerned.

When he arrived I was cooking	عِنْدَمَا وَصَلَ كنتُ أطْبُخُ
He used to write every day	كَانَ يَكْتُبُ كُلَّ يَوْم

❖

B. كَانَ *in the verbal sentence*

When كان is used in verbal sentence, it could be in the past form preceding a perfect tense, or it could be in the imperfect form preceding a perfect tense.

He had gone	كَانَ قَدْ ذهَبَ
He will have gone	يَكُونُ قَدْ ذهَبَ

C. The particle قَـدْ

If the particle قَـدْ precedes the perfect tense, then this arrangement indicates a definite execution of the action in the past or the execution of the future action is expected with certainty (as in above examples).

When the particle قَدْ precedes the imperfect tense, the arrangement indicates a possibility that the action of the verb *might* take place.

He might go	قَـدْ يَذهَبُ

Activity 1: This is the conjugation of the verb كَانَ in the past and present. Please repeat.

Imperfect (Present)	Perfect (Past)	Independent Pronoun
يَكُونُ	كَانَ	هو
تكُونُ	كَانَتْ	هي
يَكونانِ	كانا	هما
تكونانِ	كانتا	هما
يكونونَ	كانوا	هم
يَكُنَّ	كُنَّ	هنَّ
تكونُ	كُنتَ	أنتَ
تكونينَ	كُنتِ	أنتِ
تكونانِ	كُنْتما	أنتما
تكونانِ	كُنْتما	أنتما
تكونونَ	كُنْتم	أنتم
تَكُنَّ	كُنْتُنَّ	أنتنَّ
أكونُ	كنتُ	أنا
نكونُ	كُنَّا	نحنُ

Figure 11.4 - Palmyra, Syria

🎧   **Activity 2:** لَيْسَ is conjugated only in the perfect. Repeat:

Perfect (Past)	Independent Pronoun
لَيْسَ	هو
لَيْسَتْ	هي
لَيْسَا	هما
لَيْسَتا	هما
لَيْسُوا	هم
لَسْنَ	هنَّ
لَسْتَ	أنتَ
لَسْتِ	أنتِ
لَسْتُمَا	أنتما
لَسْتُمَا	أنتما
لَسْتُمْ	أنتم
لَسْتُنَّ	أنتنَّ
لَسْتُ	أنا
لَسْنا	نحْنُ

❖

Drill 1: Complete the sentences below using the correct form and tense of the verb كَانَ.

١ - أنا ـــــــــــ في لبنان الأسبوع الماضي.

٢ - هي ـــــــــــ هنا قبل ساعة.

٣ - صديقي وزوجته ـــــــــــ في المطعم أمس.

٤ - متى ـــــــــــ في المطار يا إبراهيم؟

٥ - متى ـــــــــــ في مكتبك يا أستاذة غداً؟

٦ - أين ـــــــــــ ليلةَ أمس يا مريم؟

٧ - نحن ـــــــــــ في الجامعة مساء يوم الأحد.

٨ - والدي ووالدتي ـــــــــــ في مصر بعد شهر.

Drill 2: Complete the sentences below using كَانَ or لَيْسَ. Use the correct form and tense, and vocalize the subject and the predicate.

Example: الطَّالِبُ جديدٌ - *ليس الطَّالِبُ جديداً*

1 - الرجلُ قويٌّ.

2 - المدينة بعيدة.

3 - أخي الكبيرُ مشهورٌ.

4 - المدرسة الثانوية قريبة من السوق.

5 - أختي سوزان متزوجة.

6 - الطلابُ الأمريكيونَ موجودون في الصفِّ.

7 - المديرُ رَجُلٌ طَيِّبٌ.

8 - الأستاذة الجميلة سودانية.

❖

Drill 3: Translate into English.

1 - كنتُ في السوق عندما حضر أخي.

2 - أكونُ في البيتِ كل يوم في السابعةِ مساءً.

3 - كان الكواكبي عَلَماً بارزاً من أعلام النهضةِ العربيةِ.

4 - ليست اللغة العربية صعبة.

5 - ما يزال الأستاذ يشرب القهوة في الصف كل يوم.

6 - أصبح فريدٌ طبيباً مشهوراً جداً.

❖

Drill 4: Translate into Arabic.

1. I will be at my office tomorrow morning.
2. She was a pretty woman.
3. He is not kind.
4. Our teacher was horrible last year.

5. The city is not clean.
6. The university is not big.
7. I was sick yesterday.
8. He has studied.
9. He will have studied.

❖

Drill 5: Fill in the blanks with the correct words from the comprehension text.

١- كان الكواكبي _____ _____ الحرية َ و _____ العدالة َ. دعا إلى _____ _____ الدِّين _____ الدولةِ، وإلى فصْل _____ الدينيةِ عن _____ السياسية. كان الكواكبي علْمَانيًّا، دعا إلى _____ الطوائفِ الدينية في _____ _____ في أمة واحدة. كان الكواكبي _____ الخلافةِ العثمانيةِ و _____ _____ الفسادِ العثماني. ماتَ الكواكبي _____ في القاهرة في سنة 1902.

٢- كان عبد الرحمن الكواكبي _____ بارزاً من أعلام النهضةِ العربيةِ التي _____ في القرن التاسعَ عشرَ و _____ _____ في منتصفِ القرن العشرين. ترجِعُ جذورُ عائلةِ الكواكبي في حلب إلى الإمام _____ بن أبي طالب، الخليفةِ الإسلامي _____ في التاريخ الإسلامي. وكانَ المُنَظِّرَ الأوَّلَ للقوميةِ في تاريخ _____ _____ الحديث.

❖

254

الفهم والاستيعاب: أعْلامٌ ومشاهير

كان عبد الرحمن الكواكبي علماً بارزاً من أعلام النهضةِ العربيةِ التي بدأتْ في القرن التاسع عشر وانتهَتْ في مُنتصَفِ القَرْنِ العِشْرين. تَرْجِعُ جُذورُ عَائِلةِ الكواكبي في حلب إلى سَيِّدِنـا الإمام علي بن أبي طالب، الخليفةِ الإسلامي الرابع في التاريخ الإسلامي. كان الكواكبي قَوْمِيَّاً في فِكْرِهِ، ديمقراطياً في مَبَادِئِهِ، وكانَ المُنَظِّرَ الأوَّلَ للقوميةِ العربيةِ في تاريخ العربِ الحديثِ.

كان الكواكبي يَعْشقُ الحرية ويُحِبُّ العدالةَ والمساواة. دَعَا إلى فَصْلِ الدِّين عَن الدولةِ، وإلى فَصْلِ السُّلطةِ الدينيةِ عَن السُّلطةِ السِّيَاسِيَّةِ. كان الكواكبي عِلْمَانِيَّاً، دَعَا إلى توحيدِ الطوائفِ الدينيةِ في المُجْتمع في أمَّةٍ واحدةٍ. كانَ الكواكبي ضِدَّ الفَسَادِ العُثْماني. مَاتَ الكواكبي مَسْمُومَاً في القاهرةِ في سَنَـة 1902.

Figure 11.5 - Narrated by Mahmoud Harmoush

كلمات وتعابير

nationalist	قوميًّا
he loves passionately	يَعْشـق
separation, to separate	(فصْلٌ) فصَلَ، يفصِلُ
theorist (a.p.), to theorize	(مُنَظِّرٌ) نَظَّرَ، يُنظِّرُ
his principles	مبادئه (مبادؤه)
it (f.s.) goes back	ترْجِعُ
equality	مُساواة
he called for	دَعَا إلى

الدَّرس الثَّانـي عشر

مِـصر أُمُّ الدُّنـيا

Lesson Twelve

Egypt: The Mother of the World

Figure 12.1 - Pyramids of Giza, Egypt

Lesson Twelve Contents

🎧 Vocabulary - المفردات

🎧 Words and Expressions - كلمات وتعابير

💿 Basic Text - النص الأساسي

   ❖ Come to Egypt - تعالَـوْا إلى مصر

Grammar - القواعد

   The Verbal Noun - المصدر

     A. Verbal Noun of Form I - مصادر الوزن الأول

     B. Verbal Nouns of Forms II to X

     مصادر الوزن الثاني إلى العاشر

     C. The Patterns and Their Verbs - الأوزان وأفعالها

💿 Comprehension Text - الفهم والاستيعاب

   ❖ Naguib Mahfouz - نجيب محفوظ

🎧 Let's Speak Arabic - المحادثة

   ❖ Introductions - التعارف

💿 Window into Arab Culture - من الثقافة العربية

   ❖ Umm Kulthum - أمُّ كُـلثـــوم

المفردات

مَحَبة (أَحَبَّ، يُحِبُّ)	love (verbal noun)
طِيبة (طابَ، يَطِيبُ)	goodness, pleasantness (v.n.)
كَرَمٌ (كَرُمَ، يَكْرُمُ)	generosity, noble nature (v.n.)
مُشاهدة (شاهَدَ، يُشاهِدُ)	seeing, watching (v.n.)
سِحْرٌ (سَحَرَ، يَسْحَرُ)	charm, enchantment (v.n.)
جَمَالٌ (جَمُلَ، يَجْمُلُ)	beauty (v.n.)
تَنَوُّعٌ (تَنَوَّعَ، يَتَنَوَّعُ)	diversity, variety (v.n.)
اِسْتِطاعَة (اِسْتَطاعَ، يَسْتَطيعُ)	ability, capability (v.n.)
تَقَدُّمٌ (تَقَدَّمَ، يَتَقَدَّمُ)	progress, advancement (v.n.)
بَسَاطَة (بَسُطَ، يَبْسُطُ)	simplicity (v.n.)
شَقَّة ج. شُقَقٌ	apartment, flat
مَسْرَح ج. مَسَارحُ	theater
غَنِيٌّ ج. أَغْنِياءُ	rich, wealthy
فَنٌّ ج. فُنونٌ	art
حَضَارَة ج. حَضَارَاتٌ	civilization
مَرْكَزٌ ج. مَرَاكِزُ	center
بَحْثٌ ج. بُحُوثٌ	research, study

كلمات وتعابير

كَمَا يَقولُ المِصريونَ	as the Egyptians say
أمُّ الدُّنْيَا	the mother of the world
أهْلُ مِصْر	the people of Egypt
جَامِعُ الأزْهَر	Al-Azhar mosque
تَجِدُونَ	you will find
الأهْرَامَات	the Pyramids
نَهْرُ النِّيل	the Nile River
الآثَارُ التَّارِيخِيَّة	historical ruins
التَّقْليدُ والحَدَاثة	traditions and modernity
تَعَالَوْا إلى زِيارَتِي - تعالوا لزيارتي	come to visit me
بَهجَةُ الحَيَاة	delight of life
سِيَاحَة	tourism
جَائِزة	prize, award

النص الأساسي: تَعَالَوْا إلى مِصْرَ

Figure 12.2 – Al Azhar Mosque, Cairo

أكْتُبُ لكُم مِن مِصْرَ. ومِصْرُ كما يقولُ المصريون هي أمُّ الدنيا. أهلُ مِصْرَ فيهم طيبة وكَرَمٌ ومَحَبَّة. أسْكُنُ في القاهرة. والقاهرة فيها سِحْرٌ وجَمَالٌ. مِن شقتي التي أسكنها أستطيعُ مُشَاهَدَة نَهْر النيل الرائِع وجامع الأزهرالعظيم. مِصْرُ فيها حَضَارَة عَريقة ولها تاريخٌ غَنِيٌّ. في مصرَ، تجِدُونَ المساجدَ والجامعات ومراكِزَ البُحُوثِ والمَسَارح. تجدونَ فيها الماضِيَ والحاضِرَ، القديمَ والحديث، التقليدَ والحداثة.

في مصرَ، هناكَ الأهراماتُ والآثارُ التاريخية وهناكَ الأدبُ والفنُّ والتَّـقَـدُّمُ. هناكَ الكلمة الحُلوة والبَسَاطة وبَهْجَة الحياة. وهذا التَّـنَـوُّعُ الغنِيُّ جَعَلَ مِصْرَ مركزاً سِيَاحِيّاً هامّاً في الشرق الأوسطِ.

أصدقائي الأعزاء: تعالَوْا إلى مصر، وتعالَوْا لِزيارتي.

❧❧

القواعد

The Verbal Noun - المصدر

The verbal noun (المصدر) is a noun derived from the forms of the verb. Each verb has at least one verbal noun that expresses the action of the corresponding verb. For example, the verbal noun دِرَاسَة 'studying' means 'the act of studying' and is derived from the verb دَرَسَ 'to study.'

- The verbal noun in Arabic has many appropriate English translations. It corresponds to the English gerund (noun ending in -ing) such as دِرَاسَة 'studying' and كِتَابَة 'writing.' It also corresponds to the English infinitive such as 'I went to Egypt *to study* Arabic' (ذهبتُ إلى مصر لدراسة اللغةِ العربية).

  Verbal nouns can be definite or indefinite. They can be made definite in three ways: first by using the definite article الـ as in الدراسة, second when the verbal noun comes as the first term of *idafa* as in دِراسَة اللغة, and third when the verbal noun is attached to a suffixed pronoun as in دِراسَتُـهُ.

- The verbal noun can be the subject or the predicate in a nominal sentence, or it can be the subject or the object in a verbal sentence. A verbal noun can also be the object of a preposition or the first or second term of an *idafa*.

  We will use the verbal noun عَمَلٌ 'working' that is derived from Form I عَمِلَ 'to work' to give the following examples:

Meaning	The Verbal Noun	Position in the Sentence
the work (or 'working') is interesting	العَمَلُ مُمْتِـعٌ	*subject of nominal sentence*
the work (or 'working') began yesterday	بدأ العَمَلُ أمس	*subject of verbal sentence*
I began the work yesterday	بدأتُ العَمَلَ أمس	*object of verbal sentence*

Meaning	The Verbal Noun	Position in the Sentence
I returned home after work	رجعتُ إلى البيت بعد العَمَل	*object of preposition*
the work of the student is beautiful	عَمَلُ الطالبِ جميلٌ	*first term of idafa*
the time of the work is early	وقتُ العَمَلِ مُبَكِّرٌ	*second term of idafa*

❖

A. The verbal noun for Form I - مصادر الوزن الأول

The verbal noun for Form I is unpredictable. Each verb can have several verbal nouns. It must be looked up in the dictionary, as it falls into a wide range of different patterns. Some of these patterns are common, and you will begin to recognize them quickly. Others are less common and may take longer to learn, but they must all be learned.

The student of Arabic will develop familiarity with these patterns and will be able to predict the verbal noun. It is therefore helpful to learn the verbal noun together with its verb.

Examples of the verbal nouns of Form I, which fall into a number of different patterns:

Meaning	الوزن	Verbal Noun	Meaning	Verb Form I
writing	فِعَالة	كِتَابَة	to write	كَتَبَ
hearing	فَعَال	سَمَاع	to hear	سَمِعَ
transmitting	فَعْل	نَقْل	to transmit	نَقَلَ
mentioning	فِعْل	ذِكْر	to mention	ذكَرَ
thanking	فُعْل	شُكْر	to thank	شَكَرَ
returning	فُعُول	رُجُوع	to return	رجَعَ

❖

B. *The verbal nouns of Forms II to X - مصادر الوزن الثاني إلى العاشر*

The verbal nouns of Forms II to X are predictable as they fall into fixed patterns. Below are the fixed patterns and general meanings of the verbal nouns of Forms II to X.

General Meaning of the Patterns	Verbal Noun	Imperfect	Perfect	Form
Simple action	فِـعْـل - فِـعَـالة...	يَـفْـعَـلُ	فَـعـل	I
causative, intensive	تَفْعيل، تَفْـعِلة	يُـفَـعِّلُ	فَعَّلَ	II
reciprocal	مُـفَاعَلة، فِعَال	يُـفَاعِلُ	فَاعَلَ	III
causative	إفْـعَال	يُـفْـعِلُ	أفْعَلَ	IV
reflexive of Form II	تَفَعُّل	يَـتَفَعَّلُ	تَفَعَّلَ	V
reflexive of III (mutual)	تَفَاعُل	يَـتَفاعَلُ	تَفاعَلَ	VI
passive of Form I	إنْـفِعَال	يَـنْـفَـعِلُ	إنْـفَعَلَ	VII
reflexive of Form I	إفْـتِعَال	يَـفْـتَـعِلُ	إفْـتَـعَلَ	VIII
colors and defects	إفْـعِلال	يَـفْـعَلُّ	إفْـعَلَّ	IX
reflexive of IV, causative	إسْتِـفْـعَال	يَـسْتَـفْـعِلُ	إسْتَـفْـعَلَ	X

❖

C. *The patterns and their verbs - الأوزان وأفعالها*

Below are examples of the patterns and their verbs:

الوزن	Verbal Noun	Imperfect	Meaning	Perfect	Form
فِـعْـل	عِلْم	يَـعْلَمُ	to know	عَلِمَ	I
تَفْـعيل	تَعْليم	يُـعَلِّمُ	to teach	عَلَّمَ	II
مُـفَاعَلة	مُكاتَبة	يُـكاتِبُ	to write to someone	كاتَبَ	III
إفْـعَال	إعْلام	يُـعْلِمُ	to inform	أعْلَمَ	IV
تَفَعُّل	تَعَلُّم	يَـتَعَلَّمُ	to learn	تَعَلَّمَ	V
تَفَاعُل	تَكاتُب	يَـتَكاتَبُ	to write to each other	تَكاتَبَ	VI
إنْـفِعَال	إنْكِسار	يَـنْكَسِرُ	to be broken	إنْكَسَرَ	VII

الوزن	Verbal Noun	Imperfect	Meaning	Perfect	Form
اِفْتِعَال	اِعْتِرَاف	يَعْتَرِفُ	to confess	اِعْتَرَفَ	VIII
اِفْعِلَال	اِحْمِرَار	يَحْمَرُّ	to become red	اِحْمَرَّ	IX
اِسْتِفْعَال	اِسْتِعْلَام	يَسْتَعْلِمُ	to inquire	اِسْتَعْلَمَ	X

❖

Drill 1: Change the verbs, which are preceded by (أنْ), into verbal nouns.
Example: أريد أنْ أذهبَ إلى المكتبةِ ـ أريدُ الذهابَ إلى المكتبة

1 - أحبُّ أنْ أشاهِدَ الفيلم هذه الليلة.

2 - أحبُّ أنْ أشربَ الشاي مع الليمون والسكر.

3 - سافرتُ بعد أنْ وَدَّعْتُ أستاذي.

4 - أكلتُ في المطعم بعد أنْ غادَرَتْ زوجتي.

5 - يريدُ أن يتكلمَ العربية جيداً قبل أنْ يُسافِرَ إلى عَمَّان.

6 - هل تُحِبُّ أنْ تَدْرُسَ معي اليوم؟

7 - اِجْتَمعتُ مع المدير بعد أنْ اِجْتَمَعْتُ مع الأستاذ.

8 - حضر إلى الصف بعد أنْ قابَلَ العميد.

9 - هو يدرسُ عادة بعد أنْ يَقرأ القرآن.

10 - الأستاذة الجديدة تُحِبُّ أنْ تشربَ القهوة قبل الصف.

11 - أريد أن أتحدثَ معكِ بعد أنْ أسْتَقْبِلَ الضيوف.

❖

Drill 2: Change the verbal nouns in the following sentences into verbs.
Example: أحبُّ العملَ في مكتبِ الرئيس ـ أحبُّ أنْ أعْمَلَ في مكتب الرئيس

1 - أريدُ الزواجَ من الفتاة التي أحِبُّها.

2 - دَرَّسَتْ في جامعة القاهرة قبل التدريس في جامعة كاليفورنيا.

3 - صديقتي تحبُّ الاستماع إلى الموسيقى قبل العمل.

٤ -   عائلتي تحبُّ السَّكنَ في الشرق الأوسط .

٥ -   سَكَنَتْ في السودان قبل الحضورِ إلى أمريكا.

٦ -   يذهب أخي إلى الكلية بعد قراءةِ الجريدة اليومية.

٧ -   يشاهد الطلاب برنامج الجزيرة قبل مُشاهَدَةِ الفيلم.

٨ -   تطبخ أختي الطعام قبل التحضيرِ للامتحان.

٩ -   يريد الحصول على عمل قبل التخرُّجِ من الجامعة.

١٠ -   أحبُّ أن أتناول فطوري قبل معرفةِ الأخبار.

❖

Drill 3: Write the verbal nouns, meanings, and root forms of the given verbs.

Meaning	الوزن	Verbal Noun	Verbs	Root Form
sitting	فَعُول	جُلُوس	يَجْلِسُ	جَلَسَ
			يُكْرِمُ	
			يَتَسَلَّمُ	
			يَسْتَحْضِرُ	
			يَنْتَقِلُ	
			يَعْتَرِفُ	
			يُكَتِّبُ	
			يَتَرَاسَلُ	
			يَخْضَرُّ	
			يَنْكَسِرُ	

❖

Drill 4: Translate into Arabic.

1. Teaching the Arabic language is an interesting job.
2. Life in Egypt is full of excitement.
3. There is a lot of cooperation between the American University in Cairo and the American University of Beirut.
4. President Gamal Abd Al-Nasser called for unity and independence.
5. The meeting between the President and students was useful.
6. Moving from one country to another is difficult.
7. Sameer's work is interesting.

8. Ahmad corresponded with Sameera last year.
Drill 5: Translate into English.

١ - دراسة اللغة العربية ممتعة جداً.

٢ - الاستماع إلى الموسيقى أفضل من الاستماع إلى المحاضرة.

٣ - إكرام الضَّيْف واجب.

٤ - أريد الحصول على عمل قبل التخرُّج من الجامعة.

٥ - طلبَ الأبُ من أبنائه الابتعاد عن المُخدِّرات.

٦ - أحِبُّ مساعدة أصدقائي.

٧ - صديقتي تُحِبُّ اِصْفِرارَ أوراق الأشجار في فصل الخريف.

٨ - والدي يُحِبُّ متابعة الأخبار السياسية كل يوم.

٩ - أريدُ الرَّحيل إلى البرازيل.

١٠ - طلبَ الرئيسُ من الحكومةِ العملَ على تَقَدُّم الاقتصاد.

❖

Drill 6: Use each of the following verbal nouns in a sentence.

٦ - الاسْتِسْلام		١ - الحُصُول على	
٧ - المُراسَلة		٢ - الاجْتماع	
٨ - العَمَل		٣ - الاسْتِقبال	
٩ - التَّرحيب		٤ - الإكْـرام	
١٠ - الانْتِقال		٥ - الاسْتعمار	

الفهم والاستيعاب: نجيب محفوظ

نجيب محفوظ

نجيب محفوظ هو كاتِبٌ مِصْريٌّ كبيرٌ بَلْ هو مِن أعْظَمِ الأدباءِ العربِ في العَصْرِ الحديثِ. وهو رائدُ فَنِّ الروايةِ العربيةِ الحديثةِ. وُلِدَ نجيب محفوظ في القاهرةِ القديمةِ، ونشأ فيها. ودَرَسَ الفلسفة وحَصَلَ على الإجازةِ في الآدابِ من جامعةِ القاهرةِ، وبدأ يكتبُ الروايةِ في الأربعيناتِ من القرنِ الماضي. عَمِلَ في الحكومةِ، وكتبَ المقالاتِ الأسبوعيةِ في جريدةِ "الأهرام" المِصريَّة، كَمَا عَمِلَ مُسْتَشاراً لوَزيرِ الثقافةِ.

كتبَ نجيب محفوظ عَنْ مَشاكِلِ النّاسِ الاجتماعيةِ والسِّيَاسِيَّةِ، وَعَنْ مِصْرَ والقاهرةِ وعنِ الأحياءِ الفقيرةِ. كان يَكْتُبُ ببساطةٍ ووُضُوحٍ، ورواياتُهُ مُتَرْجَمَةٌ إلى خَمْسٍ وعِشرينَ لغةً، مِن رواياتِهِ المترجمةِ إلى الإنكليزيةِ "خان الخليلي" و"زقاقُ المِدَقِ" و"اللصُّ والكلاب".

حصل نجيب محفوظ على جائزةِ نوبلِ للآدابِ في عام 1988، بَعْدَ رحْلَةٍ طويلةٍ وغنيةٍ مع الفَنِّ والأدبِ، وهو أوَّلُ كاتبٍ عربيٍّ يَحْصُلُ على جائزةِ نوبل.

🎧

كلمات وتعابير

pioneer, leader	رائِدٌ	modern times	العَصرُ الحَديث
Bachelor of Arts degree	الإجازة	the Arabic novel	الرِّواية العربيَّة
poor	فقيرٌ ـ فقيرة	the weekly articles	المَقالاتُ الأسبوعية
he obtained	حَصَلَ على	clarity	وُضوحٌ
The Thief and the Dogs	اللصُّ والكِلابُ	problems	مَشاكِلُ
Nobel Prize	جائزة نوبل	*Midaq Alley*	زقاقُ المدق

❖

🎧

المحادثة
Introductions - التعارف

Repeat the following question out loud:

Who is with you (m.s.)?	مَنْ مَعَكَ؟
Who is with you (f.s.)?	مَنْ مَعَكِ؟

Now repeat the following answer out loud:

I would like to introduce you (m.s.) to my friend	أريدُ أنْ أعَرِّفَكَ على صديقي
I would like to introduce you (f.s.) to my friend	أريدُ أنْ أعَرِّفَكِ على صديقي

Next, repeat the sentence and substitute the following words for صديقي:

my father	والِدي
my mother	والِدَتي
my cousin	ابن عَمِّي
my husband	زَوْجِي
my neighbor	جَاري

Repeat the dialogue with a classmate.

৩৯৩

Homework - الواجب

1. Listen to the comprehension text. Understand as much as you can.

2. Look up the words you do not know in the dictionary.

3. Translate one paragraph. Turn in the translation to your teacher.

4. Write a composition on Naguib Mahfouz.

Praise be to God — الحمد لله

من الثقافة العربية
أم كلثـــوم

Figure 12.3 - Umm Kulthum
(1904-1975)

The Star of the East - كَوْكَبُ الشرق

A legendary classical Egyptian singer, Umm Kulthum is one of the most distinguished Arab singers of the 20th century and a powerful symbol of pride for Egypt. As a child, she was a Qur'anic reciter, which led her to discover singing. Many of her songs were classical poems put to music. Her beautiful voice and the intense emotion with which she sang endeared her to the people. Umm Kulthum's popularity has continued decades after her death, as her songs often outsell many contemporary Arab vocalists. It is common to hear her songs on television and radio stations, and her video and audio recordings continue to be played all over the Arab world. Her funeral in 1975 was as elaborate and well attended as the funeral of President Nasser five years earlier, and millions of people poured into the streets of Cairo for her funeral.

Amongst her famous songs is *Al-Atlal* "The Ruins." Enjoy the singer's voice. Identify three words you know and write them in complete sentences. Look up three words you do not know, write down their roots and forms, and give a verbal noun for each. Identify three imperative verbs in the poem. Write a composition about Umm Kulthum or memorize two verses.

271

The Ruins - الأطلال

شعر: إبراهيم ناجي

كـانَ صَرْحاً من خيالٍ فهوى	يا فـؤادي لا تسَلْ أينَ الـهَوى
وارو عني طالما الدمعُ روى	إسْقِني واشرب على أطلاله
وحديثاً من أحاديث الـجَوى	كيف ذاك الحب أمسى خبراً
بـفم عذب المناداة رقيق	لست أنساك وقد أغريتني
من خلال الموج مدّت لغريق	ويدٍ تمتد نحوي كـيدٍ
أين في عينيك ذيّاك البريق	وبريق يـظمأ الساري له
طائر الـشـوق أغني ألمي	يا حبيباً زرت يوماً أيكه
وتجني الـقـادر الـمحتكم	لـك إبطـاء المذلّ الـمنعم
والـثواني جمرات في دمي	وحنيني لك يكـوي أضـلعي
إنني أعطيت ما استبقيت شيئا	أعطني حريتي أطلق يـديّ
لـمَ أبقيهِ وما أبقى عليَّا	آه من قـيـدك أدمى معصمي
وإلام الأسـر والـدنيا لديّا	ما احتفاظي بعهود لم تصنها

272

الدَّرس الثَّالث عشر

تونسُ الخضراءُ

Lesson Thirteen

Tunisia the Green

Figure 13.1 - Fishing boats on the Tunisian coast

Lesson Thirteen Contents

🎧 Vocabulary - المفردات

🎧 Words and Expressions - كلمات وتعابير

💿 Basic Text - النص الأساسي

  ❖ Life in Tunis - الحياة في تونس

Grammar - القواعد

  1. *Inna* and Its Sisters - إنَّ وأخَـواتـها
  2. The Difference Between إنَّ and أنَّ
  3. The Difference Between أنَّ and أنْ
  4. The Difference Between لكنَّ and لكنْ

💿 Comprehension Text - الفهم والاستيعاب

  ❖ Trip in the Desert - رحْلة في الصـحـراء

🎧 Let's Speak Arabic - المحادثة

  ❖ Profession - المِـهْنة

💿 Window into Arab Culture - من الثقافة العربية

  ❖ Modern Arabic Poetry - الشـعر العربي الحديث

المفردات

to go	ذهَبَ، يَذهبُ، ذهابٌ
to visit	زارَ، يَزورُ، زِيَارة
coast, seashore	ساحِل ج. سَواحِلُ
capital city	عاصِمَة ج. عَواصِمُ
blue	أزرقُ - زرقاءُ
to live	عاشَ، يَعيشُ، عَيْشٌ
to be located, to fall, to lie on	وَقعَ، يَقعُ، وُقوعٌ
heart, middle, center	قَلْبٌ ج. قُلوبٌ
tourist, traveler	سائِح ج. سُيّاحٌ - سُوّاحٌ
residence, home, house	مَنْـزلٌ ج. مَنازلُ
olive	زَيْـتـونٌ
lemon	لَـيْـمـونٌ
orange	بُـرتُقالٌ
million	مِلْـيُون ج. ملايينُ
trees	شَـجَـرٌ، أشْجارٌ
hotel	فُنْدُقٌ ج. فَنَادِقُ
sky, heaven	سماءٌ ج. سَمَاوَاتٌ، سَمَوَاتٌ
to extend, reach, stretch (VIII)	اِمْتَـدَّ، يَمْتَـدُّ، اِمْتِـدَادٌ
to connect, to be connected (VIII)	اِتَّـصلَ، يَتَّصِلُ، اِتِّصَالٌ
horizon, range of vision	أفُـقٌ ج. آفَـاقٌ

🎧

كلمات وتعابير

full of life and movement	مَلِيئة بِالحَياةِ والحَرَكة
The Tunisia Republic	الجُمْهوريَّة التُّونِسِيَّة
The Mediterranean Sea	البَحْرُ الأبْيَضُ المُتوَسِّطُ
it resembles the color of the sea	تُشْبِـهُ لَوْنَ البَحْر
without an end, to infinity	لا نِهاَيَةَ لَهُ
combines the past with the present	تَجْمَعُ بَيْنَ المَاضي والحَاضِر
heritage (tradition) and modernity	التُّرَاثُ والحَدَاثَة
her people are educated and open	أهْلُهَا مُثَـقَّـفُونَ ومُنْـفَـتِحُونَ
land of paradise	أرْضٌ مِنَ الجَنَّة
colors and lights	الأضواءُ والألـوانُ

Figure 13.2 - Sidi Bou Said, Tunisia

276

النص الأساسي: الحياة في تونس

Figure 13.3 - Traditional Tunisian door

إنَّ تونسَ مَدِينة مليئة بالحَياةِ والحَرَكَةِ، وهي عَاصِمَة الجُمْهوريةِ التونسيةِ. تقعُ في قلبِ البَحْر الأبيض المُتوسِّطِ، ويَذهَبُ السُيّاحُ إليها مِنْ كُلِّ مَكانٍ لِزِيَارتِهَا.

إنَّها مَليئة بالأضْواءِ والألْوان. سَواحِلُهَا زرْقاءُ، ومَنازلُهَا زرقاءُ وسَمَاؤُهَا زرقاءُ. إنَّ المدينة تُشْبهُ لَوْنَ البَحْر، وكَأنَّ الأفُقَ فيها لا نِهَايَة لَهُ، فَهْوَ يَمْتَدُّ ويَمْتَدُّ كَأنَّهُ يَتَّصِلُ بالسَّمَاءِ.

إنَّ تونسَ خضراءُ فِعْلاً. إنَّها مَلِيئة بأشجارِ الزيتون والليْمون والبُرتقال، فيها ملايينُ الأشجار الخضراء الرائعةِ التي تُعْطي المدينة جَمَالاً وسِحْراً.

إنَّ تونسَ تجْمَعُ بَيْنَ الماضي العَريق والحاضِر الحديثِ. تجمعُ بين التُراثِ والحداثةِ. إنَّ فنادقَ المدينةِ حديثة راقية، وأسواقها القديمة تقليدية وضيقة. إنَّها مليئة بالناس والزَّائِرين، وفيها المقاهي والمطاعمُ والمساجدُ وجَامِعُ الزيتونةِ العظيم.

إنَّ مهرجانات تونس الثقافية والفنية معروفة في العالم، والحياة فيها جميلة غنية. أهلُهَا مُثقفونَ ومُنفتحونَ. إنَّ تونسَ مدينة ساحِرة. إنَّكَ تشعُرُ فيها وكأنَّكَ تعيشُ في أرض مِنَ الجَنَّة.

❖

القواعد

1. *Inna* and Its Sisters - إنَّ وأخـواتـها

Inna and its sisters (إنَّ وَأَخَوَاتُهَا) are a group of particles used in the nominal sentence. They cause the subject to change from the nominative case to the accusative case. However, the predicate remains in the nominative case. For example, in the nominal sentence البيتُ جميلٌ 'The house is beautiful,' once إنَّ is introduced the subject changes from the nominative case to accusative case إنَّ البيتَ جميلٌ 'Indeed the house is beautiful.'

The sisters of إنَّ are all used in nominal sentences and all have the same grammatical function in that they change the subject from nominative to accusative. However, they have different meanings. Following are إنَّ وأخواتها and their meanings:

Meaning	Sentence	Meaning	Particle
Indeed the house is beautiful	إنَّ البَيْتَ جَمِيلٌ	indeed, that	إنَّ
I know that the house is beautiful	أعْرفُ أنَّ البيتَ جَمِيلٌ	that	أنَّ
As if the man is dead	كأنَّ الرَّجُلَ مَيِّتٌ	as if	كأنَّ
I left because the man is difficult	غادَرْتُ لأنَّ الرَّجُلَ صَعْبٌ	because	(لأنَّ)
But the test is easy	لكنَّ الامتِحَانَ سَهْلٌ	but	لكنَّ
I wish she were here	لَيْتَها هنا	would that	لَـيْتَ
Perhaps he heard the news	لَعَلَّـهُ سَمِعَ الخَبَرَ	perhaps	لَعَلَّ

As you see in the chart, the predicate of إنَّ وأخواتها could be a verb or any other word or phrase. The subject could be a suffixed pronoun.

❖

2. The Difference Between إِنَّ and أَنَّ

Both particles إِنَّ and أَنَّ correspond to the English conjunction 'that.' The difference is إِنَّ is used at the beginning of the sentence, and after the verb قَالَ 'to say' or any of its forms, such as يَقُولُ، قَائِل، قِيلَ. The particle أَنَّ is used anywhere else. Examples:

Meaning	Sentence	Particle
Indeed the girl is pretty	إِنَّ البنتَ جميلةٌ	إِنَّ
He said that the girl is pretty	قال إِنَّ البنتَ جميلةٌ	إِنَّ
I know that the girl is pretty	أعرف أَنَّ البنتَ جميلةٌ	أَنَّ

❖

3. The Difference Between أَنَّ and أَنْ

أَنَّ is a particle that introduces a nominal sentence; it is one of the sisters of إِنَّ. It is followed by a noun or a suffixed pronoun. But أَنْ is not one of the sisters of إِنَّ; it is followed by a verb. The particle أَنْ causes the verb, if it is in the present tense, to be in the subjunctive case. Example:

Meaning	Sentence	Particle
I heard that the book was difficult	سَمِعْتُ أَنَّ الكتابَ صعبٌ	أَنَّ
I heard it was difficult	سَمِعْتُ أَنَّـهُ صعبٌ	أَنَّ
I want to go to Tunis	أريدُ أَنْ أذهَبَ إلى تونس	أَنْ

❖

4. The Difference Between لكِنَّ and لكِنْ

There are two similar articles that both mean 'but.' One of these particles ends in شدّة 'shadda' and the other ends in سُكُون 'sukuun.' The particle لكِنَّ is the sister of إِنَّ. Therefore, it must be followed by a noun or a suffixed pronoun. The noun or suffixed pronoun after it serves as its subject.

The particle لكنْ is <u>not</u> a sister of إنَّ ; it is never followed by a pronoun suffix. It could be followed by a verb, a noun, or any other word. It has no effect on the word or the sentence following it. If it is followed by a noun, the noun must be in the nominative case. Example:

Meaning	Sentence	Particle
The house is big but the kitchen is small	البيتُ كبيرٌ لكنَّ المطبخَ صغيرٌ	لكنَّ
The kitchen is small but beautiful	المطبخُ صغيرٌ لكنَّهُ جميلٌ	لكنَّ
We study Arabic literature but in English	ندرسُ الأدبَ العربي لكنْ بالإنكليزيـة	لكنْ

❖

Inna and its sisters (إنَّ وأخواتها) can also be followed by a suffixed pronoun instead of a noun. Below is an example showing إنَّ followed by suffixed pronouns.

نَحْنُ	أنا	أنْتُنَّ	أنْتُم	أنْتُمَا	أنتِ	أنتَ	هُنَّ	هُمْ	هُمَا	هِيَ	هُوَ
إنَّـا	إنِّي	إنَّكُنَّ	إنَّكُمْ	إنَّكُمَا	إنَّكِ	إنَّكَ	إنَّهُنَّ	إنَّهُمْ	إنَّهُمَا	إنَّهَا	إنَّهُ

❖

Drill 1: Use either أنَّ or أنْ in the following sentences and vocalize the words in each sentence.

1 - أريدُ ـــــــــ أذهبَ إلى المطعم.

2 - أحبُّ ـــــــــ أشاهدَ الفيلمَ الجديد.

3 - ذكرتْ الأستاذة ـــــــــ المكتبة مفتوحة.

4 - قرأتُ ـــــــــ شركة الطيران مغلقة اليوم.

5 - سافرتْ صديقتي بعد ـــــــــ أخذتْ الامتحان.

6 - سنذهبُ إلى الصحراء قبل ـــــــــ نغادر تونس.

7 - علمتُ ـــــــــ الموعد فاتَ.

8 - أشعرُ بـ ـــــــــ المشكلة كبيرة.

Drill 2: Use either إنَّ or أنَّ in the following sentences. Vocalize the words.

1 - قال ــــــــ العمل في المصنع متعبٌ.
2 - ــــــــ الله يُحِبُّ البسطاء من الناس.
3 - أعرفُ ــــــــ اللغة العربية جميلة.
4 - انتقلَ إلى جامعة كاليفورنيا لـ ــــــــ أخته تسكن هناك.
5 - قرأتُ ــــــــ تونس من أجمل البلاد.
6 - قالوا ــــــــ الأستاذ سافر إلى عَمَّان.
7 - ــــــــ العمل في مصر ممتع جداً.
8 - درس اللغة العربية لـ ــــــــ زوجته عربية.

❖

Drill 3: Fill the blank with either لكنَّ or لكنْ and vocalize the words.

1 - البيتُ كبيرٌ ــــــــ المطبخ صغير.
2 - البيتُ كبيرٌ ــــــــ مطبخـه صغير.
3 - لا تدرسْ الدرسَ الأول ــــــــ السابع.
4 - خالدٌ رجلٌ غنيٌّ ــــــــ سمير بخيل.
5 - ــــــــ الكاتب مشهور.
6 - الجامعة مشهورة ــــــــ صغيرة.
7 - أحبُّ القهوة ــــــــ بدون سكَّر.
8 - المحاضِرُ ممتعٌ ــــــــ خجول.

❖

Drill 4: Compose a sentence for each sister of إنَّ.

1- كأنَّ
2- لكنَّ
3- لَيْتَ
4- لعَلَّ
5- لأنَّ

❖

281

Drill 5: Translate into English.

١ - غادر المدينة لأنَّهُ لا يُحِبُّ العملَ فيها.
٢ - الأزهر جامع ولكنَّه جامعة كذلك.
٣ - كأنَّهَا ستمطر اليوم.
٤ - إنَّ الحياة في تونس تختلفُ عن الحياة في المغرب.
٥ - لَيْتَ أصدقائي معي.
٦ - لَعلَّهَا تحْضُرُ غداً.

❖

Drill 6: Translate into Arabic.

1. I read that tourism in Tunis is very interesting.
2. He told me that he loves me.
3. Lily speaks Arabic well, but her brother does not.
4. I went there because he told me to go.
5. Perhaps she would arrive on time.
6. I wish she were here.

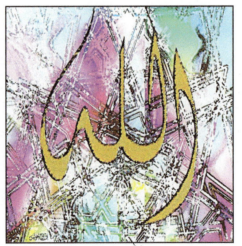

God - الله

الفهم والاستيعاب: رِحْلة في الصحراء

Figure 13.4 - The Sahara Desert, Tunisia

لا يُمْكِنُ أنْ تزورَ تونسَ دونَ أنْ تزورَ الصحراء. إنَّ الصحراءَ التونسية مُتْعَة حقيقية، تَجِدُ فيها البُحيرات المالحة والمياه العذبة والواحات وأشـجارَ النخيل والكُثْبَانَ والرمـالَ الذهبية.

يذهبُ إليها السائحُ بالسيارةِ ليُشاهدَ هذه الأرضَ الساحرة. فالصحراءُ في تونسَ لَيْسَتْ مَجَرَّدَ صَحْرَاءَ، بَلْ هي تجربة غنية ومدهشة. إنَّ الرحلة إلى الصحراء، تُزيلُ الهُمُومَ، وتبعثُ الحياة في الأرواح.

بدأتْ رِحْلتُنا إلى الجنوبِ التونسي مع الفَجْرِ وخِلالَ الرِّحْلةِ بدأت الصَّحْراءُ تتبدَّلُ. في البدايةِ، كانت الأرضُ خضراء، وسُفوحُ الجبال خضراء، والحُقولُ خضراء، ولكنْ بَعْدَ ساعةٍ من الزَّمَن، تلاشت الخُضْرة مِن الأرض لكنَّ أشجارَ الزيتون ما زالتْ خضراءَ. حين وصلنا إلى وسطِ الصحراءِ، شاهَدْنا كُثْبانَ الرِّمَال وواحاتِ النخيل، والجِمَالَ التي تمشي في الصحراء التي لا يَسْكُنُهَا أحَـدٌ.

بدأنا رحلة العودة. لقد انتهتْ الرحلة بعد أن غسِّلت الصحراءُ أرواحَنا وأعطتنا ساعاتٍ من الهدوء والسلام. في صحراء تونسَ تمَّ تصويرُ الكثير من الأفلام العالمية، منها "حرب النجوم" و"المريض الإنجليزي."

🎧

كلمات وتعابير

دُونَ	without
بُحَيْرات	lakes
أشجارُ النخيل	palm trees
كُثْبان	dunes
مُجَرد	mere, only
تجربة	experience
هُموم	anxieties, worries
أرواح	souls
بدأت الصحراءُ تتبدَّلُ	the desert began to change
حُقول	fields
عَوْدَة	return
المَريض الإنجليزي	*The English Patient*
مُتعة	joy
مَالحة	salty
واحَات	oases
رمَال	sand
بَل	rather, but
غنيَّة	rich
أعْطتنا	it gave us
فَجْر	dawn
سُفوحُ الجبال	the foothills
جِمَالٌ	camels
غَسَلتْ	it (f.s.) washed
حَرْبُ النجوم	*Star Wars*

284

🎧

المحادثة
المِـهْـنة - Profession

Repeat the following question out loud:

What do you want to be after you graduate (m.s.)?	ماذا تريدُ أنْ تصبحَ بعد أن تتخرَّج؟
What do you want to be after you graduate (f.s.)?	ماذا تريدينَ أنْ تصبحي بعد أن تتخرَّجي؟

Now, repeat aloud the following answer:

I want to become a doctor	أريد أنْ أصبحَ طبيباً

Next, repeat the sentence and substitute the following words for طبيباً.
The direct object must be in the accusative case.

teacher	أسـتاذ
lawyer	مُحامي (مُحامٍ)
engineer	مُـهَنـدِس
translator	مُـتـرجِم
ambassador	سَـفـير

Repeat the dialogue with a classmate.

୬ص୬

Homework - الواجب

1. Read and listen to the comprehension text. Identify (أنَّ) or any of its sisters. Look up the words you do not understand in the dictionary. Translate the text and write a composition about a desert trip you have taken or a geographic region of Tunisia.

2. Enjoy Nizar Qabbani's famous poem about Tunisia. Identify five words you know and put them into sentences. Look up five words you do not know, write down their roots, their forms, and their verbal nouns. Write a composition about the poem and memorize a few verses.

من الثقافة العربية
الشِّعر العربي الحديث

نزار قباني

أنا يا صديقةُ مُتْعَبٌ بعُروبتي

وعلى جبيني وردة وكتابُ	يا تونسُ الخضراءُ جئتك عـاشِقًا
فاخْضَوْضَرَتْ لِغنائِهِ الأعشابُ	إني الدِّمشقيُّ الذي احترفَ الـهوى
إنَّ الهوى أن لا يكونَ إيابُ	أحرقتُ من خلفي جميعَ مراكبي
والـمفرداتُ حِجارة وترابُ	مـاذا أقولُ؟ فمي يفتش عـن فمي
قمعٌ وحين مساؤنا إرهابُ	مِنْ أين يأتي الشِعْرُ؟ حين نهارنـا
فبأيِّ شَيءٍ يَكتبُ الكُتّابُ	سرقوا أصابعَنا وعِطْرَ حُروفِنا
وحدائقُ الشعر الجميل خَرَابُ	مِنْ أيـْنَ أدخلُ في القصيدة يا ترى؟
يُثري بِهِ الأميُّ والـنصّابُ	يا تونسُ الخضراءُ هذا عَالَـمٌ
ترتاحُ فوقَ رمـالِهِ الأعْصابُ	هل في العيون التـونسية شـاطِئٌ
فَهَل العُروبة لَعْنة وعِقابُ؟	أنـا يا صديقـةُ مُتْعَبٌ بعُروبتي
لـم يبقَ مِنْ كُتبِ السماءِ كتابُ	يا تونسُ الخضراءُ كيفَ خلاصُنا؟
أم أن حُبِّي الـتونسيَّ سَرابُ؟	هل لي بعَرْض البَحْر نِصْفُ جزيرة؟

* نزار قباني، الأعمال السياسية الكاملة، منشورات نزار قباني، 2000، بيروت.

الدَّرس الرَّابع عشر

جُبْـران خَليـل جُبْـران

Lesson Fourteen

Jubran Khalil Jubran

Figure 14.1 – Ancient ruins in Lebanon

النص الأساسي: كاتِبٌ مِنْ لبنان

Figure 14.2 - Jubran Khalil Jubran

كاتِبٌ مِنْ لبنان

جُبْران خليل جبران شاعِرٌ لُبْنانِيٌّ أمْريكِيٌّ، ورائِدُ الشِعْر العربيِّ الحَديثِ. وُلِدَ جُبْران في لُبْنانَ في عام 1883 م، ثمَّ حضَرَ إلى الولاياتِ المتحدةِ الأمْريكيةِ، وسَكَنَ في مَدينتَيْ بوسطن ونيويورك. وفي أمريكا الْتَقَى جُبْران مَعَ كاتِبٍ لبنانِيٍّ آخَرَ اسْمُهُ ميخائيل نعيمة. وسَاهَمَ هذان الكاتِبان اللُّبْنانِيَّان الكبيران في تأسيس حَرَكَةِ الحَداثةِ الأدبيَّةِ العربيَّةِ. وأسَّسا مَعَاً جَمْعِيَّة أدبيَّة وجَريدَة عَربيَّة في نيويورك، وشارَكَهُما في جَمْعِيَّتِهِمَا أدباءُ وشعراءُ وكتَّابٌ مِنَ الأمْريكِيَّتَيْن، الشَّماليَّةِ والجَنوبيَّةِ.

ألَّفَ جُبْران كتباً كثيرة، وكتبَ الشِعْرَ والرِّوايَة والقِصَّة القصيرة. وكانَ فَيْلَسُوفاً ورَسَّامَاً وأديباً في آن مَعَاً. مِنْ أشْهَر كُتُبِهِ كِتابُ (النَّبِيُّ) الذي كَتَبَهُ باللُّغةِ الإنكليزيةِ. كَمَا أنَّ رُسُومَهُ مَوْجُودَةٌ في عَدَدٍ مِنْ مَتاحِفِ العالَمِ.

تُوُفِّيَ جُبْران في نيويورك في عام 1931 م. وهُناكَ حَديقة باسْمِهِ في العاصمةِ الأمْريكية واشنطن، وفيها تِمْثالٌ لَهُ. والحَديقة قريبة مِنْ مَسْكَنِ نائِبِ الرَّئيس الأمْريكي، وتَقَعُ في المِنْطَقة الدِّبْلوماسِيَّةِ في شارع ماسَتشوسِتس.

<h1 style="text-align:center;color:purple;">القواعد</h1>

There are three categories of nouns in the Arabic language. The singular (المُفْرَد) refers to one, the dual (المُثَنَّى) refers to two, and the plural (الجَمْع) refers to three or more.

1. The Dual - المثنى

The dual (المُثنى) is formed by adding the suffix ان to the singular in the nominative case, and the suffix يْن to the singular in the accusative and genitive cases. Examples:

Dual Gen.	Dual Acc.	Dual Nom.	Meaning	Singular masc.
مُدَرِّسَيْنِ	مُدَرِّسَيْنِ	مُدَرِّسَانِ	a teacher	مُدَرِّسٌ
المُدَرِّسَيْنِ	المُدَرِّسَيْنِ	المُدَرِّسَانِ	the teacher	المُدَرِّسُ

If the noun is a singular feminine ending in تاء مربوطة, the تاء changes to تاء مفتوحة. Example:

Dual Gen.	Dual Acc.	Dual Nom.	Meaning	Singular fem.
مَدْرَسَتَيْنِ	مَدْرَسَتَيْنِ	مَدْرَسَتَانِ	a school	مَدْرَسَة
المَدْرَسَتَيْنِ	المَدْرَسَتَيْنِ	المَدْرَسَتَانِ	the school	المَدْرَسَة

If the dual is the first term of an *idafa*, or if it is attached to a suffixed pronoun, then the final ن is dropped:

The two teachers of the school came	حَضَرَ مُدَرِّسَا المَدْرَسَةِ
His two teachers came	حَضَرَ مُدَرِّسَاهُ
I saw the two teachers of the school	شاهَدْتُ مُدَرِّسَي المَدْرَسَةِ
I saw his two teachers	شاهَدْتُ مُدَرِّسَيْهِ

❖

2. Masculine Sound Plural - جمع المذكر السالم

The masculine sound plural refers to three or more. This type of plural is confined to nouns and adjectives indicating professions or habitual actions. They are called sound plurals because the words do not change internally in order to form the plural. We simply add a suffix to the singular word.

The masculine sound plural is formed by adding the suffix ـُونَ in the nominative case and the suffix ـِينَ in both the accusative and genitive cases. Examples:

Plural Gen.	Plural Acc.	Plural Nom.	Meaning	Sing. masc.
مُدَرِّسِينَ	مُدَرِّسِينَ	مُدَرِّسُونَ	teacher	مُدَرِّسٌ
المُدَرِّسِينَ	المُدَرِّسِينَ	المُدَرِّسُونَ	the teacher	المُدَرِّسُ
خَبَّازِينَ	خَبَّازِينَ	خَبَّازُونَ	baker	خَبَّازٌ
الخَبَّازِينَ	الخَبَّازِينَ	الخَبَّازُونَ	the baker	الخَبَّازُ

As in the dual, when the masculine sound plural comes as the first term of an *idafa*, or if it is attached to a suffixed pronoun, the final ن is dropped. Example:

The teachers of the school came	حَضَرَ مُدَرِّسُو المَدْرَسَةِ
His teachers came	حَضَرَ مُدَرِّسُوهُ
I saw the teachers of the school	شاهَدْتُ مُدَرِّسِي المَدْرَسَةِ
I saw his teachers	شاهَدْتُ مُدَرِّسِيهِ

❖

3. Feminine Sound Plural - جمع المؤنث السالم

Feminine sound plurals are not solely confined to female human beings. They apply to many other nouns. Also, the singular feminine does not need to end in ة 'taa` marbouta' to qualify as a feminine plural. There are many masculine words that also take the feminine plural ending. You will need to memorize which masculine words take the feminine singular ending by consulting the dictionary when introduced to new or unfamiliar vocabulary.

In general, there are two groups of the feminine sound plural. One group refers to female human beings and the second refers to nonhuman things. The feminine sound plural is formed by adding the suffix اتٌ to the singular for the nominative case and the suffix اتِ for the genitive and accusative cases.

A. Human Feminine Plurals:

Fem. Sound Plural Gen.	Fem. Sound Plural Acc.	Fem. Sound Plural Nom.	Meaning	Singular fem.
مُدَرِّسَاتِ	مُدَرِّسَاتِ	مُدَرِّسَاتٌ	teacher	مُدَرِّسَة
المُدَرِّسَاتِ	المُدَرِّسَاتِ	المُدَرِّسَاتُ	the teacher	المُدَرِّسَة
أمريكيَّاتِ	أمريكيَّاتِ	أمريكيَّاتٌ	American	أمريكيَّـة
جَميـلاتِ	جَميـلاتِ	جَميـلاتٌ	beautiful	جَميلـة

B. Nonhuman Feminine Plurals:

Fem. Sound Plural Gen.	Fem. Sound Plural Acc.	Fem. Sound Plural Nom	Meaning	Singular fem. and masc.
طاولاتِ	طاولاتِ	طاولاتٌ	table (f.)	طاولـة
مطاراتِ	مطاراتِ	مطاراتٌ	airport (m.)	مَطارٌ
ولايـاتِ	ولايـاتِ	ولايـاتٌ	state (f.)	ولايـة
مؤتمـراتِ	مؤتمـراتِ	مؤتمـراتٌ	conference (m.)	مُؤتمـر

❖

Drill 1: Use the dual form in the following sentences.

١ - علي ومحمد هما ـــــــــ ويعملان في شركة سياحية. (صديق)

٢ - ماجدة وهند هما طالبتان ـــــــــ. (خليجي)

٣ - أبو ظبي وبيروت ـــــــــ جميلتان. (مدينة)

٤ - مليسا وكاثي طالبتان ـــــــــ. (جديد)

٥ - الجامعتان الجديدتان في المدينة ـــــــــ. (صغير)

٦ - حضرتُ ـــــــــ عندما كنتُ في الشرق الأوسط. (مؤتمر)

٧ -   شاهدتُ ـــــــــ الفرنسيَّيْنِ في المطعم. (رجل)

٨ -   بحثتُ في المكتبة عن ـــــــــ عن تاريخ المغرب. (كتاب)

❖

Drill 2: Write the duals and plurals in the nominative, genitive, and accusative cases and give the meaning of the singular.

F. Sound. Pl. Acc. Gen.	F. Sound. Pl. Nom.	M. Sound. Pl. Acc. Gen.	M. Sound Pl. Nom.	Dual Acc. Gen.	Dual Nom.	Meaning	Singular
							إيطالي
			أمريكيُّــونَ				
		ذاهبــينَ					
							مُدَرِّسٌ
آنســاتٍ							
							أجنبيَّــة
	صديقــاتٌ						

❖

Drill 3: Use the dual or plural forms in the following sentences.

Example - أنا آسِــف ــ نحن آسِــفون

١ -   هو خليجيّ . هم: ـــــــ.

٢ -   الطالب مصري . الطالبتان ـــــــ.

٣ -   نحن عربٌ . هنَّ ـــــــ.

٤ -   علي شاعر من السودان. أحمد ومريم هما ـــــــ من مصر.

٥ -   كاثي طالبة امريكية . أنتنَّ ـــــــ ـــــــ ـــــــ.

٦ -   أنتَ مُدَرِّس مشهور. هما ـــــــ ـــــــ ـــــــ.

٧ -   هي طالبة أمريكية . هم ـــــــ ـــــــ ـــــــ.

❖

Drill 4: Translate into English.

1 - درستُ العربية مع الطالبين الجديدين اللذين وصلا أمس.

2 - شاهدتُ الأستاذيْن الأمريكِيَّيْنِ في الجامعة.

3 - الطالباتُ الأردنياتُ يَبْحثْنَ عن عمل في مكتب العميد.

4 - حَضَرَ والدا الأستاذِ إلى الصَّفِ.

5 - قرأتُ كتابَيْ الكاتبِ الإسباني المشهور.

6 - نحن ذاهبونَ إلى الشرق الأوسطِ اليوم.

❖

Drill 5: Translate into Arabic.

1. Our teachers went to several conferences last year.
2. The two new visitors are Egyptians.
3. The classrooms of the college are small.
4. The two American writers met with Arab writers.
5. The university's professors and students left for the holidays.
6. I saw his two teachers and his three friends.

القواعد

1. Broken Plurals - جمع التكسير

Broken plurals are not formed by adding regular endings to the singular as in the case of sound plurals. Rather, they are formed by internal changes within the word itself. The syllabic structure in the word changes by altering the long and short vowels of the singular or by adding prefixes or suffixes. The broken plural patterns are different from their singulars.

Broken plurals fall into many patterns, some with variations and exceptions within the same pattern. The most practical way to learn the plural forms for any new vocabulary term is to look up the word and its plurals in the dictionary as soon as you are introduced to the new vocabulary. Many students have found that this is the best way to learn the plurals in Arabic.

Arabic has some thirty patterns for the broken plural. The following are the most common patterns.

I. أَفْعَالٌ

Plural	Meaning	Singular
أَسْـواقٌ	market	سُـوقٌ
أَوْلادٌ	boy	وَلَـدٌ
أَمْطارٌ	rain	مَطَـرٌ
أَوْقـاتٌ	time	وَقْـتٌ
أَعْمـالٌ	job	عَمَلٌ

II. فُـعُـولٌ

Plural	Meaning	Singular
بُيُوتٌ	house	بَيْتٌ
قُـلُـوبٌ	heart	قَلْـبٌ
صُفُـوفٌ	class	صَفٌّ
دُرُوسٌ	lesson	دَرْسٌ
حُرُوفٌ	letter	حَرْفٌ

III. فِعَالٌ

Plural	Meaning	Singular
بِحَارٌ	sea	بَحْرٌ
رِجَالٌ	man	رَجُلٌ
جِبَالٌ	mountain	جَبَلٌ
طِوَالٌ	tall	طَويلٌ
كِبَارٌ	big	كَبيرٌ

IV. فُعُلٌ

Plural	Meaning	Singular
كُتُبٌ	book	كِتَابٌ
مُدُنٌ	city	مَدينة
جُدُدٌ	new	جَديدٌ
رُسُلٌ	messenger	رَسُولٌ
طُرُقٌ	road	طَريقٌ

V. أفْعُلٌ

Plural	Meaning	Singular
أنْهُرٌ	river	نَهْرٌ
أعْيُنٌ	eye	عَيْنٌ
أشْهُرٌ	month	شَهْرٌ
أرْجُلٌ	foot	رِجْلٌ
أسْهُمٌ	share of stock	سَهْمٌ

VI. فُعَلاءُ *

Plural	Meaning	Singular
سُفَرَاءُ	ambassador	سَفيرٌ
أمَرَاءُ	prince	أميرٌ
خُلَفَاءُ	caliph	خَليفة
رُؤَسَاءُ	president	رَئيسٌ
قُدَمَاءُ	old, ancient	قَديمٌ

VII. أَفْعِلاءُ *

Plural	Meaning	Singular
أَصْدِقَاءُ	friend	صَدِيقٌ
أَغْنِيَاءُ	rich	غَنِيٌّ
أَقْرِبَاءُ	relative	قَرِيبٌ
أَقْوِيَاءُ	strong	قَوِيٌّ
أَوْفِيَاءُ	faithful	وَفِيٌّ

VIII. مَفَاعِلُ *

Plural	Meaning	Singular
مَكَاتِبُ	office	مَكْتَبٌ
مَسَارِحُ	theater	مَسْرَحٌ
مَصَانِعُ	factory	مَصْنَعٌ
مَطَاعِمُ	restaurant	مَطْعَمٌ
مَرَاكِبُ	boat	مَرْكَبٌ

IX. فَعَالِيلُ *

Plural	Meaning	Singular
شَبَابِيكُ	window	شُبَّاكٌ
صَنَادِيقُ	box	صُنْدوقٌ
عَصَافِيرُ	sparrow	عُصْفورٌ
قَنَادِيلُ	lamp	قِنديلٌ
عَنَاوينُ	title, address	عُنْوانٌ

X. فُعْلانٌ

Plural	Meaning	Singular
قُضْبَانٌ	rod, rail	قَضِيبٌ
بُلْدانٌ	country	بَلَدٌ
شُجْعَانٌ	brave	شُجَاعٌ
شُبَّانٌ	young man	شَابٌّ
فُرْسَانٌ	knight	فارسٌ

* Diptotes (see next page).

2. Diptotes in the Broken Plurals - الممنوع من الصرف

The plurals of the patterns VI, VII, VIII, and IX are called diptotes (ممنوع من الصرف أو ممنوع من التنوين) . This means that these words take one *damma* instead of double *damma* in the indefinite nominative case, and *fatha* instead of *kasra* in the indefinite genitive case. The *fatha* is used for the indefinite accusative case. You will also learn more about diptotes in the next chapter.

Nonhuman Plurals: If the plural is not a human being, then the adjective and the predicate that follow must both be singular feminine.

Adjective/ Predicate	Meaning	Sentence
جميلاتٌ	The girls are beautiful	البنـاتُ جميـلاتٌ
الجديدةُ\أجميلةٌ	The tables are beautiful	الطـاولاتُ الجديدةُ جميلةٌ
العربيةُ\رائعةٌ	The Arab cities are wonderful	المدنُ العربيـة رائعـةٌ
الكبيرةُ\ مشهورةٌ	The large universities are famous	الجامعاتُ الكبيـرةُ مشهورةٌ

❖

Drill 1: Put in the correct adjective or predicate for the following sentences.

١ - المراكـزُ الثقافية ـــــــ. (هام)

٢ - الأمسياتُ الشعرية ـــــــ. (جميل)

٣ - الكتَّابُ ـــــــ اجتمعوا أمس. (مشهور)

٤ - الكاتباتُ ـــــــ حضرنَ الاجتماع. (عربي)

٥ - الشعراءُ ـــــــ وصلوا إلى الجامعة. (مصري)

٦ - الأصدقاءُ الأمريكيُونَ رَحَّبُوا بـ ـــــــ العرب. (ضيف)

٧ - الأسماء ـــــــ ـــــــ. (ألماني) (صعب)

٨ - الآنسات ـــــــ ذهَبْنَ إلى ـــــــ (جميل) (مسرح)

❖

309

Drill 2: Give the plural of each of the following words, and write down their meanings.

Meaning	Plural	Singular
		دَرَجَة
		شَيْخ
		قاعِدَة
		اِسْمٌ
		مَعْرَكَة
		مَسْجِدٌ

❖

Drill 3: Give the singular of each of the following words, and write down their meanings.

Meaning	Singular	Plural
		دُرُوسٌ
		مُدُنٌ
		جَرائِدُ
		أنْهُرٌ
		غُرَباءُ
		خرائِطُ

God - الله

الفهم والاستيعاب: شجرة الحياة

Figure 15.5 - The Tree of Life - Bahrain

شجرة الحياة

هُناكَ سِــرٌّ في تلكَ الشجرةِ التي تَقِفُ في وسطِ الصحراء في جَنوبِ البحرين وحيدة،
منعزلة، حتى بدون أيِّ شجرةٍ أخرى أو أيِّ نَبْتَةٍ أخرى بجوارها. هذِهِ الشَّجَرَةَ اِسْمُها
"شجرة الحياة" وتعيشُ وحيدة بلا مَاء، ومكانُها في الصحراء يَبْعُدُ خمسة وثلاثينَ
كيلومتراً عن العاصمةِ، المَنامَةِ.

لا أَحَدَ يعرفُ كيفَ تعيشُ هذه الشجرة المعزولة، ولا أحَدَ يعرف لماذا ليس هُناكَ أشجارٌ
أخرى بجانبها، ولا أَحَدَ يعرفُ سِرَّهَا. يزورُهَا الناسُ ويتعجَّبون. وبدأ السُّيَّاحُ يزُورُونَهَا
ويحاولونَ أن يعرفوا سِرَّها. وأصبحتْ هَذِهِ الشجرة مركزاً سِياحِيَّاً في البحرين.

يقولُ العُلماءُ والمُخْتَصُّونَ إنَّ في الشجرةِ سِــرّاً. ولكنَّهُم يعتقدونَ أنَّها تَحْصُلُ على الماء
من عُرُوقِها التي تمتدُّ في أعماقِ الأرض عِدة كيلومتراتٍ وتمتصُّ الماءَ مِنْ مَسافاتٍ
بعيدةٍ. هَكَذا تعيشُ هذِهِ الشَّجرة مُنذ مِئاتِ السِّنين.

🎧

كلمات وتعابير

it stands	تَقِفُ	secret	سِـرٌّ
alone	وَحِيدة	isolated	مُنعَزلة
its (f.s.) neighborhood	جِوارها	plant, sprout	نَبتة
they wonder, marvel	يتعجَّبُونَ	next to it (f.s.)	بجانبها
specialists	مُختصُّونَ	tourists	سُيَّاحٌ
roots, veins	عِـرقٌ ج. عُرُوقٌ	they believe	يَعْتقدونَ
bottom, depths	أعْمَـاق	it stretches into	تمتدُّ في
distances	مَسَافات	several, many	عِدَّة

❖

Drill 4: Translate into English.

١ - المسـاجدُ في الشرق الأوسط جميلة.

٢ - عناوينُ الشـوارع في المدينةِ واضحة جداً.

٣ - العصـافيرُ في الحديقةِ زرقـاءُ.

٤ - متـاجِفُ القاهرةِ كبيـرة.

٥ - عُمَّالُ المصـانِع يعملون ساعات طويلة كل يوم.

٦ - المدينة مليئة بالمسـارح والمطـاعم.

❖

Drill 5: Translate into Arabic.

1. The ambassadors of the Arab countries arrived in New York.
2. The streets are full of lights in Paris.
3. The teachers of the high schools are excellent.
4. The newspapers are in Arabic.
5. His two friends are Tunisians.
6. The writers at the conference are Americans and Arabs.

🎧   المحادثة
Transportation - المواصلات

Repeat the following question out loud:

How did you (m.s.) arrive here?	كَـيْف وَصَـلْـتَ إلى هُنـا؟
How did you (f.s.) arrive here?	كَـيْف وَصَـلْـتِ إلى هُنـا؟

Now repeat the following answer out loud:

I arrived by bus	وَصَـلْتُ بالحافلة

Next, repeat the sentence and substitute the following words for بالحافلة:

car	بالسَّـيَّـارة
plane	بالطَّـائِـرة
train	بالقِـطَـار
bicycle	بالـدَّرَّاجَــة
taxi	بسيَّـارةِ أجرة (بالتاكسي)

Repeat the dialogue with a classmate.

ৎৰৎ

Homework - الواجب

1. Read and listen to the comprehension text. Understand as much as you can.

2. Identify the plurals. Write down their singulars, and look up their meanings.

3. Translate the text or write a composition about the Tree of Life.

من الثقافة العربية
بـيت القرآن في البحـرين

بيت القرآن

بيتُ القرآن في البحرين هو من أهَمِّ المراكِز الإسلاميةِ في الخليج العربي، ويَحْتَوي على أكْثر من ستينَ ألفِ مطبوعةٍ مُتَعَلِّقَةٍ بالقرآن الكريم وعُلومِهِ. وفيه أهَمُّ الكتبِ الإسلامية في العالم. يأتي إليْهِ الباحِثونَ والدَّارسونَ من كُلِّ بُلدان العالم للاطِّلاع على مخطوطاتِ القرآن الكريم النادرةِ. أسَّسَـهُ الدكتور عبد اللطيف كانو، وهو رجلُ أعْمَال بحريني مَعْروفٌ.

ويَضُمُّ بيتُ القرآن أوَّلَ نسخةٍ للقرآن الكريم كُـتِبَتْ في عَهْدِ الخليفةِ عثمان بن عفان. والنسخة مكتوبة على شَكْـل صَحَائِفَ من دون نقاطٍ أو حركاتٍ. كما يحتوي على أوَّل نسخةٍ من القرآن مطبوعةٍ في ألمانيا في سنةِ 1694 م. وفيه كذلك أكبرُ مُصْحَـفٍ في العالم مكتـوبٍ في الهِنْد بخطِ النَّسْخ في القرن الثامِنَ عَشَرَ.

في بيتِ القرآن قاعة مُؤتمراتٍ فخمة، ومكتبة غنية متميزة. والمركزُ مفتوحٌ لجميع الجِنْسِيَّاتِ ولجميع أصْحَابِ الأدْيَـان. ويقعُ المركزُ في مِنطقةٍ تجاريَّةٍ هامَّةٍ.

❖

Try to understand as much as you can. Identify five words you know and put them into sentences. Look up five words you do not know and write down their roots, forms, and verbal nouns. Write a paragraph about Beit Al Qur`an.

الدَّرس السَّادس عشر

العـــائـــلة العربية

Lesson Sixteen

The Arab Family

Figure 16.1 - Chehabi family

Lesson Sixteen Contents

🎧 Vocabulary - المفردات

🎧 Words and Expressions - كلمات وتعابير

💿 Basic Text - النص الأساسي

    ❖ The Arab Family - العائلة العربية

Grammar - القواعد

    1. The Diptotes - الممنوع من الصرف

    2. Other Types of Diptotes

    3. Absolute Object - المفعول المطلق

💿 Comprehension Text - الفهم والاستيعاب

    ❖ Polygamy in Arab Society - تعدد الزوجات في المجتمع العربي

🎧 Let's Speak Arabic - المحادثة

    ❖ Activities - نشاطات

💿 Window into Arab Culture - من الثقافة العربية

    ❖ The Family: The Pillar of Arab Life - العائلة: ركن الحياة العربية

🎧

المفردات

family	عائِلة ج. عائِلاتٌ
corner, pillar, basic element	رُكْنٌ ج. أرْكانٌ
bond, tie, connection	رابطة ج. روابطُ
strong, powerful	قويٌّ ج. أقوياءُ
to bind, connect	رَبَط، يربُط، ربْط
to provide	وفَّر، يُوَفِّرُ، توفيرٌ
individual	فَردٌ ج. أفْرادٌ
to give, grant	أعْطى، يُعطي، إعْطاءٌ
opportunity, chance	فُرْصة ج. فُرَصٌ
to feel	شَعَرَ، يَشْعُرُ، شُعُورٌ
difficulty	صعُوبَة ج. صعُوباتٌ
problem	مُشْكلة ج. مَشاكلُ، مُشْكِلاتٌ
to derive, take, draw	اِسْتَمَدَّ، يَسْتَمِدُّ
value	قيمة ج. قِيَمٌ
tradition, custom	تقليدٌ ج. تقاليدُ
concept	مَفْهُومٌ ج. مفاهيمُ
relative	قريب ج. أقارب، أقرباءُ، أقربون
for, for the sake of	مِنْ أجْل
to help, assist	ساعَدَ، يُساعِدُ، مُساعَدة
connected, committed, bound	مُرتَبط ج. مُرتبطونَ

🎧

كلمات وتعابير

identity	هُويَّة
Arab society	المُجتمعُ العربيُّ
social life	الحياة الاجتماعية
warmth and protection	الدِفْءُ والحِمَايَة
all of the basic needs	كافة الاحْتِيَاجَات الأساسِيَّة
strong connection, close union	اِلْتِحَامٌ مَتينٌ
necessary strength	قُوَّة ضَرُوريَّة
facing life, encountering life	مُواجَهة الحَيَاة

to rely on	يَعْتَمِدُ على
principle axis, pivot point	مِحْوَرٌ رئيسيٌّ
life and culture of the Arabs	حياةُ العَربِ وثقافتُهُم
individual success	نجاحُ الفرد
alienation	اِغْتِرابٌ
a warm refuge	مَلْجأً دافِئٌ
loyalty, devotion	وَلاءٌ

النص الأساسي: العائلة العربية

العائلة العربية هي الرُّكنُ الأساسيُّ في المجتمع العربي، وهي الرابطة القوية التي تربُط الحياة الاجتماعية العربية، وتُعْطي الدِّفْءَ والحِمَايَة والحُبَّ لأفرادِ العائلةِ. والعائلة تعطي أفرادَهَا ما لا تستطيعُ الدَّولة أنْ تُعْطيَهُم. فالعائلة تُوفِّرُ العملَ والفُرصَ وكافة الاحتياجاتِ الأساسيةِ لأفرادِهَا. إنَّ العربَ مرتبطونَ بعائلاتِهِم أوَّلاً وبالمجتمع ثانياً. وهذا الالتحامُ المتينُ بينَ أفرادِ العائلةِ العربيةِ يُعْطيهِم القوة الضرورية لمواجهةِ الحياةِ وصعوباتِهَا ومشاكِلِهَا.

والعربيُّ يعتمدُ على عائلتِهِ كلَّ الاعتمادِ. كانت العائلة العربية منذ فجر التاريخ المِحْوَرَ الرئيسيَّ في حياةِ العربِ وثقافتِهِم. والمجتمعُ العربيُّ يستمدُّ قيمَهُ وهُوِيَّتَهُ، وتقاليدَهُ ومفاهيمَهُ من العائلةِ. ومن هنا فإنَّ الولاءَ لأفرادِ العائلةِ وللأقرباءِ هو قيمة هامة في المجتمع. وأفرادُ العائلةِ قَدْ يَحْرِمُونَ أنفُسَهُم من فُرَصِ الدِّراسةِ أو السَّفرِ أو العَمَلِ في الخارج مِن أجْلِ مُساعدة أخواتِهم وإخوتهم وأقربائهم. إن نجاحَ الفردِ هو نجاحٌ للعائلة كُلِّهَا. وقد يشعرُ الأفرادُ بالاغترابِ عن مجتمعِهم، إلا أنَّهُم لا يشعرونَ بالاغترابِ عن عائلاتِهم. فالعائلة هي المَلجأُ الدَّافِئُ والأوَّلُ للفردِ العربيِّ.

القواعد

1. The Diptotes - الممنــوع من الصرف

We learned that a noun in Arabic could be in one of these cases:

- Nominative case (حالة الرفع). When the noun ends in one *damma* (ـُ) or double *dammas* (ـٌ) as in الطالبُ - طالبٌ.

- Accusative case (حالة النصب). When the noun ends in *fatha* (ـَ) or double *fathas* (ـً) as in الطالبَ - طالباً.

- Genitive case (حالة الجرّ). When the noun ends in *kasra* (ـِ) or double *kasra* (ـٍ) as in (الطالبِ - طالبٍ).

We also learned that some nouns do not take تنوين 'nunation.' Those nouns are called diptotes (ممنــوع من الصرف). They take *damma* (ـُ) in the nominative case and *kasra* (ـِ) in both the *genitive* and *accusative* cases.

Diptotes include certain patterns of broken plurals (such as أفْعِـلاءُ، فُـعَـلاءُ، مَفـاعِـلُ and فَـعَـاليلُ), names of cities and countries, foreign names, feminine names, some masculine names, and other words.

❖

A. Diptotes of the broken plurals:

The following are the most common patterns of diptotes in the broken plurals:

فُـعَـلاءُ

Gen.	Acc.	Nom.	Pattern	Singular
سُـفـراءَ	سُـفـراءَ	سُـفـراءُ	فُـعَـلاءُ	سَفيرٌ

أفْـعِـلاءُ

Gen.	Acc.	Nom.	Pattern	Singular
أصْدِقـاءَ	أصْدِقـاءَ	أصْدِقـاءُ	أفْـعِـلاءُ	صديقٌ

319

The verbal noun must be in the accusative case, and it may be followed by an adjective. Examples:

I love him greatly	أُحِبُّهُ حُبًّا عظيماً
I studied the book very well	درستُ الكتابَ دراسةً جيدة
I slept deeply	نِمْتُ نَوْمًا عميقًا

The absolute object is used in Arabic for emphasis and to declare the intensity of the action. It is a powerful and beautiful style of Arabic and is used in the Qur`an and in Arabic literature.

The absolute object can come as the first term of *idafa*, or can be used with demonstratives or nouns of quantity such as بعضَ and كلَّ.

I fought like a man	قاتلتُ قِتالَ الرِّجال
I loved him such a strong love	أحْبَبْتُهُ هذا الحُبَّ القويَّ
I loved him very much	أحْبَبْتُهُ كلَّ الحُبِّ
I loved him a little	أحْبَبْتُهُ بعضَ الحُبِّ

❖

Drill 1: Vocalize the words in the following sentences.

١ - درستُ في مدارس خاصة.

٢ - حضر رجل سكران إلى الجامعة.

٣ - شاهدت كثيراً من الأصدقاء أمس.

٤ - رجعتُ إلى البيت مع عمر ليلة أمس.

٥ - أحِبُّ خديجـة.

٦ - في المدينة مطاعم عربية كثيرة.

٧ - زرتُ مصر وذهبتُ إلى مطاعم القاهرة.

٨ - حضرتُ المؤتمر وتكلمتُ مع سفراء الدول العربية.

❖

Drill 2: In each sentence, change the singular to the plural and vocalize.

١ - ــــــــ ــــــــ المدينة كبيرة. (مسجد)

٢ - يسكن الطلاب في ــــــــ جميلة. (فندق)

٣ - أكلتُ الكباب في ــــــــ شعبية في عمَّان. (مطعم)

٤ - درستُ مع ــــــــ سامي. (صديق)

٥ - أعطاني أحمد ــــــــ ثقيلة. (صندوق)

٦ - ابراهيم له ــــــــ كثيرون في اليمن. (صديق)

٧ - شاهدتُ مسرحيات رائعة في ــــــــ بيروت. (مسرح)

٨ - أعطاني ــــــــ ــــــــ السيارة الحمراء. (مفتاح)

❖

Drill 3: Translate into English.

١ - وصل عدد من الطلاب الأجانب إلى مدينة الخرطوم في السودان.

٢ - لي أصدقاء لبنانون في مدينة سياتل.

٣ - أقرباء عدنان سافروا اليوم إلى الكويت ومعهم حقائب سفر كثيرة.

٤ - قرأتُ كتاباً هاماً عن الخلفاء الراشدين.

٥ - وصل عدنان إلى بيتي مع صناديق كبيرة من الأوراق.

٦ - نشرت الجرائد أن هناك مشاكل في مدارس المدينة.

٧ - تعلمت في معاهد القاهرة وجامعاتها قبل وصولي إلى أمريكا.

٨ - أعطاني زوجي وردة حمراء في عيد ميلادي.

❖

Drill 4: Provide the absolute object for each sentence.

١ - ساعدتُها ــــــــ كبيرة.

٢ - كتبتُ الواجب ــــــــ جيدة.

٣ - سبحتُ في البحر ــــــــ طويلة.

4 - استقبلني صديقي ــــــــ رائعاً.

5 - حدثتني ــــــــ جميلاً.

6 - تقدم الاقتصاد ــــــــ واضحاً.

7 - ضربني ــــــــ شديداً.

8 - أرحِبُ بكم ــــــــ الترحيب.

❖

Drill 5: Translate into Arabic.

1. I met some foreign journalists and their friends in Jordan last week.
2. Some of my friends are rich.
3. I do not like to visit markets and mountains.
4. We saw many poor men in the streets of the city.
5. The professors moved to new offices last month.
6. There are many crazy people in the world.
7. His relatives are misers.
8. I faced problems when I crossed the border without a visa.

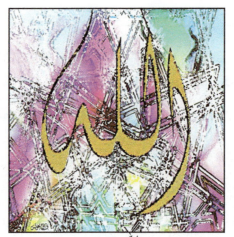

God - الله

الفهم والاستيعاب: تعدد الزوجات في المجتمع العربي

إنَّ ظاهرة تَعَدُّدِ الزَّوْجَاتِ في المجتمع العربي قديمة وترجعُ أسبابُهَا إلى ضَرورةِ خَلْق تَوازُن سُكَّانيٍّ بين الإناثِ والذكُور في المجتمع في بدايةِ ظُهور الإسلام. إنَّ مَوْتَ الرِّجَال في الحُرُوبِ المُتكرِّرَة جعلَ عددَ الإناثِ يزيدُ كثيراً على عددِ الرّجالِ في المجتمع.

لهذا جاءَتْ هذه الظاهرة الاجتماعية من أجل أنْ تُقَلِّلَ مِنْ وُجُودِ عددٍ كبير من النساء غَيْر المتزوجاتِ في المجتمع. ولهذا فوائِدُ كثيرة تنفعُ المجتمعَ وتحافِظ على قِيَمِهِ وتقاليدِهِ، وتُوَفِّرُ الحِمايَة والحاجَة للمرأةِ. ولهذا حَلَّلَ الإسلامُ الزواجَ من أربع نساءٍ لأسبابٍ اجتماعيةٍ واقتصاديةٍ وأخلاقيةٍ. وتعدُّدُ الزوجاتِ مسموحٌ بـهِ شرْعاً ولا يزالُ مقبولاً في القُرَى وعِنْدَ القبائلِ والفلاحينَ.

ومع أنَّ القرآنَ الكريمَ حَلَّلَ زواجَ الرّجُلِ من أربع نساءٍ إلا أنَّهُ وَضَعَ شُروطاً وقُيوداً صارمة لِمِثْل هذِهِ الظاهرةِ. والزواجُ في العالم العربيُّ يخضَعُ للسُّلطاتِ الشَّرْعِيَّةِ والقضائيَّة، كما يخضَعُ لقوانين الدَّولةِ. والطَّلاقُ ليس سَهْلاً، فهو يخضَعُ لشروطٍ قانونيةٍ وبراهينَ واضحة ولا يُمْنَحُ إلا عَنْ طريق القضاء. وبعضُ الدُّول العربيَّةِ تمنعُ الرَّجُلَ مِنَ الزَّواج من أكثر من امْرأة واحدة.

Figure 16.2 - Narrated by Salma Chehabi

🎧

كلمات وتعابير

necessity	ضَرُورة
balance	تَوازُن
wars	حُروب
therefore	لِهذا
it (f.s.) reduces	تُقلِّلُ
appearance	ظهور
it (m.s.) benefits	تَنفعُ
its (m.s.) values	قِيمَهُ
its traditions	تقاليدُهُ
need	حَاجَة
to permit	حَلَّلَ
severe, stern	صَارِمَة
judicial	قضائِيَّة
evidence	بَراهين
acceptable	مَقْبُول
phenomenon	ظَاهِرَة
creating	خَــلْق
reasons	أسْبَاب
benefits, virtues	فوائِد
females	إناث
males	ذكُور
death	مَوْت
existence, presence	وُجُود
it (f.s.) provides	تُوَفِّر
protection	حِمايَة
moral	أخلاقِيَّة
legally	شَرْعَاً
it (m.s.) is subjected	يَخضعُ
divorce	طلاق
it (f.s.) prevents	تَمْنَعُ

❖

المحادثة

Activities - نشاطات

Repeat the following question out loud:

| What did you (m.s.) do over the weekend? | ماذا فعلتَ في عُطلةِ نهايةِ الأسبوع؟ |
| What did you (f.s.) do over the weekend? | ماذا فعلتِ في عُطلةِ نهايةِ الأسبوع؟ |

Now repeat aloud the following answer:

| I visited my family | زُرْتُ عائلتي |

Next, substitute the following sentences for زُرْتُ عائلتي:

I saw my friends	شَاهدتُ أصدقائي
I learned to drive	تعلَّـمْتُ قِيادة السَّيارة
I got married	تزوَّجْـتُ
I bought a new computer	اِشْتَرَيْتُ حاسوباً جديداً
I rented an apartment	اِسْتأجَرْتُ شَقَّـة

Repeat the dialogue with a classmate.

Homework - الواجب

1. Read and listen to the comprehension text. Look up the words you do not understand in the dictionary.

2. Translate the text and hand it in to your professor.

3. Write a composition about the pattern of polygamy in any society.

Lesson Seventeen Contents

🎧 Vocabulary - المفردات

🎧 Words and Expressions - كلمات وتعابير

💿 Basic Text - النص الأساسي

    ❖ Tourism in Jordan - السياحة في الأردن

Grammar - القواعد

    1. Active Participle - اسم الفاعل

    2. Passive Participle - اسم المفعول

💿 Comprehension Text - الفهم والاستيعاب

    ❖ The City of Petra - مدينة البتراء

🎧 Let's Speak Arabic - المحادثة

    ❖ The Market - السوق

💿 Window into Arab Culture - من الثقافة العربية

    ❖ The Dead Sea - البحر الميِّت

المفردات

known (passive participle)	مَعْرُوفٌ (عَرَفَ، يَعْرِفُ)
guest, visitor	ضَيْفٌ ج. ضُيُوفٌ
coming, arriving; comer, arriver (a.p.)	قَادِمٌ ج. قَادِمُونَ (قَدَمَ، يَقْدُمُ)
to move, travel about (Form VIII)	اِنْتَقَلَ، يَنْتَقِلُ، اِنْتِقالٌ
visitor (a.p.)	زائِرٌ (زارَ، يَزورُ)
hill, elevation, mountain	هَضْبَةٌ ج. هِضَابٌ
located, falling (a.p.)	واقِعٌ على (وقَعَ، يَقَعُ)
inhabited, populated (a.p.)	مَسْكُونٌ (سَكَنَ، يَسْكُنُ)
hunting, hunt	صَيْدٌ (صادَ، يَصِيدُ)
to exercise, practice (Form III)	مارَسَ، يُمارِسُ، مُمارَسَةٌ
sport, practice, exercise	رياضَة ج. رِياضاتٌ
swimming	سِباحَة (سَبَحَ، يَسْبَحُ)
to be baptized (Form V)	تَعَمَّدَ، يَتَعَمَّدُ
to secure, ensure	أمَّنَ، يُؤَمِّنُ
access, passageway	مَنْفَذٌ ج. مَنافِذُ
wealth, fortune	ثَرْوَة ج. ثَرَواتٌ
to enjoy (Form V)	تَمَتَّعَ بـ، يَتَمَتَّعُ بـ، تَمَتُّعٌ بـ
landmark, site	مَعْلَمٌ ج. مَعالِمُ
banquet	وَلِيمَة ج. وَلائِمُ

كلمات وتعابير

welcome, greeting	تَرْحابٌ
genuine Arab generosity	كَرَمٌ عربيٌّ أصِيلٌ
the warmth of its (m.s.) people	حَرارة أهْلِهِ
as if (he)	كأنَّهُ
with enjoyment and pleasure/ease	بسُهُولةٍ ومُتْـعَةٍ
thousands of years ago	منذ آلافِ السِّنين
climate	مَناخٌ، مُناخٌ
weather, climate	طَقْسٌ

the Mediterranean Basin   حَوْضُ البَحْر الأبْيَض المُتَوَسِّط

water skiing   تَزَلُّجٌ على المَاء

the Messiah, Christ   السَّيِّدُ المَسيحُ

Aqaba   العَقَبَة

the Red Sea   البَحْرُ الأحْمَرُ

popular dish, national dish   طَبَقٌ شَعْبيٌّ

delicious dish   طبقٌ لَذيذٌ

meat and rice   لَحْمٌ وأرُزٌّ

people of the country   أهْلُ البلاد

taxicabs   سيَّاراتُ الأجْرةِ

full of   مَليءٌ بـ ، مَليئة بـ

comfortable and quiet   مُريحٌ وهَادِىءٌ، مُريحَة وهادِئة

salty water   مِياةٌ مَالِحَة

transportation   مُواصَلاتٌ

mild, moderate (a.p.)   مُعْتَدِلٌ

warm (a.p.)   دافِئ

port, harbor   مِيناء

Figure 17.2 - Wadi Rum, Jordan

النص الأساسي: السِّياحَة في الأردنِّ

Figure 17.3 - Ajloun, Jordan

الأرْدُنُّ بلدٌ معروفٌ بالكرمِ العربيِّ الأصيلِ، وبحَرارةِ أهلهِ وترحَابهم بالضيوفِ القادمينَ إليهِ. يَشْعُرُ القادِمُ إلى الأرْدُنِّ وكأنَّهُ في بَلَدِهِ وبَيْنَ أهْلِهِ، وينتقلُ الزائرُ بينَ المدنِ والسهولِ والجبالِ والهضابِ والصحراءِ بسهولةٍ ومتعةٍ.

والأردنُّ بلدٌ حديثٌ لكنّهُ واقعٌ على أرضٍ تاريخيةٍ مسكونةٍ بالناسِ منذ آلافِ السّنينِ. يَجْمَعُ الأردنُّ بين مناخِ حوضِ البحرِ الأبيضِ المتوسِّطِ والمناخِ الصحراويِّ، وطَقْسُهُ دافِئٌ صَيْفاً ومُعْتَدِلٌ شِتاءً. ويمارسُ السُّيّاحُ فيهِ رياضَةَ التَّزَلُّجِ على الماءِ والسِّبَاحَةِ والصَّيْدِ.

وفي الأردنِّ يقعُ البحرُ المَيِّتُ، المعروفُ بمياهِهِ المالِحَةِ، ويقعُ فيهِ نَهْرُ الأردنِّ، الذي تعمَّدَ فيهِ السَّيِّدُ المسيحُ، وهناك ميناءُ العقبةِ الذي يُؤَمِّنُ للأردنِّ مَنفذاً إلى البحرِ الأحمرِ. وهناكَ الكثيرُ مِن المواقِعِ التاريخيةِ والأثريةِ منها البتراء وجرش. وفي العاصمةِ عمَّان، يلتقي القديمُ بالحديثِ، وتَتَمَتَّعُ عَمَّانُ بثروةٍ كبيرةٍ من المَعالِمِ الأثريةِ.

والمَنْسَفُ الأردنيُّ هو الطبقُ الشعبيُّ الشَّهيرُ في الأردن، وهو طبقٌ لذيذ مُكَوَّنٌ من اللَّحْمِ والأرُزِّ، يُقَدِّمُهُ أهلُ البلادِ في الوَلائمِ وتكريماً للضُّيُوفِ. والمُواصَلاتُ في عمَّانَ سَهْلة، فشوارعُ العاصِمةِ مليئة بسياراتِ الأجْرَةِ. والفنادقُ كثيرة، والحَياة مُريحَة وهادِئة.

❦❧

القواعد

Active and Passive Participles (اسم الفاعل واسم المفعول)

The active and passive participles are derived nouns. They are used a great deal in Arabic, and students of Arabic become more familiar with them by reading texts and literature.

1. Active Participle - اسم الفاعل

Active participles are derived nouns that have the characteristics of both nouns and adjectives. The active participle refers to the 'actor' or the 'doer' of the action of the verb from which the participle is derived. It is formed from Form I on the pattern of فاعِل. Example:

Meaning	Example	Active Participle	Verb (Form I)
He is going	هو ذاهِبٌ	ذاهِبٌ	ذَهَبَ
He is riding	هو راكِبٌ	راكِبٌ	رَكِبَ
He is living here	هو ساكِنٌ هنا	ساكِنٌ	سَكَنَ

Active participles can also be replaced by imperfect verbs. Example:

Imperfect	Active Participle
هو يذَهَبُ	هو ذاهِبٌ
هو يركَبُ	هو راكِبٌ
هو يَسْكُنُ هنا	هو سَاكِنٌ هنا
هو الطالبُ الذي يسكنُ هناك	هو الطالبُ الساكنُ هناك

Active participles modify nouns in gender, definiteness, case, and number when used as adjectives:

The student (m.s.) who is living here is Egyptian	الطالبُ الساكِنُ هنا مِصريٌّ
The student (f.s.) who is living here is Egyptian	الطالبةُ الساكِنةُ هنا مِصْريةٌ
The students (m.dual.) who are living here are Egyptians	الطالبانِ الساكِنانِ هنا مِصريانِ

The students (f.dual.) who are living here are Egyptian	الطالبتانِ الساكِنتان هنا مصريتان
The students (m.pl.) who are living here are Egyptians	الطلابُ الساكِنونَ هنا مِصريونَ
The students (f.pl.) who are living here are Egyptians	الطالباتُ الساكِناتُ هنا مِصرياتٌ

Depending on the context and the verb, the active participles can have present, future, present perfect, present continuous, or past continuous meanings.

I am going now	أنا ذاهِبٌ الآن
I am going tomorrow	أنا ذاهِبٌ غداً
I was going yesterday	كنتُ ذاهِباً أمس
I have obtained the doctorate	أنا حاصِلٌ على الدكتوراه
He has succeeded in the elections	هو ناجِحٌ في الانتخابات

Active participles, like verbs, may require a direct object.

The scholar who has written a book	العالِمُ الكاتِبُ كتاباً
The student who has studied the lesson	الطالبُ الدارسُ الدَّرسَ

As previously mentioned, active participles are derived from Form I on the pattern of فاعِل, as in كاتِب 'writer,' عامِل 'worker,' and حالِم 'dreamer.' For Forms II - X, active participles are derived from their imperfect verbs by replacing the prefix of the imperfect with مُ and by placing كسرة 'kasra' before the last radical.

Active Participle	Imperfect	Perfect	Form
مُدَرِّسٌ	يُدَرِّسُ	درَّسَ	II
مُراسِلٌ	يُراسِلُ	راسَلَ	III
مُكرِمٌ	يُكرِمُ	أكرَمَ	IV
مُستَقبِلٌ	يَستَقبِلُ	استَقبَلَ	X

❖

2. Passive Participle - اسم المفعول

Passive participles refer to the recipient of the action of the derived verb. They are formed from Form I on the pattern of مَفْعُول. Example:

Example	Meaning	Passive Participle	Verb
الدرسُ مدروسٌ	studied	مَدْرُوسٌ	دَرَسَ
الكتابُ منشورٌ	published	مَنْشُورٌ	نَشَرَ
البيتُ مسكونٌ	dwelled in	مَسْكُونٌ	سَكَنَ

As with the active participle, the passive participle could be replaced in a sentence by a verb. But, the passive voice of that verb must be used.

الكتابُ الذي دُرِسَ	الدرسُ مدروسٌ
الكتابُ الذي نُشِرَ	الكتابُ المنشورُ
البيتُ الذي سُكِنَ	البيتُ مسكونٌ

Passive participles are derived from Form I on the pattern of مَفْعُول, as in مَكْتُوب 'written,' مَحْمُول 'carried,' and مَسْمُوع 'heard.' For Forms II - X, passive participles are derived from their imperfect verbs by replacing the prefix of the imperfect with مُ and placing فتحة *fatha* before the last radical.

Passive Participle	Imperfect	Perfect	Form
مُدَرَّسٌ	يُدَرِّسُ	درّسَ	II
مُعَامَلٌ	يُعَامِلُ	عامَلَ	III
مُكْرَمٌ	يُكْرِمُ	أكْرَمَ	IV
مُسْتَقْبَلٌ	يَسْتَقْبِلُ	اِسْتَقْبَلَ	X

The chart below shows Forms I-X with their active and passive participles:

Passive Part.	Active Part.	Imperfect	Perfect	Meaning	Form
مَفْعُول	فاعِل	يـفْعَلُ	فَعَلَ		I
مَدْرُوس	دارس	يَدْرُسُ	دَرَسَ	to study	Example
مُفَعَّل	مُفَعِّل	يُفَعِّلُ	فَعَّلَ		II
مُدَرَّس	مُدَرِّس	يُدَرِّسُ	دَرَّسَ	to teach	Example
مُفاعَل	مُفاعِل	يُفاعِلُ	فاعَلَ		III
مُقاتَل	مُقاتِل	يُقاتِلُ	قاتَلَ	to fight	Example
مُفْعَل	مُفْعِل	يـفْعِلُ	أفْعَلَ		IV
مُكْرَم	مُكْرِم	يُكْرِمُ	أكْرَمَ	to honor	Example
مُتَفَعَّل	مُتَفَعِّل	يتفَعَّلُ	تَفَعَّلَ		V
مُتَعَلَّم	مُتَعَلِّم	يَتَعَلَّمُ	تَعَلَّمَ	to learn	Example
مُتَفاعَل	مُتَفاعِل	يتفاعَلُ	تَفاعَلَ		VI
مُتَراسَل	مُتَراسِل	يتَراسَلُ	تَراسَلَ	to correspond	Example
مُنْفَعَل	مُنْفَعِل	ينْفَعِلُ	إنْفَعَلَ		VII
مُنْكَسَر	مُنْكَسِر	يَنْكَسِرُ	إنْكَسَرَ	to be broken	Example
مُفْتَعَل	مُفْتَعِل	يَفْتَعِلُ	إفْتَعَلَ		VIII
مُحْتَفَل	مُحْتَفِل	يحْتَفِلُ	إحْتَفَلَ	to celebrate	Example
-	مُفْعَلٌّ	يـفْعَلُّ	إفْعَلَّ		IX
-	مُحْمَرّ	يَحْمَرُّ	إحْمَرَّ	to become red	Example
مُسْتَفْعَل	مُسْتَفْعِل	يَسْتَفْعِلُ	إسْتَفْعَلَ		X
مُسْتَقْبَل	مُسْتَقْبِل	يَسْتَقْبِلُ	إسْتَقْبَلَ	to receive	Example

❖

Drill 1: Change the verbs to active participles.

١ - الأستاذ يسكنُ في مدينة بيروت.

٢ - نحن نذهبُ إلى الجامعة في الساعة التاسعة.

٣ - صديقي يعملُ في شركة.

٤ - أحمـد يدرسُ دروسَهُ.

٥ - عميد الجامعة يستقبلُ الطلاب.

6 - الرئيس يحضرُ الاجتماعَ اليوم.

7 - هنَّ يَكْتُبْنَ واجِبَ اللغة العربية.

8 - الرجالُ يجلسونَ على الأرض.

❖

Drill 2: Write the correct passive participle in each blank.

1 - الرجل ــــــــ كان سائحاً. (قتل)

2 - شباك الصف ــــــــ. (كسر)

3 - صديقتي ــــــــ في المكتبة كل الوقت. (وجد)

4 - كان الباب ــــــــ عندما دخلتُ. (فتح)

5 - الصوت في السينما لم يكن ــــــــ. (سمع)

6 - كان الطعام ــــــــ. (أكل)

7 - أعتقد أن البنت ــــــــ . (جَنَّ)

8 - مقالتي ــــــــ في الجريدة. (نشر)

❖

Drill 3: Give the active and passive participles of the verbs.

Active Participle	Passive Participle	Verb
		حَكَمَ
		اِنْتَخَبَ
		قَرَأَ
		تَرْجَمَ
		اِسْتَخْدَمَ
		اِعْتَبَرَ
		سَمِعَ
		قَدَّمَ

الفهم والاستيعاب: مدينة البتراء

Figure 17.4 - Petra, Jordan

مدينة البتراء هي مدينة قديمة، بَنَاهَا الأنْبَاطُ قَبْلَ الميلادِ، وجَعَلُوهَا عاصمَةَ لِدَوْلَتِهِم، وقلعَة لأمْنِهِم، ومَوْقِعَاً تِجارِيّاً لِحَضَارَتِهِم. كانت البتـراءُ مركزاً تجارياً وطريقاً هامّاً تسيرُ إلَيْهِ القوافلُ من الجزيرةِ العربيةِ جنوباً إلى بلادِ الشّامِ شَمَالاً. والقادِمُ إلى قلبِ المدينةِ يمشي على الأقدام عَبْرَ شَقٍّ صَخريٍّ مُدْهِش يَبْلُغُ طولُهُ أكْثر من ألف متر.

والبتراءُ تُعْتَبَرُ مِن عَجَائِبِ الدُّنيا السَّبْعِ، ومِن أشْهَر المَعَالِمِ الأثريَّةِ في الأردنِّ، وهي مدينة مبنية مِن صُخُورِ الجـبَالِ، ومعروفة باسم (المدينة الوردية) لأنَّهَا مبنية مِن الصخور ذاتِ اللَّون الوَرْدِيِّ. وهي واقعة على بُعْدِ 262 كيلومتراً إلى الجَنَوبِ مِن عَمَّانَ.

في مدينةِ البتراء هناكَ الهياكِلُ والمَعَابِدُ والقُبُورُ، والبيوتُ الصَّغيرة والكبيرة، وقَنَوَاتُ الماء، والأسواق، والبوابات القديمة التي بناها الإنسانُ القديمُ. وهناك المُدَرَّجُ الأثريُّ الذي يَتَّسِـعُ لسبعةِ آلافٍ مُتفرِّج.

وحينَ تَسْطَعُ أشِعَّة الشمس فَوْقَ صخورِ المدينةِ الطبيعيَّةِ، تَتَحَوَّلُ الصخورُ إلى لَوْن وَرْدِيٍّ جميل، وإلى مَشْـهَدٍ خَلابٍ ساحِرٍ، لا ينسَاهُ الزَّائِـرُ مَدَى الحياةِ.

🎧

كلمات وتعابير

Before Christ (B.C.)	قَبْلَ الميلاد	the Nabataeans	الأنْباط
castle, fort	قلعة	they made it	جَعَلوها
location, center	مَوْقِعاً	it walks	تَسيـرُ
the Arabian Peninsula	الجَزيرة العَربية	caravans	قوافِل
split, opening, cleavage	شَـقٌّ	greater Syria	بلادُ الشَّـام
rocky	صَخْـريٌّ	amazing	مُدْهِش
spectators	مُتَفرِّجٌ	gates	بَوَّابات
amphitheater	مُدَرَّجٌ أثريٌّ	rays of the sun	أشِعَّة الشمس
captivating	خَـلَّابٌ	scene	مَـشهَدٌ
channels	قَنَـوَاتٌ	the Seven Wonders of the World	عَجَائِبُ الدُّنيا السَّبْع

❖

Drill 4: Translate into English.

١ - أعرفُ الطالبة الساكنة في الشقة العاشرة.

٢ - أنا حاصِلٌ على الدكتوراه من جامعةِ صنعاء في اليمن.

٣ - أصدِقائي ذاهِبُونَ إلى الشرق الأوسط هذا الصيف.

٤ - المُحَاضِرونَ وصلوا قبل أسبوع من بدء المؤتمر.

٥ - نحن راغِبُونَ في الحصول على عمل في بداية الصيف.

٦ - المُسْتَشْرِقُونَ يحضرون مهرجان قرطاج في تونس.

٧ - المُرَشَّحُ الديمقراطي فاز بالانتخاب.

٨ - التدخين مَمْنُوع في المكاتب الحكومية وفي مكاتب الشركات الخاصة.

❖

Drill 5: Translate into Arabic.

1. I know the man who is known for his generosity.
2. I was living in a house on the beach.
3. The lecture by the French lecturer was interesting.
4. I met the writer of the book.
5. The American researchers visited the city streets.
6. She is the wife of the governor of New York.
7. She was present at the party.
8. He was sincere in his relationship with me.

🎧

المحادثة
السُّـوق - The Market

Repeat aloud the following question:

What did you (m.s.) buy at the market?	ماذا اِشْـتَرَيْتَ مِنَ السوق؟
What did you (f.s.) buy at the market?	ماذا اِشْـتَرَيْتِ مِنَ السوق؟

Now repeat aloud the following answer:

I bought apples	اِشْـتَرَيْتُ التُّـفَّـاح

Next, repeat the sentence and substitute the following words for التُّـفَّـاحَ:

banana	الـمَـوْز
tomatoes	البَنَـدُورة
watermelon	البَطِّـيخ
cucumber	الخِيَـار
lettuce	الخَسّ

Repeat the dialogue with a classmate.

Homework - الواجب

1. Read and listen to the comprehension text.

2. Try to understand as much as you can. Look up the words you do not understand in the dictionary.

3. Translate the text and hand it in to your instructor.

4. Write a composition about any subject concerning Jordan.

من الثقافة العربية
البـحـر المـيِّـت

البحر الميِّت

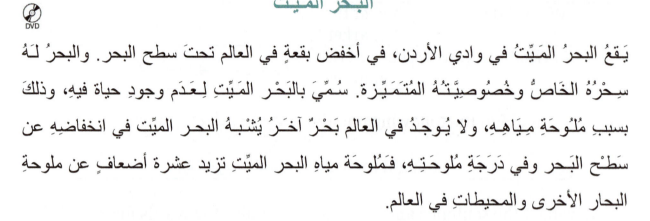

يَقعُ البحرُ المَيِّتُ في وادي الأردن، في أخفض بقعةٍ في العالم تحتَ سطح البحر. والبحرُ لَـهُ سِـحْرُهُ الخَاصُّ وخُصُوصِيَّتُهُ المُتَمَيِّزة. سُمِّيَ بالبَحر المَيِّتِ لِعَدَم وجودِ حياة فيه، وذلكَ بسببِ مُلُوحَةِ مِيَاهِهِ، ولا يُوجَدُ في العَالم بَحْرٌ آخَـرُ يُشْبهُ البحر الميت في انخفاضِهِ عن سَطْح البَحر وفي دَرَجَةِ مُلوحَتِهِ، فَمُلوحَة مياه البحر المَيِّتِ تزيد عشرة أضعافٍ عن ملوحةِ البحار الأخرى والمحيطاتِ في العالم.

وعلى الرَّغْم مِن درجةِ ملوحتِه العاليةِ وانعدام الحياة فيه إلا أنَّهُ مِن أكثر البحار جاذبية وسِـحْراً. هو يتوسَّط وادي الأردن ويُشَكِّلانَ معاً مَشْهَداً جَمَالِيّاً رائعاً، ففي أطرافِ الوادي تبدأ الأرضُ بالإرتفاع مُكَوّنَة سلسلة مِن المرتفعاتِ الجبلية، مِمّا يزيدُ المَشْهَدَ جَمَالاً.

والبحرُ المَيِّتُ يحتوي على أملاح ومعادن مفيدة في معالجةِ الأمراض الجلديَّةِ. كما أنَّ السباحة فيه سهلةٌ بسبب ملوحة مياهِه. والبحرُ يتمتعُ بالسَّكينة والهدوء. فالزائرونَ يَنْعَمُونَ باستراحاتِه وفنادقِه الحديثةِ الرَّاقِيَة. والمكانُ مِثالِيٌّ ورائعٌ لِعَقْدِ الاجتماعاتِ والمُؤتمراتِ الدُّوَلية والنَّدواتِ المحليَّة والعَالمِيَّة.

❖

Try to understand as much as you can. Identify ten words you know and put them into complete sentences. Look up words you do not know in the dictionary. Write a paper on any sea in the world.

الدَّرس الثَّامن عشر

العرب في الأندلس

Lesson Eighteen

The Arabs in Al-Andalus

Figure 18.1 - Toledo, Spain

Lesson Eighteen Contents

🎧 Vocabulary - المفردات

🎧 Words and Expressions - كلمات وتعابير

💿 Basic Text - النص الأساسي

   ❖ The Lost Paradise - الفِرْدَوْسُ المَفقـود

Grammar - القواعد

   Passive Voice - الفِعْل المبني للمجهول

     A. The Passive of the Perfect - الماضي المبني للمجهول

     B. The Passive of the Imperfect - المضارع المبني للمجهول

💿 Comprehension Text - الفهم والاستيعاب

   ❖ Arab Culture in Al-Andalus - الثقافة العربية في الأندلس

🎧 Let's Speak Arabic - المحادثة

   ❖ Activities - نشاطات

💿 Window into Arab Culture - من الثقافة العربية

   ❖ Modern Arabic Poetry - الشـعر العربي الحديث

🎧

المفردات

Umayyad	أَمَوِيٌّ ج. أَمَوِيُّونَ
Abbasid	عَبَّاسِيٌّ ج. عَبَّاسِيُّون
prince	أَميرٌ ج. أُمَراءُ
to escape, flee	هَرَبَ، يَهرُبُ، هُروبٌ
to enter	دَخَلَ، يَدخُلُ، دُخولٌ
grandson, descendant	حَفيدٌ ج. أحفادٌ
Caliph	خَليفة ج. خُلَفاءُ
army, troops	جَيْشٌ ج. جُيوشٌ
to conquer, open	فَتَحَ، يَفْتَحُ، فَتْحٌ
to arrive	وَصَلَ، يَصِلُ، وُصولٌ
palace	قَصْرٌ ج. قُصورٌ
institute	مَعْهَدٌ ج. مَعاهِدُ
net, network, system	شَبَكَة ج. شَبَكاتٌ
irrigation	رَيٌّ
complicated, complex	مُعَقَّدٌ، مُعَقَّدة
it (f.s.) was transformed (Form V)	تَحَوَّلَتْ
torch	مَشْعَلٌ ج. مَشاعِلُ
to create, bring forth	أحدَثَ، يُحْدِثُ، إحْداثٌ
to affect, influence	أثَّرَ، يُؤثِّرُ، تأثيرٌ
to dominate, control, seize	سَيْطَرَ، يُسَيْطِرُ، سَيْطَرة

☸

🎧

كلمات وتعابير

Straits of Gibraltar	مَضيق جَبَل طارق
the Eagle of Quraysh	صَقْر قُرَيْش
the Umayyad state	الدَّوْلَة الأمَوِيَّة
at the hands of	على أيْدي
the middle of the eighth century	مُنتصف القَرْن الثامِن
is known (passive)	يُعْرَفُ
was defeated (passive)	هُزِمَ

is called, nicknamed (passive) يُلَقَّبُ

was named (passive) سُمِّيَ

Atlantic Ocean المُحيط الأطلسي

before that قَبْلَهَا

the Umayyad ruler, governor الحاكِمُ الأَمَويُّ

under the leadership of بِقيادةِ

across, through, by way of عَبْرَ

was built (perfect passive voice) بُنِيَتْ

European thought الفِكْر الأوربي

European Renaissance النَّهْضَة الأوربيَّة

The Arab presence ended اِنْتَهَى الوُجُود العربي

forever إلى الأبَـد

leaving behind it تاركاً وراءَهُ

emptiness, void, gap فَـراغ

Ibn Rushd (Averroës) ابن رُشْـد

Ibn Sina (Avicenna) ابن سـيـنا

Córdoba قُـرْطُـبَة

Granada غِرناطَة

Prime Minister رئيس وزراء

advanced administrative system نِظام إداري مُتَطَـوِّر

Figure 18.2 - Southern Spain

النص الأساسي: الفِرْدَوْسُ المَفْقـود

هُـزِمَ الأمَوِيُّونَ على أَيْدِي العبَّاسِيِّينَ في مُنتصفِ القَرنِ الثامِنِ المِيلادي. إلاّ أنَّ أميراً أمَوِيًّا، اسمه عبد الرحمن بن معاوية، ويُعْرَفُ باسم عبد الرحمن الدَّاخِل، ويُلَقَّبُ بـ (صَقْـر قُـرَيش)، اِسْتَطَاعَ أنْ يَهْـرُبَ مِن دمشقَ إلى المغرب، ثم يدخلَ الأندلسَ، ويُؤسِّسَ الدولة الأموية هناك. أمَّا حَفيدُهُ، الأميرُ عبد الرحمن الثالث، فقد سَيطرعلى كلِّ الأندلس، وصار خليفة.

وقَبْـلَـهَا كانَ مُوسى بن نُصَيْر، الحاكمُ الأمويُّ في شَمالِ أفريقيا، قَدْ أرْسَلَ جيشاً لِفَتْح الأندلس، بقيادةِ طارق بن زياد، عام 711 م. وَصَلَ طارق بن زياد مع جَيْشِهِ إلى الأندلس عبـر المضيق الذي يربطُ البحرَ الابيضَ المتوسّط بالمحيطِ الاطلسي ويفصلُ المغربَ عـن إسبانيا، ولِهَذا سُمِّيَ بمضيق جبـل طـارق.

كانتْ قرطبـة، عاصمة الأندلس، أعظمَ مُدِنِ العَالمِ حضارة وعلماً. وكان لها رئيسُ وزراء ونظامٌ إداريٌّ مُتطَوِّرٌ. وكانت الأندلسُ مَمْلكة السَّلام والجَمَال والتَّسَامُح. بُنِيَتْ فيها المَسَاجِدُ والقُصُورُ والجَامِعَاتُ والمَعَاهِدُ وشَبَكاتُ الرَّيِّ المُعَقَّدَة.

تحولت الأندلسُ إلى مَشْعَلِ حَضَارَةٍ أحْدَثَ تأثيراً هامًّا في الفِكْـرِ الأوربيِّ وفي النَّهْضَةِ الأوربيِّة. وفي أواخر القرن الخامِسِ عشَـر انتهى الوجودُ العربيُّ في الأندلس، إلى الأَبَـد، تاركاً وراءَهُ فراغاً كبيراً.

ൠൠ

القواعد

Passive Voice - الفِعْل المبني للمجهول

The active verb in Arabic is called مَبْني للمَعْلوم 'known.' This means the subject of the verb is known. The passive verb is called مَبْني للمَجْهُول 'unknown,' which means the subject of the verb is unknown.

❖

A. The Passive of the Perfect - الماضي المبني للمجهول

The passive of the perfect is formed by changing the vowels of the active verb. We place *damma* over the first consonant and *kasra* before the last consonant. Examples to show the contrast:

Meaning	Passive
it was written	كُتِبَ
it was studied	دُرِسَ
it was translated	تُرْجِمَ

Meaning	Active
he wrote	كَتَبَ
he studied	دَرَسَ
he translated	تَرْجَمَ

The passive is mostly used with Forms I, II, III, IV, VIII, and X. The passive of Forms VII and IX are not used. And the passive of Forms V and VI are rarely used.

Pattern	Passive	Meaning	Active	Form
فُعِلَ	شُرِبَ	he drank	شَرِبَ	I
فُعِّلَ	دُرِّسَ	he taught	دَرَّسَ	II
فُوعِلَ	قُوبِلَ	he met	قابَلَ	III
أفْعِلَ	أكْرِمَ	he honored	أكْرَمَ	IV
أفْتُعِلَ	انْتُخِبَ	he elected	انْتَخَبَ	VIII
أسْتُفْعِلَ	أسْتُقْبِلَ	he received	اسْتَقْبَلَ	X

Normally in Arabic, the verb is followed by the subject and then the object. When using the passive voice, the subject is not mentioned and the object acts as a subject (taking the nominative case). We call the object that acts as a subject نائب فاعل 'deputy subject.'

Meaning	Passive
The book was written	كُتِبَ الكتابُ

Meaning	Active
The professor wrote the book	كَتَبَ الأستاذُ الكتابَ

❖

B. *The Passive of the Imperfect* - المضارع المبني للمجهول

The passive of the imperfect is formed by changing the vowels of the active verb. We place *damma* over the first consonant and *fatha* before the last consonant.

Pattern	Meaning	Passive
يُفْعَلُ	to be written	يُكْتَبُ
يُفَعَّلُ	it is (being) studied	يُدَرَّسُ
يُفاعَلُ	to be seen	يُشاهَدُ
يُفْعَلُ	to be honored	يُكْرَمُ
يُفْتَعَلُ	to be elected	يُنْتَخَبُ
يُسْتَفْعَلُ	to be received	يُسْتَقْبَلُ

Meaning	Active	Form
he writes	يَكْتُبُ	I
he studies	يُدَرِّسُ	II
he sees	يُشاهِدُ	III
he honors	يُكْرِمُ	IV
he elects	يَنْتَخِبُ	VIII
he receives	يَسْتَقْبِلُ	X

❖

Drill 1: Change the following verbs from active to passive.

Passive	Active
	يَعْتَبِرُ
	يَفْتَتِحُ
	أخْبَرَ
	سَلَّمَ

Passive	Active
	أرْسَلَ
	قَدَّمَ
	شاهَدَ
	سَمَحَ

❖

Drill 2: Change the following verbs from passive to active.

Active	Passive
	يُسافَرُ
	يُسْتَعْلَمُ

Active	Passive
	قُوبِلَ
	رُحِّبَ

	يُسَامَحُ		حُمِلَ
	يُعْقَدُ		أُرْسِلَ

❖

Drill 3: In each sentence, change the object to create نائِب فاعِل 'deputy subject' and the verb from active to passive.

١ - شَرِبَ الطالبُ القهوة .

٢ - عَقَدَ الرئيسُ اجتماعاً.

٣ - قدَّمَ الأستاذ اِستقالته.

٤ - تَرْجَمَ المترجِمُ البحثَ.

٥ - أرْسَلْتُ الرسالة.

٦ - أغْلَقَ المديرُ المكتبَ.

٧ - أطْعَمَ الرَّجُلُ الكلبَ.

٨ - صَوَّرَ السَّائِحُ المدينة.

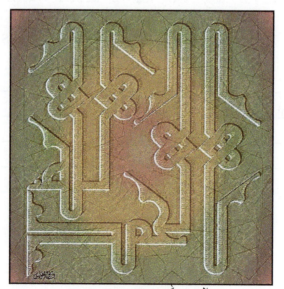

Praise be to God - الحمد لله

الفهم والاستيعاب: الثقافة العربية في الأندلس

كانت الثَّقافة العربية الإسلاميَّة في الأندلس أعظمَ ثقافةٍ في العَالـم القديم، وكانت مدينة قرطبة عاصمة العالم الثقافية. لَقَدْ جَعَلَ الأمويونَ من قرطبة أهمَّ مركز عِلمي وتعليمي في أوروبا، وكانت الجامعاتُ والمراكزُ العلمية فيها قِبـلـة للطلابِ والباحثينَ، يَحْضُرُونَ إليها من كل أنحاء أوروبا، ليدرسوا الفلسفة والعلومَ والطِّبَّ والموسيقى واللغة العربية والترجمة، وليدرسوا كذلك كُتُبَ ابن رُشْـد وابن سينا.

لقد عاشَ المسلمونَ والمسيحيونَ واليهودُ جنباً إلى جنب في إسبانيا وشاركوا في صناعة ثقافة مشتركة وشكلوا مجتمعاً أندلسيّاً مُتَمَيِّزاً.

ويُعْتَبَرُ قصْرُ الحمراء في مدينةِ غرناطة من أبرز المعالم العربيةِ في الأندلس، وهو شاهِدٌ على عَظَمَةِ الحضارةِ العربيةِ، ومِرآة تعْكِسُ الفَنَّ العَربيَّ الإسلاميَّ الرَّفيـع.

لَقَدْ أنجبت الأندلسُ عدداً كبيراً من العلماء والأدباء والشُّعراء والمُؤرِّخِين والأطِبَّاء، وظلت الأندلسُ حضارة عظيمة خلالَ القرون الثمانية التي حَكَمَهَا العربُ، وقَدْ تـقَدَّمَتْ فيها الزراعة والصناعة والتجارة والعُلومُ والآدابُ والفُنـُونُ.

ఴఝ

🎧

كلمات وتعابير

focus of attention	قِبلة	the ancient world	العَالَمُ القديمُ
researchers	بَاحِثينَ	from all parts of	مِنْ كلِّ أنحَاء
they participated in	شاركوا في	side to side	جَنباً إلى جَنب
common, collective	مُشتركة	creating	صناعَة
is considered	يُعْتَبَرُ	they formed	شَكَّلوا
witness	شاهِدٌ	Alhambra	الحَمراء
it (f.s.) reflects	تعْكِسُ	mirror	مِرْآة
agriculture	زراعَة	it (f.s.) produced	أنجَبَتْ

❖

Drill 4: Translate into English.

١ - تُرْجِمَتْ الرواية الجديدة.

٢ - شُوهِدَ في المكتبة أمس.

٣ - نُقِلَ المَكتبُ إلى مدينة بعيدة.

٤ - عُومِلَ الموظف معاملة جَيِّدة.

٥ - قُدِّم أخي للمُحاكمة.

٦ - أُخبِرْتُ عن الأمْر صباحَ اليوم.

٧ - جُمِعَ الطلابُ لمناقشة الموضوع.

٨ - شُغِلَ بدراسته.

❖

Drill 5: Translate into Arabic.

1. The window was broken.
2. The meeting was canceled yesterday.
3. The guest was honored when he visited the university.
4. He was brought to the office.
5. She was seen with him last night.
6. The money was collected to build a school.
7. They were informed of the bad news.
8. You were received like a hero.

🎧   المحادثة
                  Activities - نشاطات

Repeat the following question out loud:

Did you (m.s.) see the movie?	هلْ شَاهَدْتَ الفيلمَ؟
Did you (f.s.) see the movie?	هلْ شَاهَدْتِ الفيلمَ؟

Now repeat aloud the following answer:

| No. I did not see the movie, but I saw the play | لا. ما شَاهَدْتُ الفيلمَ ولكن شاهدتُ المسرحية |

Next, repeat the sentence and substitute the following words for المسرحية.

the soccer game	مباراة كُرَة القَدَم
the television	التِّلْفَاز
the President's speech	خِطاب الرَّئيس
the interview	المُقابلة
the concert	الحَفْلة المُوسيقِيَّة

Repeat the dialogue with a classmate.

Homework - الواجب

1. Listen and repeat the vocabulary and expressions in the basic and the comprehension texts.

2. Look up the words you do not understand in the dictionary.

3. Translate the text.

4. Write a composition about Al-Andalus.

من الثقافة العربية
الشعر العربي الحديث

نِـزار قَـبَّـانـي
أحزان في الأندلس

كتبتِ لي يا غالية
كتبتِ تسألينَ عن إسبانية
عن طارق، يفتحُ باسم اللهِ دُنْيَا ثانية
سألتِ عن أميةٍ
سألتِ عن أميرها مُعاوية
عن السَّرايا الزاهية
تحْمِلُ من دمشقَ في ركابها
حضارةً وعافية

❖

لمْ يَبْقَ في إسبانية
منَّا، ومن عُصُورنا الثمانية
غيرُ الذي يبقى من الخمر،
بجوفِ الآنية

❖

لم يبقَ من قرطبة
سوى دموعُ المئذناتِ الباكية
لم يبقَ إلا قَصْرُهم
كامرأةٍ من الرُّخام عارية
تعيشُ - لا زالتْ - على
قِصَّةِ حُبٍّ ماضية

مَضَتْ قرونٌ خمسة

مُـذ رَحَلَ (الخليفة الصغيرُ) عن إسبانية

ولمْ تزلْ أحقادُنا الصغيرة

كمَا هي

مَضَتْ قرونٌ خمسة

ولا تزال لفظةَ العروبة

كزهرةٍ حزينةٍ في آنية

كطفلةٍ جائعةٍ وعارية

مَضَتْ قرونٌ خمسة يا غالية

كأننا نخرجُ هذا اليومَ من إسبانية

❖

* نزار قباني، الأعمال السياسية الكاملة، منشورات نزار قباني، بيروت.

Figure 18.3 - Narrated by Mohamad Saadoun

Enjoy the poem, memorize a few verses, and look up the words you do not know. Write a paper on the poem's theme or a related topic.

❖

الدَّرس التَّاسع عشر

كاتبات وإعلاميات

Lesson Nineteen

Women Writers and Journalists

Fig 19.1 Alleyway in Syria

Lesson Nineteen Contents

🎧 Vocabulary - المفردات

🎧 Words and Expressions - كلمات وتعابير

💿 Basic Text - النص الأساسي

   ❖ I Become a New Woman - أصير امرأة جديدة

Grammar - القواعد

   1. The Five Nouns - الأسماء الخمسة

   2. Hollow Verbs - الفعل الأجوف

💿 Comprehension Text - الفهم والاستيعاب

   ❖ Death Is a Return - الموت عودة

🎧 Let's Speak Arabic - المحادثة

   ❖ Where Do You Live? - أين تسكن؟

💿 Window into Arab Culture - من الثقافة العربية

   ❖ The Arab Media - الإعلام العربي

المفردات

woman	اِمْـرَأَة ج. نِسَـاءٌ
to be changed, undergo change (V)	تَغَيَّرَ، يَتَغَيَّرُ، تَغَيُّرٌ
to change, alter (II)	بَدَّلَ، يُبَدِّلُ، تبديلٌ
female, feminine	أنثى ج. إناثٌ
blow, fill with air	نَفَخَ، يَنْفُخُ، نَفْخٌ
sail, tent	شِراعٌ ج. أشْرِعَة، شُرُعٌ
road, path	دَرْبٌ ج. دُرُوبٌ
to leave behind, leave (II)	خَلَّفَ، يُخَلِّفُ، تَخْلِيفٌ
strange, foreign	غَريبٌ ج. غُرَبَاءُ
imprint, fingerprint	بَصْمَة ج. بَصَمَاتٌ
glass	زُجَاجٌ
to crack, splinter	شَرَخَ، يَشْرَخُ، شَرْخٌ
storm, violent wind	عَاصِفة ج. عَواصِفُ
moment, instant	لحْظة ج. لَحَظَـاتٌ
thunder	رَعْـدٌ ج. رُعُـودٌ
to be inflamed (VIII)	الْتَهَبَ، يَلْتَهِبُ، الْتِهابٌ
to burn, ignite, catch fire (VIII)	اشْتَعَلَ
forest	غابَة ج. غابَاتٌ
to touch	مَسَّ، يَمَسُّ، مَسٌّ

كلمات وتعابير

everything	كلُّ شَيْءٍ
every day	كلُّ يَوْمٍ
a breeze of wind	هَبَّة ريح
new human being, new creature	كائِنة جَديدة
every fire	كلُّ حَريق
every death	كلُّ مَوْتٍ
sudden birth	ولادَة مُفاجِئة

every word	كلُّ كلمةٍ
it (m.s.) becomes more radiant, glow	يَزْداد تألقاً
place of my birth	مَسْـقَـط رأسِي
in my depth, deep inside me	في أعْمَاقِي
infinite formula, unfinished formula	لا صيغة نهائية لها
it (f.s.) covers, conceals	تُـغَطِّـي
wrong (telephone) number	النُّمْرَة غَلَط
telephone call	مُكالَمَة هاتِفِيَّة
it (f.s.) lost its way, went astray	ضَلَّت الطَّريـق

لا إله إلا الله

النص الأساسي: أصير امرأة جديدة*

Figure 19.2 - Ghada Samman

غـادة السـمان: أديبـة سـورية، ولدت في دمشق عام 1942، وتخرجت من جامعتها في قسـم اللغـة الإنكليزيـة.
روائية وشاعرة وصحفية، من أعمالها: عيناك قدري، وليل الغرباء، وكوابيس بيروت، وليلة المليار، والرقص مع البوم.

أصير امرأة جديدة

أصيرُ امـرأة جديدة في كُلِّ يَوْم. كُلُّ شَيْءٍ يتغيرُ، كُلُّ شَيْءٍ يُبَدِّلُني، كأنْثَى وامرأة
وكاتِبَة. كلُّ هَبَّةِ ريح تُنْفَخُ في شراعي تُغَيِّرُ دَرْبِي. كلُّ حَريق يُخَلِّقُني كائنة جديدة. كُلُّ
مَوْتٍ يفتحُ عَيْنَيَّ على ولادةٍ مُفاجئة. كلُّ كلمةٍ يَقولُهَا حبيبٌ أو غريبٌ تَتْرُكُ بَصْمَتها
على زُجَاج القلبِ المَشروخ. أتَبَدَّلُ كثيراً كأوراق الأشْجَار.

أشْعُرُ أنني كالعاصفةِ، لا صيغة نهائية لها. أنا لَحْظَة مَطَر، لحظة رَعْدٍ، لحظة صَحْو.
كلُّ ما يَمَسُّني يُبَدِّلُني. الكتابُ الذي أطالِعُهُ يُبَدِّلُني، والغيمة لحظة تُغَطِّي الشمسَ تبدّلني،
وبكاءُ طفل يبدّلني، وصوتٌ مجهول يقولُ: "النُّمرة غلط" في مُكالمةٍ هاتفيةٍ ضَلَّت الطريقَ
يُبدّلني، وخَبَرٌ عن أحِبَّائي في مسقط رأسي يبدّلني.

شَيْءٌ واحِدٌ لم يتبدّلْ في أعماقي كأنثى وامرأة وكاتبة. إنَّهُ حُبُّ الكِتابةِ. هذا وَحْدهُ الذي يبقى
ويزداد تألُّقاً في أعماقي. منذ طفولتي وأنا أشْعُرُ بذلك الغليان في أصابعي أمامَ ورقةٍ بيضاء.
ما زلْتُ ألتهبُ حِينَ ألامِسُ الورقة. ما زلتُ أشْتَعِلُ أمامَ فِعْل الكتابةِ مِثْلَ غابة.

❖

* غادة السمان، من كتاب ستأتي الصبية لتعاتبك. منشورات غادة السمان، 2009، بتصرف.

القواعد

1. The Five Nouns - الأسماء الخمسـة

In Arabic, there are five words that are called the five nouns. These nouns are أبٌ 'father,' أخٌ 'brother,' حَمٌ 'father-in-law,' فمٌ 'mouth,' and ذو 'owner' or 'possessor.' These nouns are distinct from regular nouns; thus they have special forms. When these five nouns are singular and followed by another noun in the genitive case, or followed by suffixed pronouns, they end in one of the long vowels (ي - و - ا), which serve as markers. They end in الواو when nominative, الألف when accusative, and الياء when genitive. The most used of these five nouns are أبٌ , أخٌ , and ذو . Examples:

Noun	Nominative	Meaning
أبٌ	حضـر أبـو الطالبِ	The student's father came
	حضر أبوه	His father came
أخٌ	حضر أخو الطالبِ	The student's brother came
	حضر أخوهُ	His brother came

Noun	Accusative	Meaning
أبٌ	شاهدتُ أبـا الطالبِ	I saw the student's father
	شـاهدتُ أباهُ	I saw his father
أخٌ	شـاهدتُ أخـا الطالبِ	I saw the student's brother
	شـاهدتُ أخاهُ	I saw his brother

Noun	Genitive	Meaning
أبٌ	ذهبتُ مع أبي الطالبِ	I went with the student's father
	ذهبت مع أبيهِ	I went with his father
أخٌ	ذهبتُ مع أخي الطالبِ	I went with the student's brother
	ذهبت مع أخيهِ	I went with his brother

If these nouns are singular but not followed by a genitive noun or by suffixed pronouns, then they are treated like regular nouns. Examples:

Meaning	Nominative	Noun
A father came	حضـر أبٌ	أبٌ
A father and a mother came	حضر أبٌ وأمٌّ	
A brother came	حضر أخٌ	أخٌ
A brother and a sister came	حضر أخٌ وأختٌ	

Meaning	Accusative	Noun
I saw a father	شاهدتُ أبـاً	أبٌ
I saw a father and a mother	شـاهدتُ أباً وأمًّا	
I saw a brother	شاهدتُ أخـاً	أخٌ
I saw a brother and a sister	شـاهدتُ أخـاً وأختاً	

Meaning	Genitive	Noun
I went with a father	ذهبتُ مع أبٍ	أبٌ
I went with a father and a mother	ذهبت مع أبٍ وأمٍ	
I went with a brother	ذهبتُ مع أخٍ	أخٌ
I went with a brother and a sister	ذهبت مع أخٍ وأختٍ	

The noun ذو 'owner' or 'possessor' is always followed by a genitive and used as the first term of *idafa*. The feminine of ذو is ذات. Examples:

Meaning	Nominative	Noun
The wealthy man came	حضر ذو المالِ	ذو
The wealthy woman came	حضرت ذاتُ المالِ	ذاتُ

Meaning	Accusative	Noun
I saw the wealthy man	شاهدتُ ذا المالِ	ذو
I saw the wealthy woman	شاهدتُ ذاتَ المالِ	ذاتُ

Meaning	Genitive	Noun
I went with the wealthy man	ذهبتُ مع ذي المالِ	ذو
I went with the wealthy woman	ذهبتُ مع ذاتِ المالِ	ذاتُ

❖

2. Hollow Verbs – الفعل الأجوف

The hollow verb (الفِعْل الأجْوَف) is a verb whose original middle radical is واو or ياء, as in the verb كانَ whose root is the radicals ك و ن (Lesson 11). The hollow verb زار is similar. Its root is ز و ر. The radicals of the hollow verb سارَ are the radicals س ي ر. The conjugation of a hollow verb is slightly different from the sound verb. Hollow verbs have two forms of stem in the perfect and two forms of stem in the imperfect.

A. The hollow verb whose medial radical is و, like the verb زار - يزور, has two forms of stem in the perfect. One is زار as in زارَ + تْ, and the other is زُرْ as in زُرْتُ + تْ. The imperfect also has two forms of stem. One is - زور - as in زور + يـ and, the second is زُرْ as in زُرْ + نَ.

Below are the conjugations of the hollow verb whose medial radical is و, as exemplified in the verb زار 'to visit.'

Imperative	Imperfect (Jussive)	Imperfect (Subjunctive)	Imperfect (Indicative)	Perfect (Past)	Independent Pronoun
	يَزُرْ	يزورَ	يزورُ	زار	هو
	تَزُرْ	تزورَ	تزورُ	زارتْ	هي
	يزورا	يزورا	يزورانِ	زارا	هما
	تزورا	تزورا	تزورانِ	زارتا	هما
	يزوروا	يزوروا	يزورونَ	زاروا	هم
	يَزُرْنَ	يَزُرْنَ	يَزُرْنَ	زُرْنَ	هنَّ
زُرْ	تَزُرْ	تزورَ	تزورُ	زُرْتَ	أنتَ
زُوري	تزوري	تزوري	تزورينَ	زُرْتِ	أنتِ
زُورا	تزورا	تزورا	تزورانِ	زُرْتُمَا	أنتما
زُورا	تزورا	تزورا	تزورانِ	زُرْتُمَا	أنتما
زُوروا	تزوروا	تزوروا	تزورونَ	زُرْتُم	أنتم
زُرْنَ	تَزُرْنَ	تَزُرْنَ	تَزُرْنَ	زُرْتُنَّ	أنتنَّ
	أزُرْ	أزورَ	أزورُ	زُرْتُ	أنا
	نزُرْ	نزورَ	نزورُ	زُرْنا	نحنُ

❖

B. The hollow verb whose medial radical is ي, like the verb سار – يسير , has two forms of stem in the perfect. One is سار as in سارَ + تْ, and the other stem is سِرْ as in سِرْ + تُ. The imperfect also has two forms of stem. One is سير as in يـ + سِرْ + نَ, and the second is سِرْ as in نَ + سِرْ + يـ.

Below are the conjugations of the hollow verb whose medial radical is ي, as exemplified in the verb سار 'to walk.'

Imperative	Imperfect (Jussive)	Imperfect (Subjunctive)	Imperfect (Indicative)	Perfect (Past)	Independent Pronoun
	يَسِرْ	يسيرَ	يسيرُ	سار	هو
	تَسِرْ	تسيرَ	تسيرُ	سارتْ	هي
	يسيرا	يسيرا	يسيران	سارا	هما
	تسيرا	تسيرا	تسيران	سارتا	هما
	يسيروا	يسيروا	يسيرونَ	ساروا	هم
	يَسِرْنَ	يَسِرْنَ	يَسِرْنَ	سِرْنَ	هنَّ
سِرْ	تَسِرْ	تسيرَ	تسيرُ	سِرْتَ	أنتَ
سيري	تسيري	تسيري	تسيرينَ	سِرْتِ	أنتِ
سيرا	تسيرا	تسيرا	تسيرانِ	سِرْتُما	أنتما
سيرا	تسيرا	تسيرا	تسيرانِ	سِرْتُما	أنتما
سيروا	تسيروا	تسيروا	تسيرونَ	سِرْتُم	انتم
سِرْنَ	تَسِرْنَ	تَسِرْنَ	تَسِرْنَ	سِرْتُنَّ	أنتنَّ
	أسِرْ	أسيرَ	أسيرُ	سِرْتُ	أنا
	نسِرْ	نسيرَ	نسيرُ	سِرْنا	نحنُ

❖

Drill 1: Change the verbs to imperfect jussive.

١ - كان كريم في البيت حين وصلتُ.

٢ - زرتُ الآثار القديمة في لبنــان.

٣ - عادوا إلى أمريكا بعد الدراسة في القاهرة.

٤ - سرنَ على الشـاطىء مساء أمس.

٥ - قالا لي إن دراسة العربية صعبة.

٦ - زال الفقر من العالم.

Drill 2: Fill in the blanks using the correct verb form.

1 - أريد أن _____ إن الكتاب صعب جداً. (قال)

2 - أحبُّ أن _____ أصدقائي للحفلة. (دعا)

3 - منذ حضوري من الشرق الأوسط لم _____ صديقي عدنان. (زار)

4 - أنا لن _____ إليه. (عاد)

5 - أنا لا أريد أن _____ إلى الجامعة. (سار)

6 - هي لم _____ ليلة أمس. (نام)

❖

Drill 3: Use the indicated noun in the correct form.

1 - حضر _____ صديقي. (أب)

2 - شاهدتُ _____ استاذي. (أخ)

3 - ذهبتُ مع _____ العلم. (ذو)

4 - جاء المدير إلى المطعم مع _____. (أخ)

5 - رأيتُ الفتاة _____ الشعر الأسود الطويل. (ذات)

6 - كتبت إلى الرجل _____ المال الكثير. (ذو)

7 - كنت في الشرق الأوسط مع _____ خليل. (أب)

8 - زرتُ _____كَ في المغرب. (أب)

وقل رب زدني عِلمـا - God increase my knowledge

الدَّرْسُ العِشْرُونَ

كُتَّابٌ حَدِيثُونَ

Lesson Twenty

Modern Arab Writers

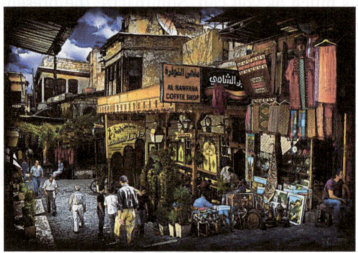

Fig 20.1 – Syrian street

Lesson Twenty Contents

🎧 Vocabulary - المفردات

🎧 Words and Expressions - كلمات وتعابير

💿 Basic Text - النص الأساسي

    ❖ Sun on a Cloudy Day - الشمس في يوم غائم

Grammar - القواعد

    Numbers - الأعداد

    1. Number One (واحد) و (واحدة)

    2. Number Two (إثنان) و (إثنتان)

    3. Numbers 3-10 (الأعداد ثلاثة إلى عشرة)

    4. Numbers 11-19 (الأعداد أحَـد عَشَرَ إلى تسعة عَشَرَ)

    5. Number 10 (عَشْـرُ) و (عَشَـرَة)

    6. Numbers 20-90 (الأعداد عشرون إلى تسعون)

    7. Hundred - (مائة) or (مئة)

    8. Thousand - (ألفٌ)

💿 Comprehension Text - الفهم والاستيعاب

    ❖ Season of Migration to the North - موسم الهجرة إلى الشمال

🎧 Let's Speak Arabic - المحادثة

    ❖ Drinks - المشروبات

💿 Window into Arab Culture - من الثقافة العربية

    ❖ The Arabic Novel - الرواية العربية

🎧

المفردات

to pass, go	مَرَّ، يَمُرُّ، مُرُورٌ
Musician	مُوسِيقِيٌّ
reed flute	شَبَّابَة
to feel	أَحَسَّ، يُحِسُّ، إِحْسَاسٌ
I was born	خُلِقْتُ
thing, something	شَيْءٌ ج. أَشْيَاءُ
to write down, record	دَوَّنَ، يُدَوِّنُ، تَدْوِينٌ
honest, trustworthy	أَمِينٌ ج. أُمَنَاءُ
lute	عُودٌ
Violin	كَمَانٌ
Mandolin	بُزُقٌ
to play a musical instrument	عَزَفَ، يَعْزِفُ، عَزْفٌ
to choose (VIII)	اِخْتَارَ، يَخْتَارُ، اِخْتِيَارٌ
to wish, desire, want	رَغِبَ، يَرْغَبُ، رَغْبَة
to discover, find out	اِكْتَشَفَ، يَكْتَشِفُ، اِكْتِشَافٌ
to be convinced, content (VIII)	اِقْتَنَعَ، يَقْتَنِعُ، اِقْتِنَاع

☸

🎧

كلمات وتعابير

typical of that age	تُنَاسِبُ ذلكَ العُمْر
within reach	تطولُهَا يَدِي
I had several interests	كانَ لي هِوايَاتٌ
to play any musical instrument	العَزْفُ على أيَّةِ آلَةٍ مُوسِيقِيَّة
young men	شَبَابٌ
beneath windows	تَحْتَ النَّوافِذِ
midnight	مُنْتَصَف الليل
to bring forth something	لاسْتِخْرَاج شَيْءٍ مَا
I could not express in words	لا أستطيعُ التعبيرَ بالكلماتِ
mainly by chance	لَمْ أَكُنْ أَقْصِدُهُ بالذات

although I took lessons	رَغْم مُثابَرَتـي على الدُّرُوس
for some time	لِبَعْض الوقتِ
it was stupid to continue	مِن السُّخْفِ أن أمْضي
I lack an ear for music	أذنِـي غَيْرُ مُوسيقيَّة
I lack the necessary patience	عَلامَتي في الصَّبْر صِفْـرٌ
easily bored	سَريعُ الضَّجَر
I flirt with his daughter	أغَازلُ ابْنَتَـهُ
tuning his instrument	يُدَوْزنُ الآلَـة
since, as, inasmuch as	طالَـمَا

الله – God

Drill 1: Fill in each blank with the correct word.

one year	١ - عـام _____
two years	٢ - عامان _____
one year	٣ - سنة _____
two years	٤ - سنتان _____
three years	٥ - _____أعـوامٍ
three years	٦ - _____ سنواتٍ
four female students	٧ - _____طالباتٍ
five male students	٨ - _____ طلابٍ
nine universities	٩ - _____ جامعاتٍ
ten books	١٠ - _____ كتبٍ

❖

Drill 2: Fill in each blank with the correct word.

13 years	١ - ثلاثةَ _____ عاماً
14 years	٢ - أربعَ _____ سنةً
15 male students	٣ - _____ عشَرَ طالباً
16 female students	٤ - _____ عَشْرَةَ طالبة
18 years	٥ - _____ ____ عاماً
19 years	٦ - _____ _____ سنةً
20 years	٧ - _____ عاماً
21 years	٨ - _____ _____ سنةً
A hundred years	٩ - _____ سنة
A thousand years	١٠ - _____ _____

❖

Drill 3: Write the correct Arabic word.

60	_____	10	عَشَـــرَة
70	سَبْعُـونَ	20	_____
80	_____	30	_____
90	_____	40	_____
100	_____	50	_____

Drill 4: Fill in each blank with the correct word.

10 - ـــــــــ عَشَرَ عاماً	11 years	1 - إحدى ـــــــــ سنةً	11 years
11 - ـــــــــ عَشَرَ عاماً	12 years	2 - ـــــــــ عَشْرَةَ سنةً	12 years
12 - ـــــــــ عَشَرَ عاماً	13 years	3 - ـــــــــ عَشْرَةَ سنةً	13 years
13 - أربعةَ ـــــــــ عاماً	14 years	4 - ـــــــــ عَشْرَةَ سنةً	14 years
14 - ـــــــــ عَشَرَ عاماً	15 years	5 - خمسَ ـــــــــ سنةً	15 years
15 - ستَّةَ ـــــــــ عاماً	16 years	6 - ـــــــــ عَشْرَةَ سنةً	16 years
16 - ـــــــــ عَشَرَ عاماً	17 years	7 - سبعَ ـــــــــ سنةً	17 years
17 - ثمانيةَ ـــــــــ عاماً	18 years	8 - ثماني ـــــــــ سنةً	18 years
18 - تسعةَ ـــــــــ عاماً	19 years	9 - ـــــــــ عَشْرَةَ سنةً	19 years

❖

Drill 5: Fill in each blank with the correct word.
Example:

Year (f) عِشرونَ سنةً		Year (m) عِشرونَ عاماً	
10 - إحدى و ـــــــــ سنة	21 years	1 - واحدٌ و ـــــــــ عاماً	21 years
11 - ـــــــــ وعشرونَ سنةً	22 years	2 - ـــــــــ وعشرونَ عاماً	22 years
12 - ثلاثٌ وعِشرونَ ـــــــــ	23 years	3 - ثلاثةٌ وعِشرونَ ـــــــــ	23 years
13 - أربعٌ و ـــــــــ سنة	24 years	4 - ـــــــــ وعِشرونَ عاماً	24 years
14 - خمسٌ و ـــــــــ سنةً	25 years	5 - ـــــــــ وعِشرونَ عاماً	25 years
15 - ـــــــــ وعِشرونَ سنة	26 years	6 - ـــــــــ وعِشرونَ عاماً	26 years
16 - سبعٌ و ـــــــــ سنةً	27 years	7 - سبعةٌ و ـــــــــ عاماً	27 years
17 - ثمانٍ وعِشرونَ ـــــــــ	28 years	8 - ثمانيةٌ وعِشرونَ ـــــــــ	28 years
18 - ـــــــــ وعِشرونَ سنة	29 years	9 - ـــــــــ وعِشرونَ عاماً	29 years

❖

Drill 6: Translate into English.

1 - مئاتٌ من السنوات.
2 - ألفُ عامٍ وعامٌ.

٣ - والدي عمره ستونَ سنة.

٤ - في السنة 365 يوماً.

٥ - عمري ثمانية عَشَرَ عاماً.

٦ - عندي مئة وخمسة عَشَرَ دولاراً.

٧ - عمري تِسْعَ عَشْرَةَ سنة.

❖

Drill 7: Translate into Arabic.

1. one male professor
2. two female students
3. three cities
4. seven companies
5. nineteen years
6. four lessons
7. seven houses
8. ten universities

بسم الله الرحمن الرحيم - In the name of God

382

الفهم والاستيعاب: مَوْسِمُ الهِجْرة إلى الشَّمَال*

الطيب صالح: كاتب سوداني، ولد عام 1929 وتوفي عام 2009. عمل إعلامياً في القسم العربي لهيئة الإذاعة البريطانية وعاش في السودان وبريطانيا وقطر. من أعماله الأدبية: عرس الزين، ودومة ود حامد، ورواية موسم الهجرة إلى الشمال.

مَوْسِمُ الهِجْرة إلى الشَّمَال*

الطيب صالح

عُدْتُ إلى أهلي يا سادتي بَعْدَ غَيْبَةٍ طويلـةٍ، عُدْتُ بعدَ سبعةِ أعْوامٍ على وَجْهِ التَّحْدِيدِ، كنتُ خِلالَهَا أَتَعَلَّمُ في أوربا. تعلَّمْتُ الكثيرَ، وغابَ عَنّي الكثيرُ، لكنَّ تِلكَ قِصّة أخرى. المُهِمُّ أنني عُدْتُ وبي شَوْقٌ عظيمٌ إلى أهْلِي في تِلكَ القَريَةِ عِنـدَ مُنْحَنى النِّيل.

سبعة أعوام وأنا أحِنُّ إليهم وأحْلُمُ بهم، ولمَّا جِئْتُهُم كانتْ لحْظَة عَجيبَة أن وَجَدْتَنِي حَقيقة قائمًا بَيْنَهُم، فَرحُوا بي وضجُّوا حَوْلِي. ولم يَمْضِ وقتٌ طويلٌ حتى أَحْسَسْتُ كأنَّ ثَلجًا يَذوبُ في دَخِيلتي، فكأنَّني مَقْرُورٌ طَلَعَتْ عليه الشَّمْسُ. فقَدْتُ دِفْءَ الحَيَاةِ في العَشيرة، فقَدْتُهُ زَمانًا في بلادٍ، تموتُ مِن البَرْدِ حِيتانُهَا.

تَعَوَّدَتْ أذنايَ أصواتِهم، وألِفَتْ عَينايَ أشكالهم مِنْ كُثْرَةِ ما فكَّرْتُ فيهِم في الغَيْبَةِ. قامَ بيني وبينهم شيء مثلَ الضَّبابِ، في أول وَهْلـةٍ رأيْتُهُم. ولكنَّ الضَّبابَ راحَ واسْتَيْقَظْتُ ثاني يوم في فراشي الذي أعْرفُهُ.

Ⲇⲟⳝⳝ

* الطيب صالح، موسم الهجرة إلى الشمال، دار العودة، بيروت، 1969، بتصرف.

🎧

كلمات وتعابير

to go, leave	رَاحَ
when I came to them	لَمَّا جئتهم
did not pass	لَمْ يَمْض
I felt	أحْسَسْتُ
cold, chilly	مَقرور
tribe	العَشيرة
time (long ago)	زَمانًا
it (f.s.) used to	تعَوَّدَتْ
fog	ضَبَاب
Season of Migration	مَوْسِم الهجرة
absence	غَيْبَة
yearning	شَـوْقٌ
until	حَتى
inside me	في دَخيلتي
warmth	دِفْءٌ
I lost	فقدْتُ
whales	حِيتان
it was accustomed to	ألِفَتْ
I woke up	اسْتيقظْتُ
my bed	فِراشـي

🎧

المحادثة
المَشـروبات - Drinks

Repeat aloud the following question:

What would you (m.s.) like to drink?	ماذا تريدُ أنْ تَشْـرَبَ؟
What would you (f.s.) like to drink?	ماذا تريدينَ أنْ تَشْـرَبي؟

Now repeat aloud the following answer:

I would like to drink coffee	أريدُ أنْ أشْـرَبَ القَهْوة

Next, repeat the sentence and substitute the following words for القهوة:

water المَاء
milk الحَـليب
orange juice عَصير البُرْتُقال
tea الشَّـاي
pepsi البِـبْـسـي

Repeat the dialogue with a classmate.

৩৶৶

Homework - الواجب

1. Watch the video and read the text.

2. Identify the words you know. Look up the words you do not know and write down their roots, forms, and verbal nouns.

3. Translate the text. Then write a composition about the author.

Lesson Twenty-One Contents

Writers and Novelists كتاب وروائيون
1.   Abdelrahman Munif - عبد الرحمن منيف
2.   Ghassan Kanafani - غسان كنفاني
3.   Nawal El Saadawi - نوال السعداوي
4.   Hanan Al-Shaykh - حنان الشيخ
5.   Mohamed Choukri - محمد شكري
6.   Ahlam Mosteghanmi - أحلام مستغانمي
7.   Zuhair Jabbour - زهير جبور
8.   Haidar Haidar - حيدر حيدر
9.   Naguib Mahfouz - نجيب محفوظ
10. Jabra Ibrahim Jabra - جبرا ابراهيم جبرا
11. Gladys Matar - كلاديس مطر

Modern Poets شـــعراء حديثــون
12. Abdul Wahab Al-Bayati - عبد الوهاب البياتي
13. Badr Shakir Al Sayyab - بدر شاكر السياب
14. Nazik Al-Mala'ika - نازك الملائكة
15. Fadwa Tuqan - فدوى طوقان
16. Adonis - أدونيس
17. Khalil Hawi - خليل حاوي
18. Lami'a Abbas Amara - لميعة عباس عمارة

Classical Poets شـعراء تقليديــون
19. Abu Al-Tayyib Al-Mutanabbi - أبو الطيب المتنبي

Classical Prose النثر التقليـدي
20. Ibn Hisham - ابن هشـــــام

Writers and Novelists

كُتَّابٌ وَرِوَائِيُّونَ

1 - النصُّ الأول

عبد الرحمن مُنيف

Abdelrahman Munif

1933 - 2004

عبد الرحمن منيف: كاتب عربي ولد في الأردن، من أم عراقية وأب سعودي. وأقام في سوريا. من أعماله الأدبية: مدن الملح، الأشجار واغتيال مرزوق، وشرق المتوسط، وسباق المسافات الطويلة.

مُـدُنُ المِلح *

Cities of Salt

إنَّـهُ وادي العُيُـون.

فَجْأَةً، وراءَ الصَّـحْراءِ القاسيةِ العنيدةِ، تَـنْـبَـثِـقُ هذهِ القِطْـعَةُ الخَضْراءُ، وَكَأَهَّا انْـفَـجَرَتْ مِنْ باطِن الأرضِ أو سَقطتْ مِنَ السَّـماءِ، فهي تختلفُ عَنْ كُلِّ ما حَوْلـها، أو بالأحْرَى ليسَ بَيْنَـهَا وبينَ ما حولها أيَّة صِلةٍ، حتى ليحار الإنسانُ ويَنْـبَهِـرُ، فيندفعُ إلى التساؤل ثُـمَّ العَجَب "كَـيْفَ انفجرتْ المِياهُ والخُضْرَةُ في مكان مِثْـلِ هذا؟" لكنَّ هذا العَجَبَ يزولُ تدريجيًّا لِـيَحُلَّ مَكانَهُ نَـوْعٌ من الإكْبارِ الغامِضِ، ثم التأمُّل. إنَّـهَا حَالَـةٌ مِنَ الحَالاتِ القليلةِ التي تُعَبِّـرُ فيها الطبيعةُ عَنْ عَبْقَرِيَّتها وجُمُوحِهَا، وتبقى هكذا عَصِيَّةً على أيِّ تفْسِـيرٍ.

وادي العيون قد يبدو بنظر الذينَ يَسْكُنُونَ فيهِ مَألوفاً، وفي بَعْض الأحْيانِ، لا يُـثِـيـرُ تَساؤلات كبيرة إلا أهُّم، يُحِسُّونَ أنَّ قُـدْرَةً مُبَارَكَـةً هي التي تَرْعَاهُم وتُـيَـسِّـرُ لهم الحَيَاة.

❖

*عبد الرحمن منيف، مدن الملح، المؤسسة العربية للدراسات والنشر، بيروت، ص ٩، بتصرف.

المفردات والتعابير

stubborn	عَنيدة
wondering, questioning	تَساؤُلٌ
it (f.s.) exploded	اِنفجَرَتْ
sky, heaven	سَماء
indeed, in fact	بالأحْرَى
connection	صِلة
is confused	يَحارُ
difficult	عَصيّة
interpretation	تفسير
sometimes	بَعْضُ الأحيان
power	قدرة
a place such as this	مَكان مثل هذا
gradually	تدريجيًّا
vague, mysterious	غامِضٌ
contemplation	تأمُّلٌ
nature	طبيعة
its (f.s.) genius	عَبْقريَّتها
valley	وادي
they feel, sense	يُحِسُّونَ
blessed	مُباركة

3 - النصُّ الثالث

نوال السعداوي

Nawal El Saadawi
(- 1931)

نوال السعداوي: كاتبة من مصر، ولدت في القاهرة في عام 1931. وتخرجت في كلية الطب. من أعمالها الأدبية: الوجه العاري للمرأة العربية وامرأة عند نقطة الصفر والمرأة والجنس.

امرأة عند نقطة الصفر *

A Woman at Point Zero

قال لي طبيبُ السِّجْن إنَّ هذه المرأةَ حُـــكِـــمَ عليها بالإعدام لأنها قتلتْ رجلاً. ولكنها ليستْ كالقاتلات المُقيمات هنا في السجن. فهي شخصية مختلفة تماماً، ولن تقابلي واحدة مثلها داخل السجن أو خارجه. إنها ترفض مقابلة أحد. وترفض أن تردَّ على أحد. وهي لا تأكلُ إلا نادراً. ولا تنام إلا عند الفجر. تراها السَّجَّانة أحياناً جالسة شاردة محدقة في الفراغ ساعات طويلة. وذات يوم طلبتْ ورقة وقلماً وقضتْ ساعات كثيرة منكفئة فوق الورقة. ولم تعرف السجانة إذا كانت تكتب رسالة إلى أحد، أم أنها لم تكتب شيئاً على الإطلاق.

وسألتُ طبيبَ السِّجْن: وهل هي ستقابلني على الإطلاق؟

وقال: سأحاولُ أن أقنعها بأن تجلسَ معكِ بعض الوقت، وربما توافق حين تعلم أنك طبيبة نفسية ولستِ محققة من النيابة. فهي ترفض الإجابة على أي سؤال.

❖

* نوال السعداوي، امرأة عند نقطة الصفر، دار الآداب، بيروت، 1979، ص 5، بتصرف.

🎧

المفردات والتعابير

prison	سِجْنٌ
she was sentenced to death	حُكِمَ عليها بالإعْدام
different personality	شخصية مختلفة
prison guard, warden	سَجَّانة
inmates, prisoners	مُقيمات في السِّجن
to stare at	حَدَّق (مُحَدِّقة)
to withdraw, retreat	اِنْكَفَأ (مُنْكَفِئة)
at all, in any respect	على الإطلاق
I will try to convince her	سأُحاوِلُ أنْ أقنعَها
investigator	مُحَقِّقة (حَقَّقَ)
public prosecutor's office	النِّيابة

4 - النصُّ الرابع

حنان الشيخ

Hanan Al-Shaykh
(1945 -)

حنان الشيخ: كاتبة من لبنان، ولدت في عام 1945. تقيم في لندن، من أعمالها الروائية: حكاية زهرة ومسك الغزال وبريد بيروت وحكايتي شرح يطول.

حكاية زهرة *

The Story of Zahra

هل تفهمين؟ أم أنَّ حُبوبَ وجهكِ تشْغِـلُـكِ عن كلامي؟ عَلاقتي بكِ بدأتْ عندما أخَذَتْ رسائِلُكِ تصلني وأنا أجيبُكِ عليها، وأنا أعْرِضُ عليكِ الجيءَ، وأنتِ تقبلينَ. علاقتي بكِ كإنسان يربطني بالوطن وبنفسي، لأنكِ أنتِ العائلة، والإنسانُ بلا عائلةٍ هو بلا نَـفَــس.

لماذا ترتجفينَ، لماذا لا تدعيني ألتصق بكِ، وأنسى الحالة المؤقتة، وأقولُ بمجيئكِ جَاءَتْ بطاقةُ السلام، وها أنا سأعودُ إلى الوطن؟

هناك شعاعٌ امتـــدَّ منكِ ودخلني وشجَّعَــني على العودة إلى الوطن. أليسَ هذا يحدث، أنْ تُعيدي لي ثقتي واشتياقي الفعلي إلى الوطن. فلا أعودُ جالساً أفكر فيهِ. أرى شفتيكِ تعصران بعضهما البعض. وأراكِ تتكومينَ وتلتصقينَ بالحائط وتقولين "ما أنا فاعـــل؟". تقولين هذا بعد وقت طويل من الصمت، وبعدها تدخلين الحمام.

❖

* حنان الشيخ، حكاية زهرة، دار الآداب، بيروت، 1989، ص 85 ، بتصرف.

المفردات والتعابير

pimples	حُبوبٌ
it reaches me, arrives	تصِلني
I offer	أعْرضُ
you shiver, tremble	ترتجفينَ
I will return	سَأعودُ
I see	أرَى
my relationship	عَلاقتي
I respond, answer	أجيبُ
you accept	تقبلينَ
I touch, connect	ألْتصِقُ
it (m.s.) encouraged me	شَجَّعَني
your lips	شفتيك (شفتاك)

5 - النصُّ الخامس

محمد شكري

Mohamed Choukri
1935 - 2003

محمد شكري: كاتب من المغرب، من أعماله الأدبية: الخبز الحافي، ووجوه، ومجنون الورد، والسوق الداخلي.

الخــبــز الحــافــي *
For Bread Alone

أبكي موتَ خالي والأطفالَ من حولي. يبكي بعضُهم معي. لم أعُـدْ أبكي فقط عندما يضربني أحدٌ او حين أفقدُ شيئاً. أرى الناسَ أيضاً يبكون. المجاعة في الريف. القحطُ والحربُ.

ذات مساء لم أستطعْ أنْ أكـفَّ عن البكاءِ. الجوعُ يُؤْلِمُـني. أمصُّ وأمصُّ أصابعي. أمي تقول لي بين لحظةٍ وأخرى:

اُسْـكُـتْ، سنهاجرُ إلى طنجة. هناكَ خبزٌ كثيرٌ. لن تبكي على الخبز عندما نبلغ طنجة. الناس هناك يأكلونَ حتى يشبعوا.

أخي عبد القادر لا يبكي.

أمي تقولُ: اُنْظُـرْ أخاك. إنه لا يبكي. وأنتَ تبكي.

أنظُـرُ إلى سَحْنَتِهِ الشاحبة وعينيه الغائرتين فأكف عن البكاء. بعد لحظاتٍ أنسى الصبرَ الذي أستمِـدُّهُ منه.

دخل أبي. وجدني أبكي على الخبز. أخذ يركُلُني ويلكُمُني.

اُسْـكُـتْ، اُسْكُتْ، اُسْكُتْ، ستأكلُ قلبَ أمِّـكَ، يا ابنَ الزنا.

❖

* محمد شكري، الخبز الحافي، دار الساقي، بيروت، 2004، ص 9، بتصرف.

المفردات والتعابير

سَحْنته	his facial expression
أَسْكُتْ	Shut up!
سَنُهَاجر	we will migrate
طنجة	Tangiers
يَلكُمُني	he punches me
ستأكلُ قلبَ أمِّكَ	you will break your mother's heart
مَجَاعَة	famine
يُؤْلِمُني	he hurts me
ذات مساء	one evening
وجَدَني	he found me
يَرْكُلُني	he kicks me
ابنُ زنا	bastard

7 - النصُّ السابع

زهير جبور

Zuhair Jabbour
(1948 -)

زهير جبور: كاتب من سوريا، ولد في مدينة القنيطرة، عام 1948. من أعماله الأدبية: موسيقا الرقاد، والحلم مرة أخرى، والورد الآن والسكين، وحصار الزمن الأخير، وبيضاء بيضاء.

بيضاء بيضاء *

White, White

لم نَـنَـمْ البارحة. خَــيَّــمَ الهدوءُ على المدينةِ لـيْلاً، وقـد ارْتفَعَـت الأعلامُ، والصورُ، والزينةُ، واليافطاتُ. وأُغْلِـقَـت الشَّــوارِعُ مِنْ قِـبَـل رِجَال شُـرْطَةِ المرور، وتَوزَّعَ رجالُ الأمْـن في كـُلِّ مَـكان. القلقُ بادٍ على الوُجُــوه، فهي الساعاتُ الصعبة جداً، حيثُ بداية النهاية، واللمساتُ الأخيرة لِكـُلِّ عَـمَـل نفَّذناهُ، وكُنّا أمْضَيْناهُ بين الضَحِـكِ، والأَلَم، والعذابِ، والشَّــــقاءِ. ولن تُنْسَى تلك الأيَّـامُ التي سَـنُوَدِّعُهَا بَعْـدَ أيَّام.

لم تتوقفْ عملياتُ التنظيفِ منذ البارحة، عُمّالٌ هنا، وهناك غسيلُ شوارعٍ. كلُّ شيءٍ هادىءٌ الآنَ في هذه الساعاتِ الصباحيةِ. زُرْتُ الفندقَ الكبيرَ، وَجَدْتُ أعضاءَ الوفودِ المُشاركةِ يتناولونَ إفطارَهُم. لا تظهرُ على وجوهِهم أيُّ مَلامح قـــلـــق، أو خوف. هم لا يفكرونَ كما نفكِّرُ.

❖

* زهيـر جبـور، روايـة بيضاء بيضاء، دار السوسن، دمشق، 2009، ص 7، بتصرف.

المفردات والتعابير

we did not sleep	لَمْ نَنَمْ
quietness, tranquility	هُدوء
banners	يَافِطات
the streets were closed	أغلِقت الشوارعُ
traffic police	شُرْطة مُرور
apparent, obvious	بادٍ (بادي)
we executed, carried out	نفَّذنا
washing	غسيل
members	أعْضاء
they eat their breakfast	يتناولونَ إفطارَهُم
yesterday	البارحَة
was raised	ارْتفعَ
decorations	زينات
by	مِن قِبَل
was dispersed	توزَّعَ
touches	لَمَسَات
cleaning	تنظيف
delegations	وُفود
participating	مُشاركة
fear	خَوْفٌ

8 ـ النصُّ الثامن

حيدر حيدر

Haidar Haidar
(1936-)

حيدر حيدر: كاتب من سوريا، ولد في سنة 1936 في حصين البحر على الساحل السوري. من أعماله الأدبية: الزمن الموحش، ووليمة لأعشاب البحر، وغسق الآلهة.

الزَّمَنُ المُوحِـــشُ *

The Desolate Time

هَلْ تُـصَدِّقُ لـو قلتُ لكَ: أتمنى أحْيَاناً لو أنني وُلِدْتُ خَارِجَ هذا الوطنِ؟

بِـهُـدُوءٍ كنتُ أسْتَـمِعُ إلَيْهَا. وقَـدْ ارْتَـدَتْ فُسْـتاناً مُعَرَّقاً ربيعيًّا، يَحْبِكُ كُلِّيَّـةً جَسَـدَهَا.

قلتُ مَازِحَاً: فُسْـتانُكِ رائعٌ. لكِنَّ جَسَدَكِ أكْـثَـرُ بَهَاءً. هل سَمِعْتِ هذا في الماضي؟ في عَيْنَيَّ ثَـبَتَتْ نظراتُـها. وبطُـفـولـةٍ مُزْدَهِرةٍ، مُفْـعَمَةٍ بالسُّخْريَةِ، ابْـتَـسَمَتْ ولم تُـجِبْ. كَـان الناسُ يَعبـرونَ فَـوْقَ الأرْصِفَـةِ، وكُـنَّـا نَرَاهُم مِنَ النَّافِذَةِ، والرِّيحُ الصَّيْفِـيَّـة الجَافَـة تُحرِّكُ أعَالي الجِـبَـال.

بهدوءٍ تقدَّمْتُ نـحْوَهَا. بَيْنَ رَاحَتَـيَّ رَفعتُ وجْهَهَا المَنْكَـبَّ على الأرضِ: لِمَاذا تَبْكِـينَ؟ بَيْنَ أناملِي انْـسَابَتْ قَـطَرَاتٌ سَاخِنَةٌ. مَسَحْتُ عَيْـنَـيْهَا بظاهِرِ كَـفِّي. وبحرَكـةٍ خفيفةٍ، دَغْـدَغْـتُ شَفَـتَـيْهَا: هَـيَّا، ابْتَـسِمِي. لَـسْتِ وَحْدَكِ الجَرِيحَة في هذا العَالَـم.

❖

* حيدر حيدر، الزمن الموحش، المؤسسة العربية للدراسات والنشر، بيروت، 1973، ص 14، بتصرف.

🎧

المفردات والتعابير

Would you believe?	هل تصَدِّقُ؟
I wish	أتمنَّى
quietly, calmly	بهُدوء
a dress	فُستاناً
to bind, tight	حَبَكَ، يَحْبِكُ
totally, completely	كُلِّية
jokingly	مَازحاً
full of	مُفعَمَة بـ
wounded	جَريحَة
irony, sarcasm	سُخريَة
dry	جَافَّة
it moves	تُحَرِّكُ
towards her	نحوها
palms of my hands	راحَتيَّ
Why do you cry?	لماذا تبكين؟
my fingers	أناملي
drops	قطرَات
smile (f.s. imp.)	إبتسِمي

9 ـ النصُّ التاسع

نجيب محفوظ

Naguib Mahfouz
1911 - 2006

نجيب محفوظ: كاتب من مصر، ولد في القاهرة. حصل على جائزة نوبل للآداب في عام 1988، من أعماله الأدبية: أولاد حارتنا، واللص والكلاب، وعبث الأقدار، وخان الخليلي.

ثرثرة فوق النيل *
Chitchat on the Nile

إبريل. شَـهْـرُ الغُبَارِ والأكاذيب. الحجْـرَة الطويلة العالية. السَّـقْفُ مَخْـزَنٌ كئيبٌ لدخان السَّجائرِ. الملفاتُ تنعَمُ برائحةِ الموتِ. ويا لها من تسلية أن تلاحظ الموظفَ من جديةِ مَظهرِهِ وهو يؤدي عملاً تافِهاً. التسجيلُ، الحِـفْـظُ في الملفات، الصَّادِرُ والوارِدُ، النَّمْلُ والصَّراصيرُ والعَـنْـكَبوتُ، ورائحة الغبار المُتَسَلِّلة مِن النوافذِ المُغلقة. وسألَـهُ رئيسُ القَـلَـمِ:

‒ هل أتـمَمْتَ البيانَ المطلوبَ؟

‒ فأجابَ بلِسانٍ مُتَـراخٍ:

‒ نعم، ورفَعْـتُهُ للمدير العام.

فـرَمَاهُ بنظرةٍ نافذةٍ لاحَتْ كإشعاع بلوريٍّ من وراء نظارتِه السميكةِ. ودَبَّـتْ حَـرَكـة عجيبة في رئيس القلم فشمَلَـتْ أعضاءَه الظاهرة فوقَ المكتبِ. راحَ ينتفخُ رُوَيْـداً، فيمتـدُّ الاِنْـتِـفَاخُ مِن الصَّـدْرِ إلى الرَّقَـبَـةِ، فإلى الوَجْـهِ ثم الرأس.

❖

* نجيب محفوظ، ثرثرة فوق النيل، مكتبة مصر، 1988، صفحة 5، بتصرف.

المفردات والتعابير

the month of dust	شَهْرُ الغبار
lies	أكاذيب
room	حُجْرة
depressed	كئيب
smoke	دُخان
cigarettes	سَجائر
files	مِلَفات
ants	نَمْل
cockroaches	صَراصير
spider	عَنكبوت
head of personnel	رئيسُ القلم
tongue	لِسَان
neck	رَقَبَة
face	وَجْه

10 - النصُّ العاشر

جَبرا ابراهيم جَبرا

Jabra Ibrahim Jabra
1920 - 1994

جبرا ابراهيم جبرا: كاتب من فلسطين، ولد في بيت لحم وتوفي في بغداد. من أعماله الأدبية: صراخ في ليل طويل، والسفينة، والبحث عن وليد مسعود، وشارع الأميرات.

شارع الأميرات *

The Street of the Princesses

كنتُ في التاسعة عشرة من عمري يوم وصلتُ إلى بور سعيد، بعد رحلة طويلة في القطار من مدينة يـــافــا. وكانتْ تلك أول مرة أخرج فيها من بلدي إلى آفاق العالم العريضة. مليئاً بالحماس لكل ما يُـــثــير في العين والحواس.

أعلنتْ إنكلترا وفرنسا الحربَ على ألمانيا يوم 3 ايلول 1939 وبدأتْ بذلك الحربُ العالمية الثانية، وذلك بعد نهاية الحرب العالمية الأولى بإحدى وعشرين سنة فقط.

ويوم أُعْلِنَتْ، كنتُ مع علي كمال (الطبيب النفساني فيما بعد) في القدس، نتسقّط الأخبار من المِذْيَاع. فتصوَّرْتُ اندلاعَها في كل مكان من أوروبا في أسبوع أو أسبوعين. وأيقنتُ أن فرصتي للسفر إلى إنكلترا في بعثة دراسية قد ضاعت دفعةً واحدةً. وكنتُ قد هَيَّأتُ نفسي لها طوال ما يقارب السنة، أعَلِّمُ في مدرسة كئيبة، وأقضي بقية وقتي في المطالعة والكتابة والترجمة. غير أنني لم أكن خائفاً وأصررْتُ على السفر.

❖

---

* جبرا ابراهيم جبرا، شارع الأميرات، المؤسسة العربية للدراسات والنشر، بيروت، 1999، ص 25، بتصرف.

المفردات والتعابير

the day I arrived	يوم وَصَلْتُ
Port Said (a seaport in Egypt)	بور سعيد
full of enthusiasm	مَليئًا بالحماس
senses, sensations	حَواس
was declared	أعْلِنَتْ
World War I	الحَرْبُ العالمية الأولى
World War II	الحرب العالمية الثانية
psychiatrist	طبيب نفساني
radio	مِذياع
I was certain	أيْقنتُ
all at once	دَفعة واحِدَة
I prepared myself	هَيَّأتُ نفسي
I insisted	أصرَرْتُ

11 - النصُّ الحادي عشر

كلاديس مطر

Gladys Matar
(1962-)

كلاديس مطر: كاتبة سورية من مواليد اللاذقية 1962، من أعمالها الأدبية: رغبة غافية، وثورة المخمل، وخارج السرب، وفرح عابر.

رغبة غافية *

Dormant Desire

مُـبَـادَرَة

قالتْ لَهُ أُحِبُّكَ. ففتحَ عَيْنيهِ على سِعَتهمَا. قالتْ: أريدُ أنْ تكونَ زَوْجِـي وأنْ نُـرْزَقَ أطفالاً يُشبهُونكَ وأنْ نَشيخَ معاً. رفعَ حاجبَيْهِ مدهوشاً، بالرَّغم مِن الحبِّ في عينيهِ، إلاَّ أنَّهُ قال: لــمْ أعرفْ امرأة تُبادِرُ في الحــبِّ ! ثم أدارَ ظهرَهُ وَرَحَـلَ.

فكـَّـرتُ: رجُلٌ آخَـرُ مِن بلادي يَـكْـرَهُ حُـرِّيـتي.

شَـــوْق

في أوج الشَّـوْقِ، وَضَعَتْ يَـدَهَا على خَـدِّهِ. وَضَعَـتْـهَا بلُـطْفٍ وهُـدوء وحبٍّ. ارْتَبَكَ وقالَ لها، بالرغم من الحب في عينيه: كمْ مرَّةً فعَلْـتِهَا من قبل مع غَـيْري ؟

فكـَّـرَتْ إنْ قالتْ له لــمْ أفعلْها أبداً فلنْ يُصَدِّقَ وإنْ قالتْ له فعلتُها أكثرَ مِن مرَّة وكلما شعرتُ بعاطفةٍ حقيقيةٍ، فإنه سينعتُها بصفةٍ أخرى أبشع. تطلعتْ إليه وقالتْ: كمْ فرصةً خَسِرْتَ أنتَ لتـغيير حياتكَ نحوَ الأفضل! ثـمَّ رَحَـلَـتْ.

❖

* كلاديس مطر، رغبة غافية، دار الحوار، اللاذقية، سوريا، 2003، ص 33، بتصرف.

🎧

المفردات والتعابير

dormant	غافِيَة
desire	رَغبَة
to be blessed with children	نُرزَقَ أطفالاً
they look like you	يُشبهُونكَ
we grow old together	نَشيخ معاً
his eyebrows	حاجبَيهِ (حاجباه)
how many times	كَمْ مرَّة
you have done it	فعَلْتَها
to believe, trust	صدَّق ، يُصَدِّقُ
astonished	مَدهوشاً
despite, in spite of	بالرَّغم مِن
to initiate	بَادَرَ، يُبادِرُ
initiative	مُبَادَرة
to turn his back	أدارَ ظهْرَهُ
to leave, depart	رَحَلَ
his cheek	خَدُّهُ
to be confused, embarrassed	إرْتَبَكَ، يَرتبكُ

Modern Poets

شُعراء حديثون

12 - النصُّ الثاني عشر

عبد الوهاب البياتي

Abdul Wahab Al-Bayati
1926 - 1999

عبد الوهاب البياتي: شاعر من العراق. من أعماله الشعرية: عيون الكلاب الميتة، والكتابة على الطين، وقصائد حب على بوابات العالم السبع، وقمر شيراز.

ســـر النـــار*
Secret of Fire

في آخر يوم، قــبَّـــلتُ يديها

عينيها، شفتيها

قلتُ لها: أنت، الآن

ناضجة مثل التفاحة

نصفكِ: امرأة

والنصف الآخر ليس له وصف

فالكلمات تهرب مني

وأنا أهرب منها

وكلانا ينهار

لطفولة هذا الوجه القمحي

وهذا الجسد المشتعل الريان

أبتهل الآن

وأقرب وجهي

413

من هذا النبع الدافق ظمآن

في آخر يوم، قلت لها:

أنت حريق الغابات

وماء النهر

وسر النار

نصفك ليس له وصفٌ

والنصفُ الآخر: كاهنة في معبد عشتار

❖

*Abdul Wahab Al-Bayati: Love, Death, and Exile. Poems Translated from Arabic by Bassam Frangieh, Georgetown University Press, 2004, p. 304.

المفردات والتعابير

last day	آخِر يَوْم
ripe	ناضِجَة
description	وَصْفٌ
to collapse	اِنهَار - يَنهارُ
the gushing spring	النبعُ الدَّافِق
priestess	كاهنة
I kissed	قبَّلتُ
half of you	نِصْفكِ
it escapes	تهرُبُ
I pray	أبتهلُ
thirsty	ظمآن
Ishtar (a goddess)	عِشتار

13 - النصُّ الثالث عشر

بـدر شاكـر السَّـياب

Badr Shakir Al Sayyab
1924 - 1964

بدر شاكر السياب: شـاعر من العراق. من أعماله الشعرية: أزهار ذابلة، وحفار القبور، والمومس العمياء، وأنشودة المطر.

أنشودة المطر *
Song of Rain

عيناكِ غابـتا نـخيـلٍ سـاعـةَ السَّـحَر

أو شُـرفتـان راحَ يَـنـأى عنـهُـما القَـمَـر

عـينـاك حـين تَـبْـسمَان تُـورِقُ الـكُـرُوم

وترقـصُ الأضواءُ كالأقـمار في نَـهر

يَـرُجُّهُ المجذافُ وَهْـنـاً ساعـة السَّـحَـر

كأنما تَـنْـبِـضُ في غَـوْرَيْـهـما، النُّـجوم

❖

وتغـرَقـان في ضَـبَـابٍ من أسـىً شفيـفْ

كالبَـحْـرِ سـرَّحَ اليـدَين فوقَـهُ المسـاء،

دفءُ الشـتـاء فيــه وارتعـاشـةُ الخـريف،

والموتُ، والميلادُ، والظلامُ، والضياء؛

فتسْتَفـيقُ مِـلءَ روحي، رعشةُ البكاء

ونـشوةٌ وحشيـةٌ تعانـق السماء

كنشوةِ الطفـل إذا خاف من القمر!

❖

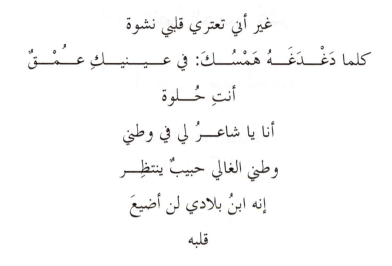

غير أني تعتري قلبي نشوة

كلما دَغْـدَغَـهُ هَمْسُـكَ: في عـيـنيكِ عـمْـقٌ

أنتِ حُـلوة

أنا يا شاعـرُ لي في وطني

وطني الغالي حبيبٌ ينتظِـر

إنه ابنُ بلادي لن أضيعَ

قلبه

❖

* فدوى طوقان، من كتاب مختارات من الشعر العربي الحديث، دار جامعة كاليفورنيا، 1974، ص 203، بتصرف.

🎧   المفردات والتعابير

like the dream	كالحُلم	coincidence	صُدْفة
distant, far away	قَصيَّة	sweet	حُلوة
it floated	طافتْ	two souls	رُوحَان
desire	رَغبة	song	غُـنوة
wealth, treasures	كُنوز	son of my native land	ابنُ بلادي
to tickle, stimulate	دَغدَغ	your whispering	هَمْسُكَ

420

16 - النصُّ السادس عشر

أدونيس

Adonis
(1930 -)

أدونيس (علي أحمد سعيد): شاعر من سوريا، ولد في عام 1930. من أعماله الشعرية: أوراق في الريح، وأغاني مهيار الدمشقي، وكتاب التحولات والهجرة في أقاليم الليل والنهار، ومفرد بصيغة الجمع.

أغـــنـــية *

A Song

من ثلاثينَ عاماً أضيعُ وأكتشفُ الآخرين

كان لي سُـــفنٌ ومرايا

في مغاورَ، حتى الصغار

يجهلون مفاتيحها

كان لي ساحران

يخطفان الهدايا

من كنوز البلاد البعيدة، من حارس البحار

❖

من ثلاثين عاماً

أضيع، وأكتشف الآخرين

حيثُ أعطيتُ وجهي للغيم، أعطيته للحقول الحزينة

حيث كُـــنَّـــا – أنا والصباح

عاشِـــقَـــيْـــن ربطنا مسافاتنا بثياب المدينة

وملأنا حقائبنا بالرياح

وجعلنا الرياح

لـــغةً وقصائدَ للآخرين.

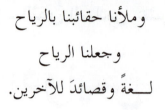

* أدونيس، الأعمال الشعرية، الجزء الثالث، دار المدى للثقافة والنشر، دمشق، 2001، ص 87، بتصرف.

المفردات والتعابير 🎧

I discover	أَكتشفُ	I disappear, get lost	أضيعُ
they are ignorant of	يَجْهَلون	caves	مَغاور
two magicians	سَاحِران	its keys	مَفاتيحها
gifts	هَدايا	they snatch	يَخطفان
I gave	أعْطَيْتُ	guard	حَارس
two lovers	عاشِقيْن	fields	حُقول
our distances	مَسافاتنا	we tied, linked	رَبَطنا
we filled	مَلأنا	clothing	ثِياب
winds	رِياح	our suitcases	حَقائبنا
poems	قصائِد	we made	جَعَلنا

422

17 - النصُّ السابع عشر

خليل حاوي

Khalil Hawi
1925 - 1982

خليل حـاوي: شـاعر من لبـنان. من أعماله الشعرية: نهر الرماد، والناي والريح، وبيادر الجوع، والرعد الجريح.

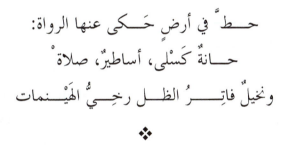

البَحَّـار والدرويش*
The Mariner and the Dervish

حـطَّ في أرضٍ حَـكى عنها الرواة:
حـانةٌ كَسْلى، أساطيرٌ، صلاةْ
ونخيلٌ فاتِـرُ الظلـلِ رخِـيٌّ الهَيْـنمات

❖

آه لو يُسْعِـفُـهُ زُهْـدُ الدروايش العُـراة
دوَّخَـتْـهـم "حَـلَـقاتُ الذكـر"
فاجتازوا الحياة
حلقات حلقات
حول درويش عتيق
شَـرَّشَتْ رجلاهُ في الوَحْـل وبات
ساكناً، يمتصُّ ما تنضحُـهُ الأرضُ المَـوات
غائِبٌ عن حِـسِّـهِ لن يَسْـتـفـيـق

❖

المفردات والتعابير

remove, take off (imp.)	أزِحْ
I look closely	أمْعِنُ
they bend, slope, lean	تميلان
clouds	سَحاب
I became	أصبحتُ
your glasses	نظارَتيْكَ
sunset	غرُوب
it undresses	تتعرَّى
for the sake of	من أجْل
shortsightedness	قِصْـرُ البَصَر

بسم الله الرحمن الرحيم - In the name of God

Classical Poets

شعراء تقليديون

19 ـ النصُّ التاسع عشر

أبو الطيِّــب المتنبي

Abu Al-Tayyib Al-Mutanabbi
(915 – 965)

أبو الطيب المتنبي: شاعر عباسي عظيـم، ولد في الكوفـة، العراق، عام 965 م.

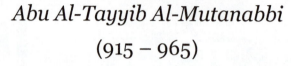

وَا حَـرَّ قَـلْبَـاهُ *

Oh, What Burning of the Heart!

وَا حَرَّ قَلْبَاهُ مِمَّنْ قَلْبُهُ شَبِمُ	وَمَنْ بجِسْمي وَحالي عِنْدَهُ سَقَمُ
مَـالي أكتِّمُ حُبّاً قَـدْ بَرى جَسَدي	وَتَـدَّعي حُبَّ سَيْفِ الدَوْلَـةِ الأمَـمُ
قَـدْ زُرتُهُ وَسُيوفُ الهِنْدِ مُغْمَـدَةٌ	وَقَـدْ نَظَـرتُ إلَيْـهِ والسُّيوفُ دَمُ
أنا الذي نَظَـرَ الأعْمَى إلى أدَبـي	وأسْمَعَتْ كَلِماتي مَنْ بِهِ صَمَـمُ
أنَامُ مِلءَ جُفُوني عن شَوارِدِها	وَيَسْهَرُ الخَلقُ جَرَّاها وَيَخْتَصِمُ
إذا رَأيْتَ نُيوبَ اللَّيْثِ بَارزَةً	فَلا تَظُنَّنَّ أنَّ اللَّيْثَ يَبْتَسِمُ
فَالخَيْلُ واللَّيْلُ والبَيْداءُ تَعْرفُني	والحَرْبُ والضَّرْبُ والقِرطاسُ والقَلَمُ
شَرُّ البِلادِ مكانٌ لا صَديقَ بِـهِ	وشَـرُّ ما يَكْسِبُ الإنْسانُ ما يَصِمُ

❖

*Bassam K. Frangieh, *Anthology of Arabic Literature, Culture, and Thought from Pre-Islamic Times to the Present*. Yale University Press, 2005, pp. 368-372.

المفردات والتعابير

Oh, what pain! Oh, what burning of the heart!	وَا حَرَّ قَلْبَـــاه
illness	سَقَـــــم
I visited him in the time of peace	قَدْ زُرتُـهُ وَسُيوفُ الهِنْدِ مُغْمَـدَة
to exhaust, tire out	بَرى
blind	أعْمَـى
sheathed	مُغْمَـدَة
paper	قِرطَاس
do not think	فَلا تَظُنَّـنَّ
to disgrace	وَصمَ، يَصِـمُ
cold	شَبِـــم
I conceal, hide	أكَتَـِّم
I saw him in the time of war	وَقَـدْ نَظَـرْتُ إليْـهِ والسُّـــيوفُ دَمُ
it (f.s.) claims, pretends	تَـدَّعي
deaf	صَمَـــم
lion	لَــيْث
fangs	نُـيُوب
evil	شَرٌّ
swords	سُيُوفٌ

God - الله

Classical Prose

النَّثر التقليدي

20- النص العشرون

Ibn Hisham

السِّيرة النَّبويَّة *

Biography of the Prophet

ابن هشـــام: أبو محمد عبد الملك بن هشـــام، مؤرخ وعالِم مصري، منحدر من جنوب الجزيرة العربية، توفي عام 834 م. وقد اعتمد ابن هشـــام على سيرة ابن اسحق الذي توفي عام 767 م.

❖

قال ابنُ إسْحاق: وحدثني وهب بنُ كَيْسـان قال: قـالَ عُـبيد: فكان رسولُ الله صلى الله عليه وسلَّم يُــجاورُ ذلك الشَّــهرَ من كـلِّ سنةٍ، يُطعِــم مَــنْ جاءَهُ من المسـاكين، فإذا قضى رسـولُ الله صلى الله عليه وسلم جِواره من شهره ذلك، كـان أوّلُ ما يـــبدأ به، إذا انصرفَ من جِواره، الكعبـــة ، قبل أنْ يدخلَ بيتَـهُ، فيطوفُ بها سَـبعاً أو ما شاءَ الله من ذلك، ثم يرجعُ إلى بيتـهِ، حتى إذا كان الشهرُ الذي أرادَ الله تعالى به فيــه ما أراد من كرامته، مِـن السَّــنَـةِ التي بعثه اللهُ تعالى فيها ؛ وذلك الشــهر (شهر) رمضان، خرجَ رسولُ الله صلى الله عليه وسلم إلى حِراء، كما كان يخرجُ لِــجِواره ومعه أهلُه، حتى إذا كانت الليلةُ التي أكْــرَمَهُ اللهُ فيها برسالته، ورَحِمَ العبادَ بها، جاءَهُ جبريلُ عليه السلام بأمر الله تعالى. قالَ رسـولُ اللهِ صلى الله عليه وسلم: فجاءني جبريـلُ، وأنا نائم، بنَـمَط من ديباج فيه كتابٌ، فقـالَ اِقـــرأ. قلتُ: ما أقرأ؟ قـالَ: فَـغَتَّـني بـه حتى ظننتُ أنَّـهُ الموت، ثم أرسلني فقـالَ: اِقـرأ. قلتُ: ما أقرأ؟ قالَ: فغتَّـني بـه حتى ظننتُ أنه الموت، ثم

أرسلني، فقال: اِقرأ. قلتُ: ماذا أقرأ؟ قالَ: فغتَّني بـه حتى ظننتُ أنـه المـوت،

ثـم أرسلني، فقال: اِقرأ.

فقـلت : ماذا أقرأ ؟ فقـالَ : " اِقـرأ باسْمِ رَبِّـك الَّـذِي خَـلَـقَ.

خَـلَـقَ الإنسانَ مِـنْ عَـلَـق. اِقرأ وَرَبُّكَ الأكْرَمُ الَّـذي عَـلَّـمَ

بالقَـلمِ . عَـلَّـمَ الإنسانَ ما لَـمْ يَـعْـلَـمْ ". قالَ: فقرأتُـها ثم انتهى فانصرفَ

عني وهـببتُ من نومي، فكأنما كُـتِـبَـتْ في قلبي كتاباً. قال: فخرجتُ حتى إذا كنتُ في وَسط

من الجبل سمعتُ صوتاً من السماء يقول: يا محمـد، أنت رسولُ الله وأنا جبريـلُ ؛ قـالَ :

فرفعـت رأسي إلى السماء أنظرُ، فإذا جبريـل في صورة رجل صافٍّ قَـدَمَـيْهِ

في أفـق السـماء يقول: يا محمـد، أنت رسولُ الله وأنا جبريـل. قـال: فوقـفت أنظر

إليه فما أتـقـدَّم وما أتـأخَّـر، وجعلت أصرِف وجهي عنه في آفاق السماء، قال: فلا أنظر

في ناحية منها إلا رأيتُـه كذلك، فما زلتُ واقفاً ما أتـقـدَّم وما أرجـع ورائي حـتى بَعَثَـتْ

خـديجـةُ رُسُـلَـها في طلبـي، فبلـغوا أعْـلـى مكة ورجعوا إليها وأنا واقـف في

مكاني ذلك؛ ثم انصرف عـني.

❖

* ابن هشـام، السيـرة النبويـة، منشورات دار إحيـاء التراث العربي، بيـروت، 1985، ص 236-241، بتصرف.

المفردات والتعابير

biography	سِيرَةٌ ج. سِيَرٌ
to tell, relate, talk about	حَدَّثَ، يُحَدِّثُ
to be in the immediate vicinity of	جَاوَرَ، يُجَاوِرُ
poor	مِسْكِينٌ ج. مَسَاكِينُ
to go around the Ka`bah	طَافَ، يَطُوفُ، طَوْفٌ / طَوَافٌ
miracle	كَرَامَةٌ ج. كَرَامَاتٌ
sort, type, kind	نَمَطٌ ج. أَنْمَاطٌ / نِمَاطٌ
silk, brocade	دِيبَاجٌ ج. دبابيج
to press, choke, suffocate	غَتَّ، يَغُتُّ، غَتٌّ
to set up in a row or line, line up	صَفَّ، يَصُفُّ، صَفٌّ
to go away, leave	اِنْصَرَفَ، يَنْصَرِفُ، اِنْصِرَافٌ

I turned my face away from him into the horizons to avoid looking at him	جَعَلْتُ أَصْرِف وجهي عنه في آفاق السماء

the holy Ka`bah in Mecca: a cubic structure that contains the black stone	كَعْبَة
the angel Gabriel, the angel of revelations who carried God's message to Prophet Muhammed	جِبْرِيل
Hira': a mountain located northwest of Mecca known also as "the mountain of light." The Prophet hid in a cave on the mountain during his flight to Medina. A spider is said to have miraculously woven a web at the mouth of the cave to dissuade the Prophet's enemies from entering to look for him since they thought the cave had been long abandoned.	حِرَاء

اِقْرَأْ باسْمِ رَبِّكَ الَّذِي خَلَقَ، خَلَقَ الإِنْسانَ مِنْ عَلَقٍ، اِقْرَأْ وَرَبُّكَ الأَكْرَمُ، الَّذِي عَلَّمَ بِالقَلَمِ. عَلَّمَ الإِنْسانَ ما لَمْ يَعْلَمْ.
Read! In the name of thy Lord who created - created man from a clinging substance. Proclaim! And thy Lord is Most Bountiful, He who taught (the use of) the pen, taught man which he knew not. *Qur'an* 96:1-5.

Section Three
القسم الثالث

Appendix and Glossary
مُلحـــق وقاموس

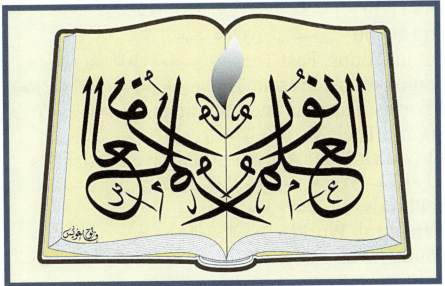

Arabic calligraphy: Knowledge is light - العلم نور

مُلحـق

Appendix

❖

Days of the Week - أيَّام الأسبوع

Saturday	Friday	Thursday	Wednesday	Tuesday	Monday	Sunday
السَّبْت	الجُمُعة	الخميس	الأرْبِعاء	الثُّلاثاء	الاثنين	الأحَد

❖

Seasons - فصول السَّنة

Winter	Fall	Summer	Spring
الشِّتاء	الْخَريف	الصَّيْف	الرَّبيع

❖

Months of the Year - شهور السَّنة

Islamic Calendar		Egypt	The Levant	English
مُحَرَّم		يَناير	كانون الثَّاني	January
صَفَر		فبراير	شُباط	February
رَبيعُ الأوَّل		مارس	آذار	March
رَبيعُ الثَّاني		إبريل	نيسان	April
جُمادى الأولى		مايُو	أيَّار	May
جُمادى الثَّانية		يُونيو	حَزيران	June
رَجَب		يُوليو	تَمُّوز	July
شَعْبان		أغُسْطُس	آب	August
رَمَضان		سبْتمبر	أيْلول	September
شَوَّال		أكْتوبر	تِشرين الأوَّل	October
ذو الْقِعْدة		نوفمْبر	تِشرين الثَّاني	November
ذو الْحِجَّة		ديسمْبر	كانون الأوَّل	December

❖

Holidays - الأعياد

The Prophet's Birthday	Eid of Breaking the Fast	Eid of Sacrifice	Easter	Christmas
عيد المَوْلِد النبوي الشريف	عيد الفِطْر (العيد الصغير)	عيد الأضحى (العيد الكبير)	عيد الفِصْح	عيد الميلاد

New Year's Day	Thanksgiving	My Birthday	Father's Day	Mother's Day
عيد رأس السنة	عيد الشكر	عيد ميلادي	عيد الأب	عيد الأم

❖

Colors and Defects - الألوان والعُيوب

Meaning	Plural	Sing. Fem.	Sing. Masc.
black	سُودٌ	سَوْداءُ	أسْوَدُ
red	حُمْرٌ	حَمْراءُ	أحْمَرُ
blue	زُرْقٌ	زَرْقاءُ	أزْرَقُ
green	خُضْرٌ	خَضْراءُ	أخْضَرُ
yellow	صُفْرٌ	صَفْراءُ	أصْفَرُ
white	بِيضٌ	بَيْضَاءُ	أبْيَضُ
deaf	طُرْشٌ	طَرْشاءُ	أطْرَشُ
lame	عُرْجٌ	عَرْجَاءُ	أعْرَجُ
blind	عُمْيٌ	عَمْيَاءُ	أعْمَى
mute	خُرْسٌ	خَرْسَاءُ	أخْرَسُ

❖

Numbers 1-10 (الأعداد من واحد إلى عشرة)

۱۰	۹	۸	۷	٦	٥	٤	۳	۲	۱	۰
عَشَرَة	تسعة	ثمانية	سبعة	ستة	خمسة	أربعة	ثلاثة	إِثنان	واحدٌ	صِفْر

❖

Numbers 11-19 (الأعداد من أَحَـد عَشَـرَ إلى تسعة عَشَرَ)

With feminine noun	With masculine noun	Numbers	Numbers
إحدى عَشْرَةَ سنةً	أَحَدَ عَشَرَ عاماً	۱۱	11
إِثْنَتا عَشْرَةَ سنةً	إِثْنا عَشَرَ عاماً	۱۲	12
ثلاثَ عَشْرَةَ سنةً	ثلاثةَ عَشَرَ عاماً	۱۳	13
أربعَ عَشْرَةَ سنةً	أربعةَ عَشَرَ عاماً	۱٤	14
خمسَ عَشْرَةَ سنةً	خَمْسةَ عَشَرَ عاماً	۱٥	15
سِتَّ عَشْرَةَ سنةً	سِتَّةَ عَشَرَ عاماً	۱٦	16
سبعَ عَشْرَةَ سنةً	سبعةَ عَشَرَ عاماً	۱۷	17
ثماني عَشْرَةَ سنةً	ثمانيةَ عَشَرَ عاماً	۱۸	18
تِسْعَ عَشْرَةَ سنةً	تِسْعةَ عَشَرَ عاماً	۱۹	19

❖

Numbers 20-90 (الأعداد عشرون إلى تسعين)

Acc. & Gen.	Nominative	Numbers	Numbers
عِشْرينَ	عِشْرونَ	۲۰	20
ثلاثينَ	ثلاثونَ	۳۰	30
أربعينَ	أربعونَ	٤۰	40
خمسينَ	خمسونَ	٥۰	50
ستينَ	ستونَ	٦۰	60
سبعينَ	سبعونَ	۷۰	70
ثمانينَ	ثمانونَ	۸۰	80
تسعينَ	تسعونَ	۹۰	90

❖

Verb Conjugations, Past Tense - تصريف الفعل الماضي

Subject Marker	Meaning	Verb Conjugation	Independent Pronoun
ـَ	he studied	دَرَسَ	هُوَ
ـَتْ	she studied	دَرَسَتْ	هِي
ـَا	they studied (m. dual)	دَرَسَا	هُمَا
ـَتَا	they studied (f. dual)	دَرَسَتَا	هُمَا
ـوا	they studied (m. plural)	دَرَسُوا	هُم
ـنَ	they studied (f. plural)	دَرَسْنَ	هُنَّ
ـتَ	you studied (m.s.)	دَرَسْتَ	أنتَ
ـتِ	you studied (f.s.)	دَرَسْتِ	أنتِ
ـتُما	you studied (m. dual)	دَرَسْتُمَا	أنتما
ـتُما	you studied (f. dual)	دَرَسْتُمَا	أنتما
ـتُم	you studied (m. plural)	دَرَسْتُم	أنتم
ـتُنَّ	you (f. plural)	دَرَسْتُنَّ	أنتُنَّ
ـتُ	I studied	دَرَسْتُ	أنا
ـنا	we studied	دَرَسْنا	نحْنُ

❖

تصريف الفعل المضارع - Verb Conjugations, Present Tense

Mood Marker	Subject Marker	Meaning	Verb Conjugation	Independent Pronoun
ـُ	يـَ	he studies	يَدْرُسُ	هو
ـُ	تَـ	she studies	تَدْرُسُ	هي
ن	يَـ + ا	they study (m. dual)	يَدْرُسَانِ	هما
ن	تَـ + ا	they study (f. dual)	تَدْرُسَانِ	هما
نَ	يَـ + و	they study (m. plural)	يَدْرُسُونَ	هم
none	يَـ + نَ	they study f. plural	يَدْرُسْنَ	هنَّ
ـُ	تَـ	you study (m.s.)	تَدْرُسُ	أنتَ
نَ	تَـ + ي	you study (f.s)	تَدْرُسِينَ	أنتِ
نِ	تَـ + ا	you study (m. dual)	تَدْرُسَانِ	أنتما
نِ	تَـ + ا	you study (f. dual)	تَدْرُسَانِ	أنتما
نَ	تَـ + و	you study (m. plural)	تَدْرُسُونَ	أنتم
none	تَـ + نَ	you study(f. plural)	تَدْرُسْنَ	أنتنَّ
ـُ	أ	I study	أدْرُسُ	أنا
ـُ	نَـ	We study	نَدْرُسُ	نحنُ

❖

441

Verbal Forms: Patterns and Meanings - أوزان الأفعال ومعانيها

General Meaning of the Patterns	Verbal Noun	Imperfect	Perfect	Form
simple action	فِعْل - فِعَالة...	يَفْعَلُ	فَعَلَ	I
causative, intensive	تَفْعيل، تَفْعِلة	يُفَعِّلُ	فَعَّلَ	II
reciprocal	مُفاعَلة، فِعال	يُفاعِلُ	فاعَلَ	III
causative	إفْعَال	يُفْعِلُ	أفْعَلَ	IV
reflexive of Form II	تَفَعُّل	يَتَفَعَّلُ	تَفَعَّلَ	V
reflexive of Form III (mutual)	تَفاعُل	يَتَفاعَلُ	تَفاعَلَ	VI
passive of Form I	إنْفِعال	يَنْفَعِلُ	إنْفَعَلَ	VII
reflexive of Form I	إفْتِعال	يَفْتَعِلُ	إفْتَعَلَ	VIII
colors and defects	إفْعِلال	يَفْعَلُّ	إفْعَلَّ	IX
reflexive of IV, causative	إسْتِفْعال	يَسْتَفْعِلُ	إسْتَفْعَلَ	X

❖

Patterns and Their Verbs - الأوزان وأفعالها

الوزن	Verbal Noun	Imperfect	Meaning	Perfect	Form
فِعْل	عِلْم	يَعْلَمُ	to know	عَلِمَ	I
تَفْعيل	تَعْليم	يُعَلِّمُ	to teach	عَلَّمَ	II
مُفاعَلة	مُكاتَبة	يُكاتِبُ	to write to someone	كاتَبَ	III
إفْعال	إعْلام	يُعْلِمُ	to inform	أعْلَمَ	IV
تَفَعُّل	تَعَلُّم	يَتَعَلَّمُ	to learn	تَعَلَّمَ	V
تَفاعُل	تكاتُب	يَتَكاتَبُ	to write to each other	تَكاتَبَ	VI
إنْفِعال	إنْكِسَار	يَنْكَسِرُ	to be broken	إنْكَسَرَ	VII
إفْتِعال	إعْتِراف	يَعْتَرِفُ	to confess	إعْتَرَفَ	VIII
إفْعِلال	إحْمِرار	يَحْمَرُّ	to become red	إحْمَرَّ	IX
إسْتِفْعال	إسْتِعْلام	يَسْتَعْلِمُ	to inquire	إسْتَعْلَمَ	X

❖

Forms I-X with Their Active and Passive Participles
أوزان الأفعال العشرة مع اسم الفاعل واسم المفعول لكل منها

Passive Part.	Active Part.	Imperfect	Perfect	Meaning	Form
مَفْعُول	فاعِل	يَفْعَلُ	فَعَلَ		I
مَدْرُوس	دارِس	يَدْرُسُ	دَرَسَ	to study	Example
مُفَعَّل	مُفَعِّل	يُفَعِّلُ	فَعَّلَ		II
مُدَرَّس	مُدَرِّس	يُدَرِّسُ	دَرَّسَ	to teach	Example
مُفاعَل	مُفاعِل	يُفاعِلُ	فاعَلَ		III
مُقاتَل	مُقاتِل	يُقاتِلُ	قاتَلَ	to fight	Example
مُفْعَل	مُفْعِل	يُفْعِلُ	أفْعَلَ		IV
مُكْرَم	مُكْرِم	يُكْرِمُ	أكْرَمَ	to honor	Example
مُتَفَعَّل	مُتَفَعِّل	يَتَفَعَّلُ	تَفَعَّلَ		V
مُتَعَلَّم	مُتَعَلِّم	يَتَعَلَّمُ	تَعَلَّمَ	to learn	Example
مُتَفاعَل	مُتَفاعِل	يَتَفاعَلُ	تَفاعَلَ		VI
مُتَراسَل	مُتَراسِل	يَتَراسَلُ	تَراسَلَ	to correspond	Example
مُنْفَعَل	مُنْفَعِل	يَنْفَعِلُ	انْفَعَلَ		VII
مُنْكَسَر	مُنْكَسِر	يَنْكَسِرُ	انْكَسَرَ	to be broken	Example
مُفْتَعَل	مُفْتَعِل	يَفْتَعِلُ	افْتَعَلَ		VIII
مُحْتَفَل	مُحْتَفِل	يَحْتَفِلُ	احْتَفَلَ	to celebrate	Example
-	مُفْعَلٌّ	يَفْعَلُّ	افْعَلَّ		IX
-	مُحْمَرٌّ	يَحْمَرُّ	احْمَرَّ	to become red	Example
مُسْتَفْعَل	مُسْتَفْعِل	يَسْتَفْعِلُ	اسْتَفْعَلَ		X
مُسْتَقْبَل	مُسْتَقْبِل	يَسْتَقْبِلُ	اسْتَقْبَلَ	to receive	Example

❖

<u>Broken Plurals</u> - جموع التكسير (Most Common Patterns)

I. أَفْعَالٌ

Plural	Meaning	Singular
أَسْـواقٌ	market	سُوقٌ
أَوْلادٌ	boy	وَلَـدٌ
أَمْطارٌ	rain	مَطَـرٌ
أَوْقـاتٌ	time	وَقْتٌ
أَعْمـالٌ	job	عَمَلٌ

II. فُعُولٌ

Plural	Meaning	Singular
بُيُوتٌ	house	بَيْتٌ
قُلُوبٌ	heart	قَلْبٌ
صُفُوفٌ	class	صَفٌّ
دُرُوسٌ	lesson	دَرْسٌ
حُرُوفٌ	letter	حَرْفٌ

III. فِعَالٌ

Plural	Meaning	Singular
بِحَارٌ	sea	بَحْرٌ
رِجَالٌ	man	رَجُـلٌ
جِبَالٌ	mountain	جَبَلٌ
طِوَالٌ	tall	طَـويلٌ
كِبَارٌ	big	كَـبيرٌ

IV. فُعُلٌ

Plural	Meaning	Singular
كُتُبٌ	book	كِتَابٌ
مُدُنٌ	city	مَدينة
جُدُدٌ	new	جَديدٌ
رُسُلٌ	messenger	رَسُولٌ
طُرُقٌ	road	طَريقٌ

V. أَفْعُلٌ

Plural	Meaning	Singular
أَنْهُرٌ	river	نَهْرٌ
أَعْيُنٌ	eye	عَيْنٌ
أَشْهُرٌ	month	شَهْرٌ
أَرْجُلٌ	foot	رِجْلٌ
أَسْهُمٌ	share of stock	سَهْمٌ

VI. فُعَلاءُ*

Plural	Meaning	Singular
سُفَرَاءُ	ambassador	سَفِيرٌ
أُمَرَاءُ	prince	أَمِيرٌ
خُلَفَاءُ	caliph	خَلِيفة
رُؤَسَاءُ	president	رَئِيسٌ
قُدَمَاءُ	old, ancient	قَدِيمٌ

VII. أَفْعِلاءُ*

Plural	Meaning	Singular
أَصْدِقَاءُ	friend	صَدِيقٌ
أَغْنِيَاءُ	rich	غَنِيٌّ
أَقْرِبَاءُ	relative	قَرِيبٌ
أَقْوِيَاءُ	strong	قَوِيٌّ
أَوْفِيَاءُ	faithful	وَفِيٌّ

VIII. مَفاعِلُ*

Plural	Meaning	Singular
مَكَاتِبُ	office	مَكْتَبٌ
مَسَارِحُ	theater	مَسْرَحٌ
مَصَانِعُ	factory	مَصْنَعٌ
مَطَاعِمُ	restaurant	مَطْعَمٌ
مَرَاكِبُ	boat	مَرْكَبٌ

IX. فَعَالِيلُ*

Plural	Meaning	Singular
شَبَابِيكُ	window	شُبَّاكٌ
صَنَادِيقُ	box	صُنْدوقٌ
عَصَافِيرُ	sparrow	عُصْفورٌ
قَنَادِيلُ	lamp	قِنديلٌ
عَنَاوِينُ	title, address	عُنْوانٌ

X. فُعْلانٌ

Plural	Meaning	Singular
قُضْبَانٌ	rod, rail	قَضِيبٌ
بُلْدانٌ	country	بَلَدٌ
شُجْعَانٌ	brave	شُجَاعٌ
شُبَّانٌ	young man	شابٌّ
فُرْسَانٌ	knight	فارسٌ

*Diptotes are in red.

Map of the Arab World - خريطة العالم العربي

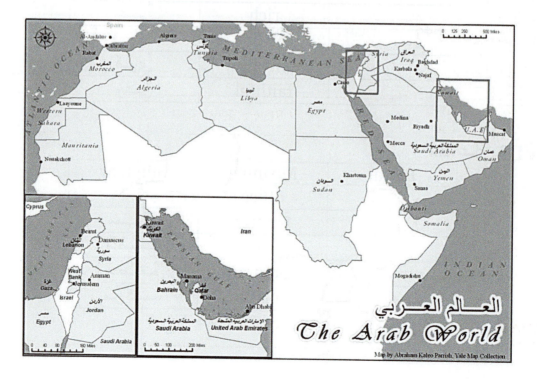

Arab Countries and Capital Cities - الدول العربية وعواصمها

العلم	Capital	العاصمة	Country	الدولة
	Cairo	القاهرة	Arab Republic of Egypt	جمهورية مصر العربية
	Baghdad	بغداد	Republic of Iraq	الجمهورية العراقية
	Damascus	دمشق	Syrian Arab Republic	الجمهورية العربية السورية
	Beirut	بيروت	Lebanese Republic	الجمهورية اللبنانية
	Amman	عَمَّان	Hashemite Kingdom of Jordan	المملكة الأردنية الهاشمية
	Riyadh	الرياض	Kingdom of Saudi Arabia	المملكة العربية السعودية
	Sana'a	صنعاء	Republic of Yemen	الجمهورية اليمنية
	Tripoli	طرابلس	Great Socialist People's Libyan Arab Jamahiriya	الجماهيرية العربية الليبية الشعبية الاشتراكية العظمى
	Khartoum	الخرطوم	Republic of the Sudan	الجمهورية السودانية
	Rabat	الرباط	Kingdom of Morocco	المملكة المغربية
	Tunis	تونس	Tunisian Republic	الجمهورية التونسية
	Kuwait City	الكويت	State of Kuwait	دولة الكويت
	Algiers	الجزائر	Republic of Algeria	الجمهورية الجزائرية
	Manama	المنامة	Kingdom of Bahrain	مملكة البحرين
	Doha	الدوحة	State of Qatar	دولة قطر
	Abu Dhabi	أبوظبي	United Arab Emirates	الإمارات العربية المتحدة
	Muscat	مسقط	Sultanate of Oman	سلطنة عُمان

Handwritten Letters - رسائل خطيّة

حيدر حيدر
Haidar Haidar – Novelist

❖

في الرسالة التي أرسلتها إليك لم ألمح إليك عن النسخة التي طلبتها لعدم توافرها آنذاك. منذ أسبوع حصلت على نسخة وحيدة أرسلتها إليك آمل أن تكون وصلتك وأرجو أن تخبرني عن وصولها لأنني أرسلتها مسجلة لأضمن وصولها.

في المستقبل آمل لو نلتقي هنا على شاطئنا الجميل لنمضي أياماً لا تنسى بين البحر والجبل والصيد حيث أعيش منذ أربع سنوات بعيداً عن ضوضاء المدن وبازارات الثقافة الراهنة.

عبد الرحمن منيف

Abd al-Rahman Munif – Novelist

❖

لذلك أرى التفكير بالروايات الأخرى: الأشجار واغتيال مسعود، حين تركنا الجسر، قصة حب مجوسية، سباق المسافات الطويلة، فإذا بدا لك أنَّ أياً من هذه الروايات تروق لك وللترجمة، فيمكن أن تتخذ الخطوات العملية لذلك.

آسف أن ليس تحت يدي الآن نسخ من الروايات، لكن سأحاول تأمينها في أقرب فرصة، أو سأشعر الناشر بإرسالها إلى عنوانك.

أرجو أن تبلغ الأخ محمد الجاسر تحياتي الحارة، وتقبل، سيدي، كل المودة والتقدير.

حنا مينه

Hanna Mina – Novelist

❖

قبل ذلك أصدرتُ رواية "حمامة زرقاء في السحب" وهي تعالج قضية اعتبرها أكثر القراء مؤلمة، لأنها تتناول موقف الإنسان حيال الموت، هذا اللغز الأبدي، الذي لم يُكتب عنه، كما لم يُكتب عن البحر والغابة والجبل والثلج والمعركة الحربيّة، إلا القليل في أدبنا العربي الحديث. وإنني أعمل على روايتين: "النجوم تحاكم القمر" أي أنَّ الشخصيَّات الأدبية تحاكم مبدعها، وهي رواية صعبة قد تستغرق وقتاً طويلاً، لذلك أرجأتُ إتمامها وبدأتُ بكتابة رواية "الرحيل عند الغروب" ذات المهاد الرومانتيكي، والتي آمل أن أنجزها هذا العام.

أدونيس

Adonis – Poet

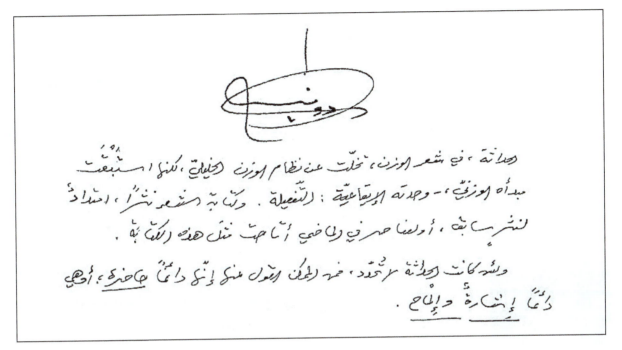

❖

الحداثة، في شعر الوزن، تخلَّتْ عن نظام الوزن الخليلي، لكنها استَبْقَتْ مبدأه الوزني، وحدته الإيقاعيَّة: التفعيلة. وكتابة الشعر نثراً، امتدادٌ لنثرٍ سابقٍ، أو لعناصر في الماضي أتاحت مثلَ هذه الكتابة. ولئن كانت الحداثة لا تُحدَّد، فمن الممكن القول عنها إنَّها دائماً حاضرة، أو هي دائماً إشارةٌ وإلْماح.

Adonis

451

Student Letters – رسائل الطلاب

وَفَــاء

مرحباً، أنا وفاء. اِسمي العربي وفاء، واسمي الأمريكي أوليفيا، أنا طالبةٌ في كُلِّيةِ كليرمُونت مكِّينا، أنا أَدْرُسُ اللُّغَةَ الْعَرَبِيَّةَ وَدِراسَات الشَّرْق الْأَوْسَطِ. أنا مِنْ مَدِينَةِ لوس أنجلوس في وِلاَيَةِ كاليفورنيا. أُريدُ أَنْ أُسافِرَ إلى الشَّرْق الْأَوْسَطِ. أنا أُحِبُّ الشَّرْقَ الأوسط، وأحب الْعَرَبَ، وأحب الطَّعامَ الْعَرَبِيَّ وَخاصَّة الْحُمُّص واللَّبْنَة والْفَلافِل والْكَبَاب. أُريدُ أَنْ أَسْكُنَ في الشرق الأوسط.

Olivia Uranga

نــور

Krysten Hartman

السَّلامُ عليكم. اسمي نور في اللُّغَةِ الْعَرَبِيَّةِ، وَلَكِنْ اِسمي الْأَمْريكي هُوَ كرسْتِن. أَنا طَالِبَةٌ في كُلِّيةِ كليرمُونت مكِّينا. أنا مُتَخَصِّصَةٌ في السِّيَاسَةِ وفي دِراسَاتِ الشَّرْق الْأَوْسَطِ. أنا أصلاً مِنْ مَدِينَةِ بُوسْطُن لكِنِّي أَسْكُنُ الآنَ في ولاَيَةِ كاليفورنيا. أُحِبُّ السَّفَرَ والْكِتَابَةَ وَقَضَاءَ الْوَقْتِ مَعَ عَائِلَتِي وَأَصْدِقَائِي. كُنْتُ في الْمَغْرِب في الْعَام الْمَاضِي، وَسَأُسَافِرُ إلى عُمَّان وعَمَّان في الْعَام الْقادِم لِلدِّرَاسَةِ والْعَمَلِ.

أبو صَخْر

اِسمي ريو فيشر، ولقبي العربي هو أبو صخر. أنا أدرسُ الفلسفة ودراسات الشرق الأوسط في كلية صغيرة جميلة في ولاية كاليفورنيا، اِسمها كليرمونت مكِّينا، بعد أن درسْتُ اللغة العربية فيها لمدة عامين، ذهبتُ إلى الأردن لدراسةِ اللغة العربية في الصَّيْف. وهذه أَوَّلُ مرَّة أزورُ فيها دولة عربية في حياتي. أنا أحب الشِّعْرَ العربيَّ. شعرائي المفضَّلون هم أبو الطيب المتنبي ونزار قباني وعبد الوهاب البياتي.

Rio Fischer

كامِلة

أنا اسْمِي كامِلَة، وكامِلة هو اسْمِي الْعَرَبِيّ، أمّا اسْمِي الأمريكي فَهْوَ كَمِيل. أنا طالبةٌ في كُلِّيَةِ بُومُونا وَمُتَخَصِّصَةٌ في السِّياسَةِ وفي دِراساتِ الشَّرقِ الْأوْسَطِ. أنا حَصَلتُ كَذلِكَ على شَهادَةٍ في الطَّيَران الْمَدَنيِّ، أي أنَّني الآنَ طَيَّار مَدَني. أنا من ولايةِ نيوجِرْزِي ولكِن أُفَضِّلُ أنْ أسْكُنَ في ولايةِ كاليفورنيا. عِنْدِي أُخْتٌ اسْمُها مَيا وهي سَتَذْهَبُ إلى الجامعة هذه السنة. وفي فَصْلِ الرَّبيعِ سَأذْهَبُ إلى سُوريَّة.

Camille Cole

أمُّ جَمَال

مرحباً. أنا ربيكا بِنـــز، واسمي في اللغة العربية أمُّ جَمَال. أنا من ولايَةِ أوريغان في الوِلاياتِ الْمُتَّحِدَةِ الأمْريكيَّةِ. أدرسُ في كلية كليرمونت مكينا، وأنا مُتَخَصِّصَة في التَّاريخ والحكومة. حصلتُ على منحة (فولبرايت) هذا العام، وسَأذْهَبُ إلى الأردن، وسَأُدَرِّسُ اللُّغَةَ الإنكليزِيَّةَ هناك. عائلتي صغيرة، أُمي مُمَرِّضَة، وأبي مهندس حاسوب. عندي أُخت واحدة، تسكن في ولاية ماساشوستس، وتعمل في دار نشر. أنا أُحِبُّ القِراءَة وكُرَةَ القَدَم واليوغا.

Rebekah Binns

داود

قَـــرَّرْتُ أنْ أتَعَلَّمَ اللُّغَةَ العربيَّةَ بينما كُنْتُ أمْشِي في الحديقة المركزيَّة في مدينة نيويورك. بدأت دراسة اللغة العربية أوَّلاً في المدرسة الثانوية. وحين اِلتحقتُ بالجامعة لم تكن دراسة العربية متوفرة، لذا سافرت إلى مصر لمدة فصل دراسي حتى أدرسَ العربية، وحين رجعت كانت الجامعة قد بدأت بتدريس العربية فتابعت دراستي فيها. أعتقد أنه من المستحيل أن يتقن الطلاب اللغة قبل أربع سنوات من الدراسة. الشعر هو أهم شيء في الثقافة العربية.

David Franzel

مليسا

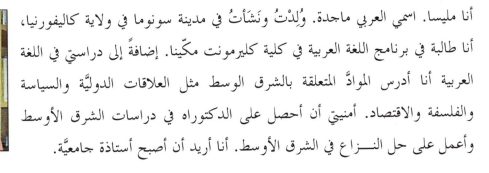

أنا مليسا. اسمي العربي ماجدة. وُلِدْتُ ونَشَأتُ في مدينة سونوما في ولاية كاليفورنيا، أنا طالبة في برنامج اللغة العربية في كلية كليرمونت مكّينا. إضافةً إلى دراستي في اللغة العربية أنا أدرس الموادَّ المتعلقة بالشرق الوسط مثل العلاقات الدوليَّة والسياسة والفلسفة والاقتصاد. أمنيتي أن أحصل على الدكتوراه في دراسات الشرق الأوسط وأعمل على حل النِّـــزاع في الشرق الأوسط. أنا أريد أن أصبح أستاذة جامعيَّة.

Melissa Carlson

قاموس

Glossary

- ❖ English - Arabic Glossary – قاموس إنكليزي - عربي –
- ❖ Arabic - English Glossary – قاموس عربي - إنكليزي –
- ❖ Words and Expressions – كلمات وتعابير –
- ❖ Let's Speak Arabic – المحادثة –

❖

قاموس إنكليزي – عربي

A

Abbasid	عَبَّاسِيٌّ ج. عَبَّاسِيُّون
ability, capability (v.n.)	إسْتِطاعَة (إسْتَطاعَ، يَسْتَطيعُ)
abyss	هاوِية
you accept	تقبلين
access, passageway	مَنْفَذٌ ج. مَنافِذْ
activity	نَشاطٌ ج. أَنْشِطَة – نَشاطاتٌ
advanced	مُتَقَدِّمٌ
to affect, influence	أثَّرَ، يُؤثِّرُ، تأثيرٌ
after that (prep.)	بَعْدَها
age	عُمْرٌ
I am used to	تَعَوَّدْتُ
American	أمْريكِيٌّ – أمْريكِيَّة
among them	مِنْهُم
and	وَ
another	آخَرُ ج. آخَرونَ
ants	نَمْل
apartment, flat	شَقَّةٌ ج. شُقَقٌ
apparent, obvious	بادٍ (بادي)
appointment	مَوْعِدٌ ج. مواعِدُ / مواعِيدُ
they are ignorant of	يَجْهَلون
army, troops	جَيْشٌ ج. جُيوشٌ
to arrive	وَصَلَ، يَصِلُ، وُصولٌ
I arrived	وَصَلْتُ
art	فَنٌّ ج. فُنونٌ
as far as the eye could see	على امْتِدادِ البَصَر
astonished	مَدهوش
at all, in any respect	على الإطلاق
to author	ألَّفَ، يُؤلِّفُ، تأليفٌ
authority, power	سُلْطَةٌ ج. سُلْطاتٌ

B

Baghdad	بَغْداد
banners	يَافِطات
banquet	وَليمَة ج. وَلائمُ
bastard	ابنُ زِنا
to bathe	إسْتَحَمَّ – يَسْتَحِمُّ
to be (I)	كانَ – يَكُونُ
to be baptized (V)	تَعَمَّدَ، يتَعَمَّدُ
to be changed, undergo change (V)	تَغَيَّرَ، يَتَغَيَّرُ، تَغَيُّرٌ
to be confused	يَحارُ
to be confused, embarrassed	ارتَبَكَ، يَرتَبكُ
to be convinced, content (VIII)	إقْتَنَعَ، يقْتنِعُ، إقْتِناع
to be in the immediate vicinity of	جاوَرَ، يُجاوِرُ
to be inflamed (VIII)	إلْتَهَبَ، يَلْتَهِبُ، إلْتِهابٌ
to be located, fall, lie on	وقعَ، يَقعُ، وُقوعٌ
to be separated (VII)	إنْفَصَلَ، يَنْفَصِلُ
to be unified (V)	تَوَحَّدَ، يَتَوَحَّدُ
beautiful	جَميلٌ – جَميلة
beauty (v.n.)	جَمالٌ
I became	أصبحتُ
because of	بسَبَبِ
to become	أصْبَحَ، يُصْبِحُ
before (prep.)	قَبْلَ
before that (prep.)	قَبْلَها
before, ago	قَبْلُ
to begin, start	بَدَأ، يبدأ
to believe, trust	صدَّق ، يُصدِّقُ
they bend, slope, lean	تميلان
big, large	كَبير – كَبيرة
to bind, connect	رَبَط، يربُط، ربْط

455

English	Arabic		English	Arabic
to bind, tight	حَبَكَ، يَحْبِكُ		it (f.s.) claims, pretends	تَدَّعِي
biography	سِيرَةٌ ج. سِيَرٌ		class	صَفٌّ ج. صُفُوفٌ
blessed	مُبَارَكة		cleaning	تنظيف
blind	أعْمَى		clothing	ثِياب
to blow, fill with air	نَفَخَ، يَنْفُخُ، نَفْخٌ		clouds	سَحاب
blue	أزرقُ - زرقاءُ		club	النَّادي ج. النَّوادي - الأنْدِية
bond, tie, connection	رابطة ج. روابطُ		coast, seashore	سَاحِل ج. سَواحِلُ
boring (adj.)	مُمِلٌّ - مُمِلَّة		cockroaches	صَراصير
bread	خُبْزٌ		coffins	أكْفان
breakfast	فطورٌ		coincidence	صُدْفة
to breathe	تَنَفَّسَ		cold	شَبَم
brother	أخٌ ج. إخْوَة		cold (adj.)	بَارِدٌ
to build	بَنَى، يَبْني		to collapse	إنْهَارَ، يَنهارُ
I bump into	أصْطَدِمُ		collective spiritual chanting (Sufism)	حَلَقاتُ الذِّكر
to burn, ignite, catch fire (VIII)	اِشْتَعَلَ		to come to an end	إنْتَهَى، يَنْتَهي
but	لكِنْ		to come back, return	عَادَ، يَعُودُ
by	مِن قِبَل		coming, arriving (AP)	قَادِمٌ ج. قَادِمُونَ (قَدَمَ، يَقدُمُ)

C

cafeteria, snack room, buffet	مَقْصَفٌ ج. مَقاصِفُ		company	شركةٌ ج. شركاتٌ
caliph	خَليفة ج. خُلَفاءُ		you (m.s.) complete (Imp. IV)	أكْمِلْ
to call (III)	نادَى - يُنادِي		complicated, complex	مُعَقَّدٌ، مُعَقَّدة
to call for	دَعَا إلى		I conceal, hide	أكَتِّمُ
to cancel (IV)	ألغَى، يُلْغِي		concept	مَفْهُومٌ ج. مفاهِيمُ
capital	عَاصِمَة ج. عَواصِمُ		conference	مُؤْتَمَرٌ
caves	مَغاور		to connect, be connected (VIII)	اتَّصَلَ، يَتَّصِلُ، اتِّصالٌ
center	مَركَزٌ ج. مَرَاكِزُ		connected, committed, bound	مُرتَبِط ج. مُرتبطونَ
to change, alter (II)	بَدَّلَ، يُبَدِّلُ، تبديلٌ		connection	صِلة
charm, enchantment (v.n.)	سِحْرٌ (سَحَرَ - يَسْحَرُ)		to conquer, open	فَتَحَ، يَفْتَحُ، فَتْحٌ
cheese	جُبْنٌ - جُبْنة		contemplation	تأمُّلٌ
child, baby	طِفْلٌ ج. أطْفالٌ		to continue, go on (X)	اِسْتَمَرَّ، يَسْتَمِرُّ
to choose (VIII)	اِخْتارَ، يَخْتارُ، اخْتِيارٌ		to continue, remain	ظلَّ
Christian	مَسِيحِيٌّ ج. مَسِيحِيُّونَ		to contribute	سَاهَمَ، يُسَاهِمُ، مُسَاهَمة
cigarettes	سَجائر		corner, pillar, basic element	رُكْنٌ ج. أرْكانٌ
city	مَدينة		courageous, brave	شُجَاعٌ ج. شُجْعانٌ
civilization	حَضَارَة ج. حَضَارَاتٌ		to crack, splinter	شَرَخَ، يَشْرَخُ، شَرْخٌ

I create	أَخلُقُ
to create, bring forth	أَحْدَثَ، يُحْدِثُ، إِحْدَاثٌ
to create, form	لأَصوغ
to criticize	نَقَدَ، يَنْقُدُ

D

darkness	الظلام
daughter	اِبْنَةٌ
dawn, early morning	سَحَر
deaf	صَمَم
dean	عَمِيدٌ ج. عُمَداءُ
decorations	زينات
Definite Article	الـ
delegations	وُفود
denied me, disowned me	أَنْكَرَني
to depart, recede	نَأى، يَنْأى
they departed (m. pl.)	رَحَلوا
depressed	كَئيب
to derive, take, draw	اِسْتَمَدَّ، يَسْتَمِدُّ
dervish	دَرْويشٌ ج. دَراويش
description	وَصْفٌ
the desert was there	جاءَتْ الصَّحراءُ
desire	رَغبة
despite, in spite of	بالرَّغم مِن
they died (m. pl.)	ماتوا
different personality	شخصية مختلفة
difficult	صَعْبٌ - صَعْبَة
difficult	عَصِيّة
difficulty	صُعُوبَةٌ ج. صُعُوباتٌ
dinner	عَشاءٌ
I disappear, get lost	أَضيعُ
I discover	أكتشفُ
to discover, find out	اِكْتَشفَ، يَكْتَشِفُ، اِكْتِشافٌ
to disgrace	وَصم، يَصِمُ
distant, far away	قَصِيّة
distinguished personality, great	عَلَمٌ ج. أَعْلامٌ

figure	
district, quarter	حيٌّ ج. أَحْياءٌ
diverse	مُتَنَوِّعٌ
diversity, variety (v.n.)	تَنَوُّعٌ (تَنَوَّعَ، يَتَنَوَّعُ)
do not think	فَلا تَظُنَّنَّ
doctor	طبيبٌ ج. أَطبّاءُ
to dominate, control, seize	سَيْطَرَ، يُسَيْطِرُ، سَيْطَرة
dormant	غافية
dreadful, horrible	مُريع
dress	فُستان
to drink	شرِبَ، يشربُ
drops	قطرات
dry	جافّة

E

easy	سَهْلٌ - سَهْلة
to eat	أكَلَ، يَأكُلُ
economy, economics	إِقْتِصاد
empire	إمبَراطوريّة
to encourage (II)	شجَّعَ، يُشَجِّعُ
it encouraged me	شَجَّعَني
end	نهاية ج. نهَاياتٌ
to enjoy (V)	تَمَتَّعَ بـ، يَتَمَتَّعُ بـ، تَمَتُّعٌ بـ
to enter	دَخَلَ، يَدْخُلُ، دُخُولٌ
to escape, flee	هَرَبَ، يَهْرُبُ، هُروبٌ
it escapes	تهرُبُ
to establish, found (II)	أَسَّسَ، يُؤَسِّسُ، تَأْسِيسٌ
evil	شَرٌّ
except for us, save us	سِوانا
to exercise, practice (III)	مارَسَ، يُمارِسُ، مُمارَسَة
to exhaust, tire out	بَرى
it (f.s.) exploded	اِنفَجَرَتْ
to extend, reach, stretch (VIII)	اِمْتَدَّ، يَمْتَدُّ، اِمْتِدادٌ
eye	عَيْنٌ ج. عُيُونٌ

English	Arabic
to listen, hear	سَمِعَ، يَسْمَعُ
to live	عَاشَ، يَعيشُ، عَيْشٌ
I live, reside	أَسْكُنُ
I lived, resided	سَكَنْتُ
living creature	مَخلوقاً يَتَنَفَّسُ
located, falling (a.p.)	واقِعٌ على (وَقَعَ، يَقَعُ)
location	مَوْقِعٌ ج. مَواقِعُ
logic	مَنْطِقٌ
I look closely	أَمْعِنُ
they look like you	يُشبهُونَكَ
lost, confused	حَيْرانُ
to love (IV)	أَحَبَّ، يُحِبُّ
love (v.n.)	مَحَبة
I love, like	أُحِبُّ
lunch	غَدَاءٌ
lute	عُودٌ

M

it made them dizzy	دَوَّخَتْهم
to make	صَنَعَ، يَصْنَعُ
man	رَجُلٌ ج. رِجَالٌ
manager, director	مُديرٌ - مُديرة
mandolin	بُزُقٌ
market, bazaar	سُوقٌ ج. أَسْواقٌ
I masked	قَنَّعْتُ
to meet (VIII)	الْتَقَى، يَلْتَقِي، الْتِقاءٌ
you meet (imp. VIII)	اجْتَمِعْ
you (m.s.) meet me (imp. III)	قابِلْني
members	أَعْضاء
mighty	جَبَّارة
million	مِلْيُونُ ج. ملايينُ
Minarets, lighthouses	مَنارات
ministry	وزارة ج. وزارات
minor cuts	خُدوش
miracle	كَرامَةٌ ج كَرامَاتٌ
modest, humble	مُتواضِعٌ ج. مُتواضِعُونَ

English	Arabic
moment, instant	لَحْظةٌ ج. لَحَظَاتٌ
most of, the majority	مُعْظَم
mother	أُمٌّ ، وَالِدَة
to move, travel about (VIII)	انْتَقَلَ، يَنْتَقِلُ، انْتِقالٌ
I moved, transferred	انْتَقَلْتُ
it moves	تُحَرِّكُ
much, many	كَثيرٌ ج. كَثيرونَ
mud	وَحْلٌ
musician	مُوسيقيٌّ
Muslim	مُسْلِمٌ ج. مُسْلِمُونَ
my age	عُمْري
my conscience	ضَميري
my father	أَبي ، والِدي
my fingers	أنامِلي
my mother	أُمِّي / والِدَتي
my name	اسْمي
my relationship	عَلاقتي
my wife	زَوْجَتي
mysterious	غامِضاً

N

naked (pl.)	عُراة
name	اسْمٌ
to name (II)	سَمَّى، يُسَمِّي
narrators	رُوَاة
nature	طبيعة
neck	رَقَبة
net, network, system	شَبَكةٌ ج. شَبَكاتٌ
newspaper	جَريدةٌ ج. جَرائِدُ
no, does not	لا
normal, usual (adj.)	عَاديٌّ

O

of course	طَبْعاً
I offer	أَعْرِضُ
oil	نَفْطٌ، زَيْتٌ

English	Arabic
okay, agreeable	طيِّب
old, ancient	قديمٌ
old, ancient	عَتيق
olive	زَيْتونٌ
one	واحِدٌ - واحِدَة
one by one	واحداً وراءَ الآخر
one evening	ذات مساء
openness	إنْفِتاحٌ
opportunity, chance	فُرْصَة ج. فُرَصٌ
orange	بُرْتُقالٌ
our distances	مَسافاتنا
our suitcases	حَقائبنا

P

English	Arabic
painter, artist, draftsman	رَسّامٌ ج. رَسّامُونَ
palace	قَصْرٌ ج. قُصُورٌ
palms of my hands	راحتيَّ
paper	قِرطاسٌ
participating	مُشاركة
to pass, go	مَرَّ، يَمُرُّ، مُرُورٌ
passion	عِشق
period of time	فترة ج. فترات
philosopher	فَيْلسوف ج. فلاسِفَة
physician	طَبيبٌ - طَبيبة
pimples	حُبوبٌ
pioneer	رائِدٌ ج. رُوّادٌ
place such as this	مَكان مثل هذا
to play a musical instrument	عَزَفَ، يَعْزِفُ، عَزْفٌ
poems	قصائد
poet	شاعِرٌ ج. شُعَراءُ
poetry	شِعْرٌ
poor	مِسْكينٌ ج. مَساكينُ
power	قدرة
I pray	أبتهلُ
president	رَئيسٌ ج. رُؤَساءُ
to press, choke, suffocate	غَتَّ، يَغُتُّ، غَتٌّ

English	Arabic
priestess	كاهِنة
prince	أميرٌ ج. أمَراءُ
prison	سِجْنٌ
prison guard, warden	سَجّانة
problem	مُشْكلة ج. مَشاكِلُ، مُشْكِلاتٌ
professor	أسْتاذٌ ج. أسَاتِذة
progress, advancement (v.n.)	تقدُّم (تَقَدَّمَ، يَتَقَدَّمُ)
to provide	وفَّر، يُوَفِّرُ، توفير
psychiatrist	طبيب نفساني
public prosecutor's office	نِيَابة
he punches me	يَلكُمُني

Q

English	Arabic
quiet, calm	هادِئٌ - هادِئة
quietly, calmly	بهُدوء
quietness, tranquility	هُدوء

R

English	Arabic
radio	مِذياع
rain	مَطَرٌ ج. أمْطارٌ
it reaches me, arrives	تصِلني
rebellious	مُتمرِّد
to recognize (VIII)	إعْتَرَفَ، يَعْتَرِفُ
reed flute	شَبّابَة
relative	قريب ج. أقارب، أقرباء، أقربون
religion	دينٌ ج. أدْيانٌ
remove, take off (imp.)	أزِحْ
renowned, famous	مَشْهورٌ ج. مَشاهيرُ
to represent (II)	مَثَّلَ، يُمَثِّلُ، تَمْثيلٌ
research, study	بَحْثٌ ج. بُحوثٌ
residence, home, house	مَنْزلٌ ج. مَنازلُ
I respond, answer	أجيبُ
restaurant	مَطْعَمٌ
revolution	ثَوْرة ج. ثَوْراتٌ

rich, wealthy	غَنِيٌّ ج. أغْنِيَاءُ
ripe	ناضِجَة
rise and fall	يَعْلو ويَهْبُط
road, path	دَرْبٌ ج. دُرُوبٌ

S

road, street	طَرِيقٌ / شارع
to rock, shake	رجَّ، يَرُجُّ
rocks	صُخورٌ
room	حُجرة
root	جَذرٌ ج. جُذورٌ
sail, tent	شِراعٌ ج. أشْرعَة - شُرُعٌ
secular (adj.)	عِلْمَانيٌّ
to secure, ensure (II)	أمَّنَ، يُؤَمِّنُ
I see	أرَى
seeing, watching (v.n.)	مُشاهدة (شاهدَ، يُشاهِدُ)
senses, sensations	حَواس
to set up in a row or line, line up	صفَّ، يَصُفُّ، صَفٌّ
shade, shadow	ظِلٌّ
sheathed	مُغْمَدَة
you shiver, tremble	ترتجفينَ
shivering	ارتعاشة
shortsightedness	قِصرُ البَصَر
Shut up!	اسْكُتْ
silk, brocade	ديبَاجٌ ج. دبابيج
silvery	الفِضِّيُّ
simple, modest	بَسِيطٌ ج. بُسطاءُ
simplicity (v.n.)	بَساطَة (بَسَطَ، يَبْسُطُ)
since, ago (prep.)	مُنذُ
they sink	تَغْرَقان
sister	أخْتٌ ج. أخَواتٌ
to sit	جَلَسَ، يَجْلِسُ
the sky closed in on him	أطبقتْ السَّماءُ فوقه
sky, heaven	سماءٌ ج. سَمَاوَاتٌ
small, little	صَغيرٌ
they smile	تَبْسِمَان

smile (f.s. Imp.)	إبتسمي
smoke	دُخان
they snatch	يَخطفان
soil, dust	تُرَابٌ
sometimes	بَعضُ الأحيان
son	إبنٌ
song	غُنوة
sort, type, kind	نَمَطٌ ج. أنْماطٌ / نِمَاطٌ
space	فضاء
specialist, specialized	مُتَخَصِّصٌ - مُتَخَصِّصَةٌ
spider	عَنكبوت
sport, practice, exercise	رِياضَة ج. رِيَاضَاتٌ
to stare at (II)	حَدَّق (مُحَدِّقة)
state	ولايَة
state	دَوْلَةٌ ج. دُوَلٌ
statue	تِمْثالٌ ج. تَمَاثيلُ
stones	حِجارة
storm, violent wind	عاصِفة ج. عَواصِفُ
strange, foreign	غَريبٌ ج. غُرَبَاءُ
street	شارعٌ ج. شوارعُ
strong, powerful	قويٌّ ج. أقوياءُ
stubborn	عَنيدة
student (f.s.)	طالِبَةٌ
student (m.s.)	طالِبٌ
I studied	دَرَسْتُ
he studies	يَدْرُسُ
she studies	تَدْرُسُ
I study	أدْرُسُ
suddenly	فَجْأة
Sunday	الأحْد
sunset	غروب
sweet	حُلوة
swimming	سِبَاحَة (سَبَحَ، يَسْبَحُ)
swords	سُيُوفٌ

T

English	Arabic
you (m.s.) talk (imp. V)	تَحَدَّثْ
to talk, narrate	حَكى
Tangiers	طنجة
tavern	حَانة
teacher	مُدَرِّس - مُدَرِّسة
to tell, relate, talk about (II)	حَدَّثَ، يُحَدِّثُ
tepid, lukewarm	فاتِر
thank you	شُكْراً
theater	مَسْرَحٌ ج. مَسَارِحُ
their depth, bottom	غَوْرَيْهما
then, furthermore	ثُمَّ
then, therefore	إذن
thing, something	شَيْءٌ ج. أشْيَاءُ
thirsty	ظمْآن
this (f.s.)	هَذِه
this (m.s.)	هَذا
thought (noun)	فِكْرٌ ج. أفْكَارٌ
it throbs/palpitates	تَنْبِضُ
thunder	رَعْدٌ ج. رُعُودٌ
to tickle, stimulate	دَغْدَغ
today	اليَوْم
tongue	لِسَان
it took roots	تَشَرَّشَتْ
torch	مَشْعَلٌ ج. مَشَاعِلُ
totally, completely	كُلِّيَّةً
to touch	مَسَّ ، يَمَسُّ، مَسٌّ
I touch, connect	ألتصِقُ
touches	لَمَسَات
to tour, walk around (V)	تَجَوَّلَ، يَتَجَوَّلُ
tourist, traveler	سَائِح سُيَّاحٌ - سُوَّاحٌ
towards her	نحوها
tradition, custom	تقليدٌ ج. تقاليدُ
traffic police	شُرْطة مُرور
transparent	شفيف
I traveled	سَافَرْتُ
trees	شَجَرٌ، أشْجَارٌ
he turned his back	أدارَ ظهْرَهُ
twenty	عِشْرُونَ
two (f. dual)	إثْنَتَانِ
two (m. dual)	إثْنانِ
two balconies, terraces	شُرْفتان
two lovers	عاشِقيْن
two magicians	سَاحِران
two souls	رُوحَان

U

Umayyad	أمَويٌّ ج. أمَويُّونَ
she undresses	تتعرَّى
university	جامِعَة
usually (adv.)	عَادَةً

V

vague, mysterious	غامِضٌ
valley	وادي
value	قيمة ج. قِيَمٌ
vase	إناءٌ
very much	جدًّا
good	جَيِّد
vineyards, orchards	كُروم
violin	كَمانٌ
to visit	زارَ، يَزورُ، زيَارة
visitor (a.p.)	زائِرٌ
Vocative Particle	يا

W

you (f.s.) wait for me (imp. VIII)	إنْتَظِريني
I was born	خُلِقْتُ
I was certain	أيْقَنتُ
was declared	أعْلِنَتْ
was dispersed	توزَّع
was raised	إرْتَفعَ

to talk, narrate	حكى
collective spiritual chanting (Sufism)	حلَقاتُ الذِكْر
sweet	حلوة
senses, sensations	حواس
lost, confused	حيْران
district, quarter	حيٌّ ج. أَحْيَاءٌ

خ

we imagined it	خِلْناهُ
bread	خبْزٌ
his cheek	خدُّهُ
minor cuts	خدوش
I was born	خلِقْتُ
to leave behind, leave (II)	خلَّفَ، يُخَلِّفُ، تَخْلِيفٌ
caliph	خليفة ج. خُلفاءُ
fear	خوْفٌ

د

to enter	دخَلَ، يَدْخُلُ، دُخُولٌ
smoke	دخان
I studied	درَسْتُ
road, path	درْبٌ ج. دُرُوبٌ
dervish	درْويش ج. دَراويش
to call for	دعَا إلى
to tickle, stimulate	دغدَغ
state	دوْلَة ج. دُوَلٌ
it made them dizzy	دوَّخَتْهُم
to write down, record (II)	دوَّنَ، يُدَوِّنُ، تدْوينٌ
silk, brocade	ديباجٌ ج. دبابيج
religion	دينٌ ج. أدْيَانٌ

ذ

one evening	ذات مساء

hungry (adj.)	جائِعٌ - جَائِعَة
cheese	جُبْنٌ - جُبْنة
mighty	جبَّارة
grandfather, forefather	جدٌّ ج. أجْدادٌ
much, very	جدًّا
root	جذرٌ ج. جُذورٌ
wounds, injuries	جراحٌ
wounded	جريحَة
newspaper	جريدةٌ ج. جَرَائِدُ
island	جزيرة ج. جُزُرٌ
we made	جعَلنا
to sit	جلَسَ، يَجْلِسُ
beauty (v.n.)	جمَالٌ (جَمُلَ، يَجْمُلُ)
beautiful	جميلٌ - جَميلة
army, troops	جيْشٌ ج. جُيُوشٌ
good	جيِّد

ح

fields	حُقول
his eyebrows	حاجبَاهُ
guard	حارس
tavern	حانة
to bind, tight	حبَكَ، يَحْبِكُ
pimples	حبوبٌ
stones	حجارة
room	حجْرة
to tell, speak, talk (II)	حدَّثَ، يُحدِّثُ
to stare at (II)	حدَّق (مُحَدِّقة)
freedom, liberty	حرِّيَّة ج. حُرِّيَّاتٌ
his senses	حسُّهُ
civilization	حضارَة ج. حَضَارَاتٌ
he landed	حطَّ
grandson, descendant	حفيدٌ ج. أحفادٌ
our suitcases	حقائبنا
she was sentenced to death	حكِمَ عليها بالإعْدام

to go	ذَهَبَ، يَذهبُ، ذَهابٌ

ر

bond, tie, connection	رابطة ج. روابطُ
palms of my hands	راحَتيَّ
pioneer	رائدٌ ج. رُوّادٌ
admirable, wonderful	رائعٌ - رائِعَة
to bind, connect	ربط، يربطُ، ربط
we tied, linked	ربطنا
man	رجُلٌ ج. رجالٌ
his two legs	رجْلاه
to rock, shake	رجَّ، يَرُجُّ
to leave, depart	رحَلَ
they departed (m. pl.)	رحَلوا
painter, artist, draftsman	رسّامٌ ج. رَسَّامُونَ
thunder	رعْدٌ ج. رُعُودٌ
to wish, desire, want	رغبَ، يَرْغَبُ، رَغْبَة
desire	رغبة
neck	رقَبَة
corner, pillar, basic element	ركْنٌ ج. أرْكانٌ
narrators	رُوَاة
two souls	روحان
sport, practice, exercise	رياضَة ج. رِيَاضَاتٌ
irrigation	ريٌّ
winds	رياح
president	رئيسٌ ج. رُؤَسَاءُ

ز

to visit	زارَ، يزورُ، زِيَارة
visitor (a.p.)	زائرٌ (زارَ، يزورُ)
glass	زجاجٌ
my wife	زوْجَتي
olive	زيتُونٌ
decorations	زينات

س

two magicians	ساحران
coast, seashore	ساحِلٌ ج. سَواحِلُ
to help, assist (III)	ساعَدَ، يُساعِدُ، مُسَاعَدَة
I traveled	سافَرْتُ
to contribute (III)	ساهَمَ، يُساهِمُ، مُسَاهَمَة
tourist, traveler	سائِحٌ ج. سُيَّاحٌ ، سُوَّاحٌ
I will try	سأحَاوِلُ
I will try convince her	سأحاوِلُ أنْ أقنعَها
I will return	سأعودُ
swimming	سباحَة (سبَحَ، يَسْبَحُ)
prison	سجْنٌ
prison guard, warden	سجَّانة
cigarettes	سجائر
dawn, early morning	سحَر
charm, enchantment (v.n.)	سحْرٌ (سحَرَ، يَسْحَرُ)
his facial expression	سحْنته
clouds	سحاب
irony, sarcasm	سخريَة
happy	سعيدٌ - سَعيدة
illness	سقَم
I lived, resided	سكَنْتُ
authority, power	سلْطَة ج. سُلْطَاتٌ
to listen, hear	سمعَ، يَسْمَعُ
to name (II)	سمَّى، يُسَمِّي
sky, heaven	سماءٌ ج. سَمَاوَاتٌ، سَمَوَاتٌ
we will migrate	سنُهَاجِر
year	سنةٌ ج. سَنَواتٌ
easy	سهْلٌ - سَهْلة
except for us, save us	سوانا
market, bazaar	سوقٌ ج. أسْواقٌ
swords	سيُوفٌ
to dominate, control, seize	سيْطَرَ، يُسَيْطِرُ، سَيْطَرة
biography	سيرةٌ ج. سِيَرٌ

English	Arabic
cockroaches	صراصير
difficulty	صُعُوبَة ج. صُعُوباتٌ
difficult	صَعْبٌ - صَعْبَة
small, little	صغيرٌ
class	صفٌّ ج. صُفوفٌ
to set up in a row or line, line up	صفَّ، يَصُفُّ، صَفَّ
connection	صلة
deaf	صمَم
to make	صنعَ، يصْنعُ
hunting, hunt	صيْدٌ (صادَ، يَصيِدُ)

ض

my conscience	ضميري
guest, visitor	ضيْفٌ ج. ضُيُوفٌ

ط

to go around the Ka`bah	طافَ، يَطوفُ، طوْفٌ
it floated	طافتْ
student (m.s.)	طالبٌ
student (f.s.)	طالِبَةٌ
of course	طبْعًا
physician	طبيبٌ - طَبيبة
doctor	طبيبٌ ج. أطبّاءُ
psychiatrist	طبيب نفساني
nature	طبيعة
street road	طريقٌ / شارع
child, baby	طفْلٌ ج. أطْفالٌ
Tangiers	طنجة
okay, agreeable	طيِّب
goodness, pleasantness (v.n.)	طيبة (طابَ، يطيبُ)

ظ

shade, shadow	ظلٌّ

ش

street	شارعٌ ج. شوارعُ
poet	شاعِرٌ ج. شُعَراءُ
net, network, system	شبَكَة ج. شَبَكاتٌ
cold	شبِم
reed flute	شبّابَة
courageous, brave	شجَاعٌ ج. شُجْعَانٌ
to encourage (II)	شجّعَ، يُشَجِّعُ
it (m.s.) encouraged me	شجّعَني
different personality	شخصية مختلفة
to crack, splinter	شرَخَ، يَشْرَخُ، شَرْخٌ
to drink	شربَ، يشرَبُ
traffic police	شرْطة مُرور
two balconies, terraces	شرْفتان
evil	شرٌّ
it took roots	شرَّشَتْ
sail, tent	شراعٌ ج. أشْرعَة - شُرُعٌ
company	شركةٌ ج . شركاتٌ
to feel	شعَرَ، يَشْعُرُ، شُعُورٌ
poetry	شِعرٌ
your lips	شفتيك
transparent	شفيف
apartment, flat	شقّةٌ ج. شُقَقٌ
thank you	شكرًا
famous	شهيرٌ- شهيرة
thing, something	شيْءٌ ج. أشْياءُ

ص

health	صحَّة
rocks	صخورٌ
coincidence	صدْفة
to believe, trust (II)	صدَّق، يُصَدِّق
friend	صديقٌ ج. أصدِقاءُ

age	عمْرٌ
her age	عمْرُهَا
his age	عمْرُهُ
my age	عمْري
I have	عندي
spider	عنكبوت
stubborn	عنيدة
lute	عودٌ
eye(s)	عيْنٌ ج. عُيُونٌ

غ

forest	غابَةٌ ج. غابَاتٌ
dormant	غافِيَة
vague, mysterious	غامِضٌ
to press, choke, suffocate	غتَّ، يَغُتُّ، غَتٌّ
lunch	غدَاءٌ
sunset	غرُوب
strange, foreign	غريبٌ ج. غُرَبَاءُ
Gaza	غزَّة
washing	غسيل
rich, wealthy	غنِيٌّ ج. أغْنِياءُ
song	غنوة
their depth, bottom	غوْرَيْهما

ف

silvery	الفِضِّيُّ
tepid, lukewarm	فاتِر
to conquer, open	فتَحَ، يَفْتَحُ، فَتْحٌ
period of time	فترة ج. فترات
suddenly	فجْأة
individual	فردٌ ج. أفرادٌ
opportunity, chance	فرْصة ج. فُرَصٌ
dress	فستان
space	فضاء

continue, remain	ظلَّ
thirsty	ظمْآن

ع

Iraq	العِراق
to come back, return	عادَ، يَعُودُ
usually (adv.)	عادةً
normal, usual (adj.)	عادِيٌّ
to live	عاشَ، يَعيشُ، عَيْشٌ
two lovers	عاشِقيْن
storm, violent wind	عاصِفة ج. عَواصِفُ
capital	عاصِمةٌ ج. عَواصِمُ
family	عائِلة ج. عائِلاتٌ
its (f.s.) genius	عبْقرِيَّتها
Abbasid	عبَّاسِيٌّ ج. عبَّاسِيُّون
old, ancient	عتيق
justice	عدالة
naked (pl.)	عراة
Iraqi	عراقيٌّ - عِراقِيَّة
to play a musical instrument	عزَفَ، يَعْزِفُ، عزْفٌ
dinner	عشَاءٌ
twenty	عشْرُونَ
Ishtar	عشتار
passion	عشق
ages	عصُور
difficult	عصيّة
distinguished personality, great figure	علَمٌ ج. أعْلامٌ
secular (adj.)	علْمَانِيٌّ
my relationship	علاقتي
at all, in any respect	على الإطلاق
as far as the eye could see	على امْتِدادِ البَصر
job, work, business	عمَلٌ ج. أعْمَالٌ
to work for	عمِلَ على
I worked	عمِلْتُ
dean	عمِيدٌ ج. عُمَداءُ

English	Arabic
like the dream	كَالْحُلم
like blood	كَالدَّم
to be (I)	كَانَ، يَكُونُ
priestess	كَاهِنة
big, large	كَبِير - كَبِيرة
much, many	كَثِيرٌ ج. كَثِيرونَ
miracle	كَرَامَةٌ ج. كَرَامَاتٌ
generosity, noble nature (v.n.)	كَرَمٌ (كَرُمَ، يَكْرُمُ)
vineyards, orchards	كروم
lazy (f. s. adj.)	كَسْلى
totally, completely	كُلِّيَّةً
violin	كَمانٌ
wealth, treasures	كنوز
how	كَيْفَ
depressed	كَئِيب

ل

no, does not	لا
without end	لا انتهاء
to create, form	لأصوغ
Lebanon	لُبْنان
Lebanese	لُبْنانِيٌّ - لُبْنانِيَّة
moment, instant	لَحْظة ج. لَحَظَاتٌ
tongue	لِسَان
kind	لَطِيف - لَطِيفة
I wrapped	لَفَفْتُ
but	لٰكِنْ
touches	لَمَسَات
we did not sleep	لَمْ نَنَمْ
he will never wake up	لن يَسْتفيق
I have	لي
lion	لَيْث
its ordinary night	لَيْلها العادِيُّ
lemon	لَيْمُونٌ

English	Arabic
breakfast	فطورٌ
you have done it	فَعَلْتَها
thought (noun)	فكرٌ ج. أفْكَارٌ
do not think	فلا تَـظُنَّنَّ
hotel	فنْدُقٌ ج. فَنَادِقُ
art	فنٌّ ج. فُـنونٌ
in	في
philosopher	فَيْلسوف ج. فلاسِـفَة

ق

you (m.s.) meet me (imp. III)	قابِلْـنِي
coming, arriving; comer or arriver (a.p.)	قادِمٌ ج. قادِمُونَ (قَـدَمَ، يَقدُمُ)
leader, chief	قائِدٌ ج. قُـوَّاد - قادَة
before, ago (prep.)	قبْلَ
before that (prep.)	قبْلَـهَا
I kissed	قبَّلتُ
power	قدرة
old, ancient	قديمٌ
paper	قرطَاس
relative	قريب ج. أقارب، أقرباء، أقربون
distant, far away	قصِيَّة
palace	قصرٌ ج. قُـصُورٌ
shortsightedness	قصْـرُ البَصَر
poems	قصائِد
drops	قطرَات
heart, middle, center	قلْبٌ ج. قُـلُوبٌ
I masked	قنَعْتُ
strong, powerful	قويٌّ ج. أقوياءُ
value	قيمة ج. قِـيَمٌ

ك

writer	كاتِبٌ ج. كُـتَّابٌ
like the hungry (pl.)	كالجِياع

م

what	ما
they died (m. pl.)	ماتوا
what	ماذا
to exercise, practice (III)	مارَسَ، يُمَارِسُ، مُمَارَسَة
jokingly	مازِحاً
initiative	مبَادَرة
blessed	مباركة
specialist, specialized	مُتَخَصِّصٌ - مُتَخَصِّصَةٌ
advanced	مُتَقَدِّمٌ
diverse	مُتَنَوِّعٌ
rebellious	متمرِّد
modest, humble	متواضِعٌ ج. مُتواضِعُونَ
when	متى
represent	مثَّلَ، يُمثِّلُ، تَمْثيلٌ
famine	مجَاعَة
love (v.n.)	محَبة (أحَبَّ، يُحِبُّ)
investigator	محَقِّقَة (حَقَّقَ)
living creature	مخلوقاً يَتَنَفَّسُ
teacher	مدَرِّس - مُدَرِّسة
city	مدِينَة
astonished	مدهوش
manager, director	مدِيرٌ - مُدِيرة
radio	مذياع
dreadful, horrible	مريع
hello	مرْحَباً
center	مرْكَزٌ ج. مَراكِزُ
to pass, go	مرَّ، يَمُرُّ، مُرُورٌ
connected, committed, bound	مرتَبِط ج. مُرتَبِطونَ
water spouts	مزاريبُ
in the evening (adv.)	مسَاءً
Christian	مسِيحيٌّ ج. مَسِيحيُّونَ
impossible (pl.)	مسْتحيلات
theater	مسْرَح ج. مَسَارحُ

inhabited, populated (a.p.)	مسْكُونٌ (سَكَنَ، يَسْكُنُ)
poor	مسْكينٌ ج. مَسَاكينُ
Muslim	مسْلِمٌ ج. مُسْلِمُونَ
to touch	مسَّ، يَمَسُّ، مَسٌّ
our distances	مسافاتنا
torch	مشْعَلٌ ج. مَشَاعِلُ
problem	مشْكلة ج. مَشاكِلُ، مُشْكِلاتٌ
renowned, famous	مشْهُورٌ ج. مَشاهيرُ
participating	مشاركة
seeing, watching (v.n.)	مشاهدة (شاهَدَ، يُشاهِدُ)
rain	مطَرٌ ج. أمْطارٌ
kitchen	مطْبَخٌ ج. مَطابِخُ
restaurant	مطْعَمٌ
complicated, complex	معقَّدٌ، مُعَقَّدة
known (passive participle)	معْرُوفٌ (عَرَفَ، يَعْرفُ)
most of, the majority	معْظَم
landmark, site	معْلَمٌ ج. مَعالِمُ
institute	معْهَدٌ ج. مَعاهِدُ
sheathed	مغْمَمَدَة
caves	مغاور
concept	مفْهُومٌ ج. مفاهيمُ
its keys	مفاتيحها
full of	مفعَمة بـ
cafeteria, snack room, buffet	مقْصَفٌ ج. مَقاصِفُ
inmates, prisoners	مقيمات في السِّجن
library	مكْتَبَة ج. مَكْتَبَاتٌ
place such as this	مكان مثل هذا
files	ملَفات
million	ملْيُونٌ ج. ملايينُ
we filled	ملأنا
boring (adj.)	مملٌّ - مُملَّة
from	من
for, for the sake of	من أجْل
since, ago (prep.)	منْذُ

كلمات وتعابير

Lesson 1

English	Arabic
Are you a student (f.s.)?	هَلْ أنتِ طالِبَة؟
Are you a student (m.s.)?	هَلْ أنتَ طالِبٌ؟
delighted, honored	تَشَرَّفْنا
English literature	الأَدَبُ الإنْكِليزي
excellent	مُمْتاز ـ مُمْتازة
good-bye	مَعَ السَّلامة
How are you?	كَيْفَ الحَالُ؟
I am in a hurry	أنا عَلَى عَجَلة
I am sorry (f.s.)	أنا آسِفة
I am sorry (m.s.)	أنا آسِف
I must go now	يَجِبُ أنْ أذهَبَ الآنَ
I study economics	أنا أدْرُسُ الاقتِصَاد
international relations	العَلاقاتُ الدُّوَلِيَّة
Jordan	الأرْدُنُ
Kingdom of Saudi Arabia	المَمْلَكَة العَرَبِيَّة السُّعُودِيَّة
So long!	إلى اللقاء
the State of California	ولاية كاليفورنيا
United States of America	الولايَاتُ المُتَّحِدَة الأمْريكيَّة
very good, praise be to God	بخَيْر، الحَمْدُ لله
Welcome! Hello!	أهلاً وسَهْلاً
What do you (f.s.) study?	ماذا تَدْرُسِينَ؟
What do you (m.s.) study?	ماذا تَدْرُسُ؟
What is your (f.s.) name?	ما اسمُكِ؟
What is your (m.s.) name?	ما اسمُكَ؟
Where are you (f.s.) from?	مِنْ أَيْنَ أنتِ؟
Where are you (m.s.) from?	مِنْ أَيْنَ أنْتَ؟

476

Lesson 2

Future Particle	سَـ
God willing	إنْ شاءَ الله
hello, welcome	أهْلاً، أهْلاً
homework, duty	واجِبٌ ج. واجِبَاتٌ
I came	حَضَرْتُ
I go	أذهَبُ
In which university do you (f.s.) study?	في أيِّ جامِعَةٍ تَدْرُسِينَ؟
laboratory	مُخْتَبَرٌ
Masters in Business Administration	ماجِسْتير في إدارَة الأعْمَال
mosque	مَسْجِدٌ
Really! Truly!	حَقًّا
This is a beautiful coincidence	هَذِهِ مُصادَفَة جَمِيلة
Will I see you (m.s.) tomorrow?	هَلْ أراكَ غداً؟
Yes, I will see you (f.s.) tomorrow	نعَم، أراكِ غداً
you do (f.s.)	تَفْعَلِينَ
you do (m.s.)	تَفْعَلُ

Lesson 3

Arab origin	أصْلٌ عَرَبيٌّ
assistant	مُساعِدٌ
Columbia University	جامِعَة كولومبيا
Damascus	دِمَشْق
eighteen years	ثمانيةَ عَشَرَ عاماً
he was born	وُلِدَ
he works	يَعْمَلُ
high school	مَدْرَسَة ثانويَّة
I grew up / was raised	نشأتُ
I have two sisters	لي أختان اِثنتان
I love my family	أنا أحِبُّ عائِلَتي

the diplomatic quarter	المِنْطَقة (المَنْطِقة) الدِّبْلوماسِيَّة
the novel	الرِّواية
the Prophet	النَّبِيُّ
the short story	القِصَّة القصيرة
the two Americas (North and South)	الأمْريكِيَّتَيْن
Vice President	نائِبُ الرَّئيس

Lesson 15

coexistence and tolerance	تَعَايُشٌ وتَسَامُحٌ
commercial center	مَرْكَزٌ تِجاريٌّ
cultural movement	حَرَكَـة ثَقافِيَّة
dawn of history	فَجْرُ التَّاريخ
Gilgamesh	جِلْجَامِش
in addition to	بالإضَافةِ إلى
in love and harmony	بِمَحَبَّة وانْسِجَام
land of ancient civilizations	أرْضُ حَضاراتٍ عَريقة
literary societies	مُجْتَمَعاتٌ أدَبِيَّة
mankind, human being	بَشَرٌ
secret of eternity	سِـرُّ الخُـلُود
the ancient ages, ancient times	أقْدَمُ العُصُـور
the Gulf	الخلِيـج
to search for	يَبْحَثُ عَنْ

Lesson 16

a warm refuge	مَلْجَأً دافئ
alienation	إغْتِرابٌ
all of the basic needs	كافة الاحْتِياجَات الأساسِيَّة
Arab society	المُجْتَمعُ العربيُّ
facing life, encountering life	مُواجَهَة الحَيَاة
identity	هُويَّة

individual success	نَجاحُ الفَردِ
life and culture of the Arabs	حياةُ العَربِ وثقافتُهُم
loyalty, devotion	وَلاءٌ
necessary strength	قُوَّة ضَرُوريَّة
principle axis, pivot point	مِحْوَرٌ رئيسِيٌّ
social life	الحياة الاجتماعية
strong connection, close union	الْتِحَامٌ مَتينٌ
to rely on	يَعْتَمِدُ على
warmth and protection	الدِفْءُ والحِمَايَة

Lesson 17

Aqaba	العَقَبَة
as if (he)	كَأنَّهُ
climate	مَنَاخٌ، مُنَاخٌ
comfortable and quiet	مُريحٌ وهَادِىءٌ، مُريحَة وهادِئة
delicious dish	طبقٌ لَذيذٌ
full of	مَلِيءٌ بـ، مَلِيئة بـ
genuine Arab generosity	كَرَمٌ عربيٌّ أصِيلٌ
meat and rice	لَحْمٌ وأرُزٌ
mild, moderate (a.p.)	مُعْتَدِلٌ
people of the country	أهْلُ البلادِ
popular dish, national dish	طبَقٌ شَعْبيٌّ
port, harbor	مِيناء
salty water	مِيَاةٌ مَالِحَة
taxicabs	سيَّاراتُ الأجْرةِ
the Mediterranean Basin	حَوْضُ البَحْرِ الأبْيَضِ المُتَوَسِّط
the Messiah, Christ	السَّيِّدُ المَسِيحُ
the Red Sea	البَحْرُ الأحْمَرُ
the warmth of its (m.s.) people	حَـرارة أهْلِهِ
thousands of years ago	منذ آلافِ السِّنينِ

485

transportation	مُواصَلاتٌ
warm (a.p.)	دافِئٌ
water skiing	تَزَلُّجٌ على المَاء
weather, climate	طَقْسٌ
welcome, greeting	تَرْحابٌ
with enjoyment and pleasure/ease	بسُهُولةٍ ومُتْعَةٍ

Lesson 18

across, through, by way of	عَبْرَ
advanced administrative system	نِظام إداري مُتَطَوِّر
at the hands of	على أيْدي
Atlantic Ocean	المُحيط الأطلسي
before that	قَبْلَهَا
Córdoba	قُرْطُبَة
emptiness, void, gap	فَراغ
European renaissance	النَّهْضَة الأوربيَّة
European thought	الفِكْر الأوربي
forever	إلى الأبَد
Granada	غِرناطَة
Ibn Rushd (Averroës)	ابن رُشْد
Ibn Sina (Avicenna)	ابن سينا
is called, nicknamed (passive)	يُلَقَّبُ
is known (passive voice)	يُعْرَفُ
leaving behind it	تاركاً وراءَهُ
Prime Minister	رئيس وزراء
Straits of Gibraltar	مَضيق جَبَل طارق
the Arab presence ended	إنْتَهَى الوُجُود العربي
the Eagle of Quraysh	صَقْر قُرَيْش
the middle of the eighth century	مُنتصف القَرْن الثامِن
the Umayyad Ruler, Governor	الحاكِمُ الأمَوِيُّ

486

the Umayyad State	الدَّوْلَة الأَمَوِيَّة
under the leadership of	بِقِيادةِ
was built (perfect passive voice)	بُنِيَتْ
was defeated (passive)	هُزِمَ
was named (passive)	سُمِّيَ

Lesson 19

a breeze of wind	هَبَّة ريح
a moment	لَحْظَة
every day	كلُّ يَوْمٍ
every death	كلُّ مَوْتٍ
every fire	كلُّ حَريق
every word	كلُّ كلمةٍ
everything	كلُّ شَيْءٍ
in my depth, deep inside me	في أَعْمَاقِي
infinite formula, unfinished formula	لا صيغة نهائية لها
it (f.s.) covers, conceals	تُغَطِّي
it (f.s.) lost its way, went astray	ضَلَّت الطَّريق
it (m.s.) becomes more radiant, glow	يَزْداد تَأَلُّقًا
new human being, new creature	كائِنة جَديدة
place of my birth	مَسْقَط رأسِي
sudden birth	وِلادَة مُفاجِئة
telephone call	مُكالَمَة هاتِفِيَّة
wrong (telephone) number	النُّمْرَة غَلَط

Lesson 20

although I took lessons	رَغْم مُثابَرَتي على الدُّروس
beneath windows	تَحْتَ النَّوافِذِ
easily bored	سَريعُ الضَّجَر
for some time	لِبَعْض الوقتِ

to go around the Ka'bah	طَافَ، يَطُوفُ، طَوْفٌ / طَوَافٌ
miracle	كَرَامَةٌ ج. كَرَامَاتٌ
sort, type, kind	نَمَطٌ ج. أَنْمَاطٌ / نِمَاطٌ
silk, brocade	دِيبَاجٌ ج. دبابيج
to press, choke, suffocate	غَتَّ، يَغُتُّ، غَتٌّ
to set up in a row or line, line up	صَفَّ، يَصُفُّ، صَفٌّ
to go away, leave	إِنْصَرَفَ، يَنْصَرِفُ، إِنْصِرَافٌ

I turned my face away from him into the horizons to avoid looking at him	جَعَلْتُ أصرف وجهي عنه في آفاق السماء

the holy Ka'bah in Mecca: a cubic structure that contains the black stone	كَعْبَةٌ
the Angel Gabriel, the angel of revelations who carried God's message to Prophet Muhammed	جِبْرِيل
Hira': a mountain located northwest of Mecca known also as "the mountain of light". The Prophet hid in a cave on the mountain during his flight to Medina. A spider is said to have miraculously woven a web at the mouth of the cave to dissuade the Prophet's enemies from entering to look for him since they thought the cave had been long abandoned.	حِرَاء

إِقْرَأْ بِاسْمِ رَبِّكَ الَّذِي خَلَقَ، خَلَقَ الإِنْسَانَ مِنْ عَلَقٍ، إِقْرَأْ وَرَبُّكَ الأَكْرَمُ، الَّذِي عَلَّمَ بِالقَلَمِ. عَلَّمَ الإِنْسَانَ مَا لَمْ يَعْلَمْ.
Read! In the name of thy Lord who created- created man from a clinging substance. Proclaim! And thy Lord is Most Bountiful, He who taught (the use of) the pen, taught man which he knew not. *Qur'an 96:1-5*

Let's Speak Arabic (English - Arabic)

English	Arabic
I am afraid, scared	أنا خائِف ـ أنا خائِفة
Africa	أفريقِيا
ambassador	سَفير
apartment	شَقَّة
Asia	آسيا
Australia	أستراليا
banana	المَوْز
basketball	كُرة السَّلَّة
beach	الشَّاطِئ
bicycle	الدَّرَّاجَة
black	الأَسْوَد
blouse	بُلوزة
blue	الأَزْرَق
boxing	المُلاكَمة
bread	الخُبْز
Bristol Street	شَارِع بريستول
brown	البُنِّي
I brush my teeth	أنَظِّفُ أسناني
car	بالسَّيَّارة
cereal	الحُبُوب
cheese	الجُبْنة
chicken	الدَّجَاج
class	الصَّف
cloudy	غَائِمٌ
coffeehouse	المَقهى
cold	بَارِدٌ
cucumber	الخِيَار
cup of coffee	فِنجان قهوة
dance	أرقصَ
dress	فُستان
I eat my breakfast	أتناولُ فُطوري
engineer	مُهَندِس
Europe	أوروبا
falafel	الفَلافِل
fish and rice	سَمَك وَرُزّ (أرزّ)
football	الفوتبول الأمريكي
I go out to dinner	أذهبَ إلى العَشاء
I go out to the party	أذهبَ إلى الحَفْلة

I go to church	أذهبَ إلى الكنيسـة
green	الأخْضَر
grilled beef	لَحْم بَقَر مَشوي
grilled chicken	فَرُّوج مَشوي
history	التَّارِيخ
hospital	المُسْتَشْفى
hot	حَارٌّ
house	بَيْت
humid	رَطْبٌ
I am hungry	أنا جُوعَان - أنا جُوعَانة
I bought a new computer	اِشْتَرَيْتُ حاسوباً جديداً
I got married	تَزَوَّجْتُ
I learned to drive	تَعَلَّمْتُ قِيادة السَّيارة
I rented an apartment	اِسْتأجَرْتُ شَقَّة
I saw my friends	شَاهدتُ أصدقائي
lawyer	مُحامي (محامٍ)
lettuce	الخَسّ
I listen to music	أستمعَ إلى الموسيقى
literature	الأدب
medicine	الطِّبّ
milk	الحَلِيب
my cousin	ابن عَمِّي
my father	وَالِدي
my husband	زَوْجِي
my mother	وَالِدَتي
my neighbor	جَاري
orange	البُرْتُقالي
orange juice	عَصِير البُرْتُقال
pants	بَنطلون
Pepsi	البِيْسي
philosophy	الفَلْسَفة
ping-pong	كُرة الطَّاوِلة
plane	بالطَّـائِرة
plate of kabaab	صَحْن كَباب
put on makeup	أضَعُ المِكيَاج
I put on my clothes	ألْبَسُ مَلابسي
rainy	مُمْطِرٌ
I am sad	أنا حَزِين - أنا حَزِينَة
science	العُلُوم

500

English	Arabic
I shave	أَحْلِقُ
shirt	قَميص
skirt	تَنُّورة
South America	أمريكا الجَنوبية
swimming pool	المَسْبَح
taxi	سيّارةِ أجرة (التاكسي)
tea	الشَّاي
teacher	أستاذ
the city of Claremont	مَدينة كليرمُونت
the concert	الحَفْلة المُوسيقِيَّة
the interview	المُقابلة
the President's speech	خِطـاب الرَّئيس
the soccer game	مباراة كُرَة القَدَم
the state of California	ولاية كاليفورنيا
the television	التِّلْفاز
I am thirsty	أنا عَطْشَان ـ أنا عَطْشَانة
I am tired	أنا تَعْبَان ـ أنا تَعْبَانة
tomatoes	البَنَدُورة
train	القِطَـار
translator	مُترجِم
volleyball	كُرة الطَّائِرة
water	المَاء
watermelon	البَطِّيخ
white	الأبْيَض
yellow	الأصْفَر

تمَّ بعون الله

PHOTO CREDITS

Section One, p. 80, Julie McAleer, Karin Weston. Photograph courtesy of Bassam Frangieh.

Section One, p. 85, Fayeq Oweis. Photograph courtesy of Fayeq Oweis.

Section Two, Lesson One, p. 88, Figure 1.1, Claremont McKenna College. Photograph courtesy of CMC.

Section Two, Lesson One, p. 95, Figure 1.2, Dhekra Toumi and Abdulaziz Abu Sag. Ccourtesy of Abdulaziz al-Zu'abi.

Section Two, Lesson One, p. 96, Figure 1.3, Hala Nazzal and Faisal Al-Salloum. Courtesy of Abdulaziz al-Zu'abi.

Section Two, Lesson One, p. 101, Figure 1.4, Nizar Qabbani. Photograph courtesy of Nizar Qabbani.

Section Two, Lesson One, p. 103, Figure 1.5, Joumana Nammour. Photograph courtesy of Abdulaziz al-Zu'abi.

Section Two, Lesson Two, p. 104, Figure 2.1, Claremont McKenna College. Photograph courtesy of CMC.

Section Two, Lesson Two, p. 108, Figure 2.2, Claremont, CA. Photograph courtesy of CMC.

Section Two, Lesson Three, p. 116, Figure 3.1, Claremont, CA. Photograph courtesy of CMC.

Section Two, Lesson Three, p. 120, Figure 3.2, Northern Lebanon. Photograph courtesy of Tariq Frangieh.

Section Two, Lesson Four, p. 132, Figure 4.1, Najran, Saudi Arabia. Photograph courtesy of Dohan Hamad Al-Salem.

Section Two, Lesson Four, p. 135, Figure 4.2, Claremont McKenna College. Photograph courtesy of CMC.

Section Two, Lesson Four, p. 136, Figure 4.3, Dohan Hamad Al-Salem. Courtesy of Dohan Hamad Al-Salem.

Section Two, Lesson Four, p. 145, Figure 4.4, Shams Ismael. Photograph courtesy of Shams Ismael.

Section Two, Lesson Five, p. 147, Figure 5.1, Imam Ali Shrine. Photograph courtesy of George Farag.

Section Two, Lesson Five, p. 150, Figure 5.2, Dany Doueiri. Photograph courtesy of Rio Fischer.

Section Two, Lesson Five, p. 161, Figure 5.3, Joumana Nammour. Photograph courtesy of Abdulaziz al-Zu'abi.

Section Two, Lesson Six, p. 162, Figure 6.1, Damascus, Syria. Photograph courtesy of Samer Kassawat.

Section Two, Lesson Six, p. 165, Figure 6.2, Ayman Ramadan. Photograph courtesy of Rio Fischer.

Section Two, Lesson Seven, p. 178, Figure 7.1, Damascus. Photograph courtesy of Samer Kassawat.

Section Two, Lesson Seven, p. 182, Figure 7.2, Majida Hourani. Photograph courtesy of Olivia Uranga.

Section Two, Lesson Seven, p. 192, Figure 7.3, Joumana Haddad. Photograph courtesy of Joumana Haddad.

Section Two, Lesson Eight, p. 194, Figure 8.1, Umayyad Mosque. Photograph courtesy of Samer Kassawat.

Section Two, Lesson Eight, p. 197, Figure 8.2, Umayyad Mosque. Photograph courtesy of Tariq Frangieh.

Section Two, Lesson Eight, p. 208, Figure 8.3, Souq al-Hamidiyyeh. Photograph courtesy of Tariq Frangieh.

Section Two, Lesson Eight, p. 211, Figure 8.4, Fairuz. Photograph courtesy of 3B Media, Inc.

Section Two, Lesson Nine, p. 213, Figure 9.1, Nile River in Cairo. Photograph courtesy of George Farag.

Section Two, Lesson Ten, p. 229, Figure 10.1, Damascus. Photograph courtesy of Samer Kassawat.

Section Two, Lesson Ten, p. 232, Figure 10.2, Coffeehouse in Syria. Photograph courtesy of Jawad Frangieh.

Section Two, Lesson Ten, p. 241, Figure 10.3, Nizar Qabbani. Photograph courtesy of Nizar Qabbani.

Section Two, Lesson Eleven, p. 243, Figure 11.1, Castle in Aleppo, Syria. Photograph courtesy of Salma Chehabi.

Section Two, Lesson Eleven, p. 246, Figure 11.2, Aleppo, Syria. Photograph courtesy of Samer Kassawat.

Section Two, Lesson Eleven, p. 247, Figure 11.3, Abd Al-Rahman Al-Kawakibi. Courtesy of Lina Al-Kawakibi.

Section Two, Lesson Eleven, p. 251, Figure 11.4, Palmyra. Photograph courtesy of Samer Kassawat.

Section Two, Lesson Eleven, p. 255, Figure 11.5, Mahmoud Harmoush. Photograph courtesy of Rio Fischer.

Section Two, Lesson Twelve, p. 258, Figure 12.1, Sphinx and Pyramid. Photograph courtesy of George Farag.

Section Two, Lesson Twelve, p. 261, Figure 12.2, Al Azhar. Photograph courtesy of George Farag.

Section Two, Lesson Thirteen, p. 273, Figure13.1, Fishing boats on the Tunisian coast. Courtesy of Abdulwahab Qadri.

Section Two, Lesson Thirteen, p. 276, Figure 13.2, Sidi Bou Said, Tunisia. Photograph courtesy of Anna Bittman.

Section Two, Lesson Thirteen, p. 277, Figure 13.3, Traditional Tunisian door. Photograph courtesy of Anna Bittman.

Section Two, Lesson Thirteen, p. 283, Figure 13.4, Sahara Desert in Tunisia. Courtesy of Abdulwahab Qadri.

Section Two, Lesson Fourteen, p. 287, Figure 14.1, Ancient Ruins in Lebanon. Photograph courtesy of Tariq Frangieh.

Section Two, Lesson Fourteen, p. 296, Figure 14.3, Lebanese Cedar Tree. Photograph courtesy of Jawad Frangieh.

Section Two, Lesson Fifteen, p. 301, Figure 15.1, Manama, Bahrain. Photograph courtesy of the Embassy of Bahrain.

Section Two, Lesson Fifteen, p. 303, Figure 15.2, Bahrain Bridge. Photograph courtesy of Embassy of Bahrain.

Section Two, Lesson Fifteen, p. 304, Figure 15.3, Traditional crafts, Bahrain. Courtesy of Embassy of Bahrain.

Section Two, Lesson Fifteen, p. 305, Figure 15.4, Bahrain Roundabout. Photograph courtesy of Embassy of Bahrain.

Section Two, Lesson Fifteen, p. 311, Figure 15.5, Tree of Life, Bahrain. Photograph courtesy of Embassy of Bahrain.

Section Two, Lesson Sixteen, p. 315, Figure 16.1, Chehabi Family. Photograph courtesy of Salma Chehabi.

Section Two, Lesson Sixteen, p. 325, Figure 16.2, Salma Chehabi. Photograph courtesy of Rio Fischer.

Section Two, Lesson Sixteen, p. 328, Figure 16.3, Joumana Nammour. Photograph courtesy of Abdulaziz al-Zu'abi.

Section Two, Lesson Seventeen, p. 329, Figure 17.1, Amman, Jordan. Photograph courtesy of Rio Fischer.

Section Two, Lesson Seventeen, p. 332, Figure 17.2, Wadi Rum. Photograph courtesy of Rio Fischer.

Section Two, Lesson Seventeen, p. 333, Figure 17.3, Ajloun. Photograph courtesy of Rio Fischer.

Section Two, Lesson Seventeen, p. 339, Figure 17.4, Petra. Photograph courtesy of Rio Fischer.

Section Two, Lesson Eighteen, p. 343, Figure 18.1, Toledo, Spain. Photograph courtesy of Raquel Vega-Duran.

Section Two, Lesson Eighteen, p. 346, Figure 18.2, Southern Spain. Photograph courtesy of Raquel Vega-Duran.

Section Two, Lesson Eighteen, p. 355, Figure 18.3, Mohamad Saadoun. Photograph courtesy of Bassam Frangieh.

TEXT CREDITS

p. 448, Letter from Haider Haider to Bassam Frangieh, courtesy of Bassam Frangieh.
p. 449, Letter from Abd al-Rahman al-Munif to Bassam Frangieh, courtesy of Bassam Frangieh.
p. 450, Letter from Hanna Mina to Bassam Frangieh, courtesy of Bassam Frangieh.
p. 451, Letter from Adonis to Bassam Frangieh, courtesy of Bassam Frangieh.
p. 452, Letter from Olivia Uranga to Bassam Frangieh, courtesy of Bassam Frangieh.
p. 452, Letter from Krysten Hartman to Bassam Frangieh, courtesy of Bassam Frangieh.
p. 452, Letter from Rio Fischer to Bassam Frangieh, courtesy of Bassam Frangieh.
p. 453, Letter from Camille Cole to Bassam Frangieh, courtesy of Bassam Frangieh.
p. 453, Letter from Rebekah Binns to Bassam Frangieh, courtesy of Bassam Frangieh.
p. 453, Letter from David Franzel to Bassam Frangieh, courtesy of Bassam Frangieh.
p. 453, Letter from Melissa Carlson to Bassam Frangieh, courtesy of Bassam Frangieh.

ILLUSTRATION CREDITS

All illustrations throughout the textbook are courtesy of Dr. Fayeq Oweis.

❖